*Buffy* Meets the Academy

D1605893

# Buffy
# Meets the Academy

*Essays on the Episodes
and Scripts as Text*

*Edited by*
KEVIN K. DURAND

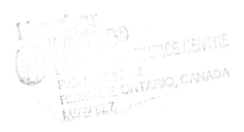

McFarland & Company, Inc., Publishers
*Jefferson, North Carolina, and London*

LIBRARY OF CONGRESS CATALOGUING-IN-PUBLICATION DATA

Buffy meets the academy : essays on the episodes and scripts
as text / edited by Kevin K. Durand.
        p.      cm.
Includes bibliographical references and index.

ISBN 978-0-7864-4355-0
softcover : 50# alkaline paper  ∞

1. Buffy the Vampire Slayer (Television program)
I.  Durand, Kevin K., 1967–
PN1992.77.B84B825    2009
791.45'72 — dc22                                    2009018617

British Library cataloguing data are available

Front cover by TG Design

Manufactured in the United States of America

*McFarland & Company, Inc., Publishers*
  *Box 611, Jefferson, North Carolina 28640*
  *www.mcfarlandpub.com*

# Table of Contents

v

# Introduction

## Pop Culture Meets the Academy

KEVIN K. DURAND

*"I'd call that a radical interpretation of the text"*
— Oz in "Doppelgangland"

Since those fateful moments when Plato expelled the poets from the ideal city and criticized the Siskels, Eberts, and Roepers of his day as know-nothing charlatans, the stage has been set for the dramatic tension between critic and artist/author, between critical theory and literature, and between theorist and theorist. Plato began the discipline that has come to be known as Literary Criticism in the context of pondering such questions of moment as Truth, Knowledge, and Virtue. While he could not have anticipated Foucault, Adorno, Lacan, Kristeva, or hooks, all literary critics owe the founding of our art to Plato.

As Plato could scarcely have anticipated the works of his descendents, one suspects he would have been even more startled to see some of the descendents of Homer. How, for example, might Plato have reacted to *Buffy* or *Angel*? Would he have found them to be interesting trifles? Radical storytelling? Something to follow the poets out of the ideal society? Whatever his reaction to them as works of art and entertainment, one thing is clear — he would have taken them seriously. Whether Homer or *Buffy*, Aristophanes or *Angel*, the works of popular culture are works to be engaged.

Bemused looks, skepticism, and, at times, outright laughter were, and oftentimes are, the reactions to the scholar who announces that he studies *Buffy*, *The Simpsons*, *The Sopranos*, or *M\*A\*S\*H*. "Why don't you study something important?" Or, in a bit of stuffy dismissiveness, "I don't watch television." To the latter minor critic, I offer David Bianculi's response at the 2004 Slayage Conference, "So, you choose to be illiterate?!?" It is indeed the case that much of that which is on television is mindless drivel. Let us imagine that no more than ten percent is worthwhile. Given that each year sees the publication of tens of thousands of books, precious few of which have a fraction of the import of direct to cable movies of the week, perhaps ten percent is not so bad.

The response to the former dismissal develops somewhat from the response to the latter. As a matter of importance and meaning, there is no question that popular culture vehicles are among the most effective for exploring topics of critical importance. *Maude* gave us one of the most gripping discussions of issues and arguments surrounding abortion. *M\*A\*S\*H* transformed post–Vietnam malaise into fodder for comedy while putting forward some of the most powerful and poignant views of war and its cost. Archie Bunker brought questions of race and racism into the homes of millions and was quietly and comedically subversive of the "separate but equal" and "not in my backyard" mind-set that endured in good health well into the 1970s and 80s despite *Brown v. Board of Education* twenty years previously. Television lampoons, critiques, subverts, and, at times, undergirds our deepest cultural concerns, questions, and commitments. In the process, like its ancestor, the *Lysistrata* of twenty-five centuries prior, television shows can provide a thoughtful place for reflection, a kind of "jumping off" spot for philosophical investigation, and even fairly sophisticate views to be added to the intellectual structure of our conversations.

Having argued for taking popular culture seriously, it is of some importance to examine why, even among those sympathetic to the foregoing argument, popular culture studies tend to languish. I shall argue that the primary reason for this is the shape of popular culture studies itself.

There is no universally accepted approach to popular culture studies. In itself, this is not problematic. There is no universally accepted approach to Socratic studies either. However, when one engages Plato or St. Thomas or William Faulkner, there is a seriousness or *gravitas* that pervades the analysis. (And, let us not forget Faulkner's own foray into the world of Hollywood, screenwriting, and moving pictures.) Scholars engage the text under examination in a deliberative fashion whatever critical framework is being employed by the scholar. This is, unfortunately, not the case in popular culture studies. However, to say that such seriousness is not universally present is not to say that it is wholly absent. Indeed, there are very thorough and deliberate scholars and some outstanding scholarship in the field. Too often, they are drowned out by fluff.

As I survey the field of popular culture studies, the various conversations tend to fall into five general sorts: Critical Engagement, Theory Exemplar/ Corrective, Point of Departure, Cultural Solipsism, and "Isn't that neat?" Taking these in reverse order, let us begin with the last.

Imagine this scene. Four or five friends gather for a night of television. Rather than succumbing to the weak ninety percent, they opt for *Buffy*. Let us also imagine that the group is fairly well-read, well-versed in critical theory, and quite well-informed with regard to the history of television and movies. As one episode moves into another, dinner and popcorn and drinks are consumed, and the hour grows late, the friends begin to note allusions to other works, homages to great television of the past, and/or false cognates of the same that just seem interesting. Before long, the gathering and viewing becomes a self-congratulatory exercise in the self-referential pointing out of neat connections or clever turns of phrase or interesting references. The result is something more than a drinking game but something somewhat less than scholarship.

At times, popular culture studies seems little more than "Isn't that neat?" At those times, when it does seem a little more, it can appear as little more than Cultural Solipsism. One of the easiest papers to write is the one that traces elements of some show or other to other shows that it references. Then, one takes those references and traces them to still others. In some rare cases, the trace comes full circle to the original program under consideration. One could fairly easily take, for example, Ray Stevens's "Dudley Dooright," trace the characters to earlier Stevens songs (e.g., "The Mississippi Squirrel Revival," "The Streak," and "The Haircut Song"). If one were particularly energetic, one could perhaps trace the influence of Jerry Clower, Grady Nutt, Grandpa Jones, and Minnie Pearl on Stevens. And, as it happens, there are elements of Ray Stevens's early material that influence the later work of these other luminaries. So, with little trouble, a Six Degrees of Ray Stevens could well be pulled together. While a good bit of fun, perhaps, such work would hardly be considered either original or particularly worthwhile. It is this sort of Cultural Solipsism that often makes popular culture studies seem less than serious and somewhat less than scholarly.

A third sort of popular culture criticism, and one that is more profitable than the preceding ones, is the Point of Departure approach. One sees this approach in many of the lounges and study rooms of departments of television studies, English, philosophy, psychology, and more. Having seen last night's episode, the "water cooler" conversation takes on the air of a somewhat more sophistication as the participants rehash the episode's more intriguing points. It is a short trip from rehashing the episode to noting that one feature or another of it can be used helpfully in advancing one's own views. Thus, Xander's behind the scenes actions in "The Zeppo Effect" become a vehicle for discussing the dynamics of exclusion from a group, of self-sacrifice, or of a coming of age arc. Similarly, one might use the empowerment of the Slayers in "Chosen" as a point of departure for discussing the nature of patriarchy, the state of feminism(s) in contemporary political and social philosophy, or the role of the heroine in an epic tale.

The Point of Departure approach to analysis is helpful, as far as it goes. Unfortunately, it does not go very far. Indeed, it is not a way of shedding light on the popular culture text before us at all. Instead, it is a way of using the popular culture event as a way of, at best, shedding light on some topic or theoretical framework in a wholly separate setting. The highly popular Philosophy and Popular Culture series generally follows this model, using the popular culture moment as an illumination of the work of some great philosopher. So, Buffy becomes an illustration to reflect on the existentialism of Kierkegaard, for example, in *Buffy and Philosophy: Fear and Trembling in Sunnydale*. The issue for the popular culture critic is this. In this model, the critical attention is not given to *Buffy* or *The Simpsons*, rather the attention is Kierkegaard and *Buffy* is a convenient, but wholly dispensable, foil. *Buffy* becomes just an interchangeable example. This approach to popular culture criticism has the often unintentional consequence of self-negation. If the subject under study is merely an interchangeable and, thus, essentially unimportant feature of a broader conversation, then it is much easier to conclude that *Buffy*, for example, is essentially unimportant. One can extend this to the breadth of the field of popular culture studies as a critique of the way in which much of it proceeds. Such an approach is most substantive than the others, but it still fails to take the text itself seriously enough to justify a separate scholarly investigation of it.

A fourth approach commonly found in popular culture critical circles is the Theory Exemplar model. It is very much akin to the Point of Departure model, however it has at least one distinguishing characteristic that makes it a superior, if still flawed, method of analysis. While the Point of Departure model simply uses *Buffy* as a starting point of the conversation, a starting point that is quickly abandoned for *serious* discussion of *weightier* texts, the Theory Exemplar approach grants a greater measure of *gravitas* to the popular culture text. To use *Buffy* as an example of a philosophical or psychological or literary theory, one must seriously engage the *Buffy* text. Scholars of Kant, for example, will be quick to note the inadequacies of using *Buffy* as an example of deontological duties if, in fact, the popular culture critic has done an inadequate job of justifying the view.

The difficulty with the Theory Exemplar view is similar to the Point of Departure view in that one still uses *Buffy* or any other popular culture artifact as a vehicle for illuminating a text other than itself. However, in the serious work that must be done to provide a clear comparison, some measure of critical worth is imputed to the popular culture illumination. At the same time, the text is still largely instrumental and its value is largely that of illuminative tool. One still fails to discern whether or not the text itself communicates anything of value.

The vast majority of popular culture studies fall into one of these four models. For these reasons, popular culture studies is often relegated to secondary status within the academy and seen as merely an interesting adjunct or sidebar to other disciplines. This volume is itself a critique of that approach to popular culture studies. Further, and more importantly, it is a bit of advocacy for another approach to popular culture texts. Let us call this approach the Critical Engagement approach.

Some of the essays in this volume fit nicely into the Theory Exemplar approach to popular culture studies. Most of them, however, stand as independent examinations of *Buffy* (and *Angel*) as texts in themselves and thus employ a Critical Engagement approach. A scholar critically engages a text when she brings her considerable training to the text and asks of the text what it is arguing. The approach is not a matter of discerning ways in which the text may be of instrumental use in some other venue, but rather of asking what intrinsic value may be found. In approaching *Buffy* this way, one is not asking "How can *Buffy* be used to discuss feminism or power?" Instead, one is asking, "What is it that *Buffy*, as a text, is arguing about feminism or power or whatever? What arguments are to be found within it?" One might conclude that the arguments are flawed, that the theories are specious, or that the text is unworthy of serious scholarly engagement. However, such conclusions would be based on the engagement with the text itself, and thus would represent the same sort of scholarship one expects of the philosopher who analyzes Aristotle's *Nicomachean Ethics* or the literary critic who explores Stoker's *Dracula*.

The Critical Engagement approach is the one most rarely seen in contemporary popular culture scholarship. Why this is something of a mystery to me. That it is mysterious, however, in no way detracts from the view that one should expect the same level of scholarly rigor from critics of popular culture that one expects from historians of Tudor/Stuart England or from archaeologists of ancient Troy. Popular culture studies will continue to suffer from second-class citizen status within contemporary academic scholarship until the majority of the scholarly work is done in this latter way. Failure to engage the text itself reduces the text and its importance to mere instrument. Such self-negating approaches have the deleterious effect of implying the negation of the entire field. The vast wealth of material to be gleaned from the study of popular culture is reason enough to commend its study and to indicate its own intrinsic value. This was the view of Plato and of Aristotle, the founders of perceptive critical and analytical theory. The choice for the modern critic is the same as the choice for our ancient ancestors— a serious engagement with the text or a capitulation to the view that popular culture studies are, at best, an adjunct to true scholarship, or, at worst, a trifling diversion unworthy of scholarly time and attention. It is the hope of the contributors to this volume that the choice to engage *Buffy* (and *Angel*) as a text is in keeping with the former choice.

Kevin K. Durand
Arkadelphia, Arkansas

# PART I. POWER AND THE *BUFFY* CANON

# Canon Fodder
## *Assembling the Text*

KEVIN K. DURAND

> ANYA: *Come on. Let's go assemble the cannon fodder.*
> XANDER: *That's not what we're calling them, sweetie.*
> ANYA: *Not to their faces. What am I — insensitive?*
> —"Choices"

Critical analysis of contemporary popular culture presents the scholar with many of the same difficulties faced by the scholar of Plato or the New Testament; difficulties not encountered by the one studying, for example, Bram Stoker's *Dracula* (the text, not the movie). For the critic of much of contemporary literature (or, for that matter, of literature of the last few hundred years), the first question faced by scholars of ancient philosophy and literature is largely absent. That question, "What is the text?," is a given, for the most part. With very few exceptions, literary critics whose field falls within the last few hundred years have little concern for matters of source criticism, redaction criticism, text criticism, or any of those fields concerned with the way in which the text before us came to be in its present form. There is simply the one version, and any alternate version or variant texts are almost always the product of the original authors. The question of what constitutes the canonical body of the author's work is a minor concern, if it rises to that level. This is clearly not the case for scholars of more ancient writings, nor, oddly enough, for scholars of contemporary popular culture.

To be sure, the cause of the difficulty of canonical inclusion and textual reconstruction differs from the ancient world to the present. Except in very special circumstances, the contemporary critic does not have to contend with the loss of manuscripts to the passage of time and the vagaries of political, religious, or tribal squabbles. Walt Disney's work is not put to the torch by angry mobs or buried in clay jars in the sand awaiting discovery by intrepid archaeologists. However, while the cause of the problem differs from then to now, the problem itself is strikingly similar. Given the variety of the works in a particular area, how does one determine which, among the competing texts, has canonical priority over the others. The case of *Buffy, the Vampire Slayer* is perhaps a perfect example of this scholarly conundrum.

Surveying the *Buffy* corpus, one is first met with the episodes as they aired, first on The WB and later on Fox. One might immediately suppose that these are the most accessible features of the textual Buffyverse and therefore that they may lay first claim to canonical priority. However, these are not the most widely accessible. The episodes air differently in original release and in syndication. Given the vastness of their popularity and their wide syndication, one might conclude that these shortened syndicated versions have canonical primacy if one were to use only the accessibility criterion as a measurement. With the release of the seven seasons on DVD, complete with commentary from the principals, including Whedon, one might suppose these to be canonically prior to any of the others. However, even these collections of episodes presented as originally aired fail in one very important respect as I will suggest a bit later in this essay.

The two aired versions of the text are not the only candidates for inclusion in the canon. Indeed, the recently released *Season Eight* Buffy comic books have been called canonical by Joss Whedon, himself. Further, there is the infamous Buffy movie which, though sharing a creator with the television show, is only loosely connected to it. The high school senior Buffy, played by Kristy Swanson in the *Buffy* movie is transmogrified into the sophomore Buffy, played by Sarah-Michelle Gellar, that we meet in "Welcome to the Hellmouth." In addition to all of these sources, we have the transcripts of the episodes on any number of internet sites and script books. These transcripts are the most widely cited source in scholarly work, apart from the aired episodes themselves. Behind all of these works, are the shooting scripts. Perhaps the least accessible of all of the elements of the textual Buffyverse, I argue that there is considerable reason to suppose that these least accessible elements are, in fact, the leading candidate for canonical primacy. To reach this conclusion, however, it is necessary to first consider the ways in which the canonical primacy problem of contemporary popular culture shares both form and possible solutions with its ancient counterpart. To carry the argument along, an analysis of a particularly pivotal scene from season seven will be helpful.

Perhaps the most obvious factor that accounts for the diversity in the textual variations of any television show is the rather rigid constraint placed upon the series by the medium and the economics that support it. The hour-long episode of prime time television in actuality amounts to roughly forty-two to forty-five minutes; the rest is taken with commercials. This time is divided into a "teaser" and four roughly equal parts. Syndication imposes more commercial time and thus further cuts to the episode as originally aired are required.

The *Buffy* franchise feels the cuts particularly acutely. One of the most critically acclaimed, innovative, and popular episodes of the series aired only once in its "as originally aired" format. "Once More, with Feeling," the *Buffy* musical, ran several minutes longer than the hour-long limit (closer to forty-eight minutes). Once. In rerun, it was cut to fit the regular time allotted. In syndication, it was cut even further. It would seem odd indeed to consider the "as originally aired" moment, ephemeral as it was, as the canonical mode of the series. Considering the DVD collection as canonically prior overcomes this difficulty because the episode as originally aired is not trimmed for time here. At least, it is not trimmed to fit the TV-hour time constraint. Unchanging, however, in this cutting and recutting is the shooting script. For the popular culture scholar, such a common text is to be preferred as expressing canonical primacy.

A recent addition has been made to the canonically sensitive scholar's difficulties. *Season Eight*, the comic version of *Buffy*, has been written and taken to press by Whedon. He, himself, distinguishes this text from all of the other many *Buffy* novels, articles, and fanfic by naming it the canonical continuation of the series. Only the comic series carries the imprimatur of the creator, leaving the field of canonization and priority within the canon open to considerable argument. No one seriously argues that the episodes as aired, the transcripts of those episodes, the DVD collections, and the shooting scripts are *not* canonical. The arguments are more a matter of emphasis and primacy — which is basic and foundational in the development of the scholarly interpretation of the Buffyverse. The argument that the shooting scripts should be taken as having canonical priority proceeds from external issues like air time and syndication to an examination of the series internally; that is, to an examination of the show with respect to its texts and the ways in which the texts contribute to a narrative beyond themselves. To defend the controversial and perhaps counterintuitive thesis that the shooting scripts ought to be considered canonically primary, it is instructive to look to perhaps *the* pivotal moment of season seven — Buffy's "Choices" speech in "Chosen."

Even the most cursory survey of the two versions of the "Choices" speech reveals significant variations. The question becomes whether or not those variations are substantial. I think it rather clear that they are.

Not all of the variants are substantial in the sense that they introduce a different interpretation of the text of the Buffyverse. For example, in the shooting script, Buffy says, "I hate that there's evil, that it's growing, and I hate that I was chosen to fight it." That the evil is growing is absent from the episode as aired. However, nothing important is lost with this omission as the entire arc of season seven expresses this dilemma faced by the Scooby gang. On the other hand, there are four variations from the shooting script that can be read as substantial alterations of the aired text. Three are omissions and one is a substitution.

The first omission has to do with Buffy having been chosen to replace her never named predecessor. She says, in the shooting script concerning her choice, "I never had one. I was chosen. And I accept that. I'm not asking you to accept anything. I'm asking you to make your own choice." Among the most controversial issues in the analysis of the Buffyverse and Whedon's vision has to do with the anti–patriarchal/female empowerment/feminist story arc. The scene of the unexpected empowerment of oppressed women and girls is emotionally satisfying. In the context of overthrowing the legacy of the psychical/metaphysical rape of the first slayer by the Shadow Men, it is even moreso. However, many have noted that there is a troubling undercurrent. Has Buffy substituted one expression of patriarchal power (her own) for that of the Shadow Men and the Watchers? I argue in a later essay in this volume, "Are You Ready to Finish This?," that this is not case. However, I must also acknowledge those who suggest that what I take to be a moment of empowerment is actually somewhat less positive.

Central to my own interpretation there was the overthrow of the patriarchal legacy of the Shadow Men and the Watchers, on the one hand, and the mutual sharing of power through the magic of the scythe, on the other. Such an interpretation, however, suffers significantly if those who are empowered have no more choice than Buffy or the First Slayer. With the power of the Slayer comes the responsibility of facing the forces of evil and a radically altered understanding of the world in which the new Slayer lives—the things that go bump in the night have more form and substance than they previously did. Such radical alterations in worldview can be supremely destabilizing, an issue Whedon faces in *Angel* when Angel finds he must face a slayer who has been imprisoned in a mental institution because she has suffered greatly with this new power, a power with which she cannot cope.

In one sense, I would argue that this is one of the consequences of the fact that surviving the apocalypse and literally reforming the power structure of the world is never neat and clean and problem-free. But that argument would ring hollow if the restructuring was a bartering of one form of patriarchy for another. The rejection of that sort of restructuring turns on a fundamental feature—choice.

While in both the shooting script and the episode as aired Buffy seems to give those with her a choice, that choice is not nearly so robust in the episode. In both cases, the "Choices" speech ends with, "So, here's the part where you make a choice." In the episode, though, it does not seem nearly as strong. In fact, it seems almost rhetorical. In the shooting script, however, the line is magnified. There, Buffy recognizes that she is one of a long line of girls who never had a choice. She says, "But this isn't about wishes. This is about choices. I never had one." Present in the shooting script, but absent from the episode is the following, "I was chosen. And I accept that. I'm not asking you to accept anything. I'm asking you to make your own choice." Whether or not she accepts this state of affairs, although she says that she does, is not completely relevant. What is relevant is that she extends to others a choice that she did not have. She will not make them accept a role that was forced on her. She does not coerce them; she persuades. In this persuasion, she honors the self-direction and autonomy of each of the potentials. Indeed, they are no longer potentials; they are individual girls and women who are recognized as full human beings, fully capable of making self-determining decisions.

The line, "I'm not asking you to accept anything. I'm asking you to make a choice" forms a frame, along with the "here's the part where you make a choice," that brackets the discussion of evil, plans, and the dilemma facing them all. It gives a weight and substance to what, without it, can simply be seen as a fig leaf covering up a power grab. The omission of the shooting script text from the episode certainly makes it more difficult to defend the view that the season seven arc is a text of empowerment and anti-patriarchy from the suggestion that a more sinister subtext permeates the episode.

Having addressed the first omission, let us turn to a textual shift, the change of an "it" to a "this." At first read, a change of this sort would seem relatively unimportant. However, even such a small change can have significant import. In the shooting script, Buffy says, "Tomorrow morning, I'm opening the Seal. I'm going down into the Hellmouth and I'm going to finish it once and for all." In the aired episode, the line has the "this" for "is"— "Tomorrow morning I'm opening the Seal. I'm going down into the Hellmouth and I'm finishing this once and for all."

When Buffy says that she is going to "finish *this*" (emphasis mine) in the episode, one is given to understand that the referent of "this" is much broader than the current Big Bad. The First Evil is the most pressing incarnation of evil, to be sure, but "this" seems to have a much broader scope. As the season comes to its apocalyptic and cataclysmic conclusion, "this" seems to refer to the Buffy arc itself, to the patriarchal imposition upon the slayer line, to the First Evil gathering an army, and to the wait to take the fight to them. In this case, the text shift seems to provide further support for the interpretation that the preceding omission supports.

On the other hand, reading the "it" does not argue against the prior interpretation, but it does limit the sweep of Buffy's speech. "It" has a very clear antecedent. "I believe we can beat this evil.... I'm going to finish it." Here, the "it" referred to can only pick out the "evil" and given that the "evil" is specified, it must refer to the First Evil, the one gathering an army beneath the Seal, the one that Buffy aims to finish. An earlier omission from the shooting script in the episode seems to support this narrower reading. As Buffy opens her "Choices" speech in the shooting script, she says that "I hate that there's evil, *that it's growing*, and I hate that I was chosen to fight it (emphasis mine). The "it" that is growing is clearly the evil that opposes the Slayer and her friends. That the pattern repeats, "evil" followed by "it" making the reference to the "evil" tends, in this case to focus the speech on the matter at hand.

If the episode followed this pattern, the disquieting undercurrent would be even more problematic. "I'm going to finish it once and for all" is the cry of the hero out to slay the dragon; it is a claim of power and dominance. The episode has to have the more sweeping "this" and its broadening of scope to the patriarchal problem in order to avoid the overly simplistic and predictable final battle between the champions of good and evil. There is no new structure of power and responsibility here — only the continuation of a timeless (and hierarchical) power structure and struggle. This seems a much more pedestrian aim than the sweeping and radical overthrow of the power of oppression itself.

The shooting script has considerably more nuance and depth to it. While the particular "it" has a quite narrow focus, the broader speech does not. It is both an expression of the narrow conflict with the First *and* the universal conflict with patriarchy within which the particular battle is situated. In the shooting script, "it" is bracketed with the claims about choosing and a recapitulation of the choiceless history of the Slayer line. Thus, the "it" of this attempt by the First is seen as a part of a more significant and sinister whole, one that the empowerment of the Slayers is imagined to overcome. So, the shift does not harm the shooting script or the interpretation of the shooting script as the canonical foundation because it is situated within a more nuanced whole. At the same time, it points to how very precarious the episode's balance is. Preserving the "it" from the shooting script into the episode would, in fact, detract, perhaps disastrously, from the positive empowerment arc.

The third difference between the shooting script and the episode, and the second omission from the latter present in the former, is of the least importance of any. In the shooting script, Buffy lists her assets, "I've got strong allies: warriors, charms, sorcerers, and I'll need them all. But I'll also need you. Every single one of you." While it seems like it should enhance the claim Buffy makes that the slayers-to-be are of great importance, it rather seems to diminish them. This diminution is not mitigated by the reiterated statement of need. At the same time, this passage is consistent with the interpretation that the moment of choice is more about cosmic restructuring than a single moment of conflict with the Big Bad of the month.

The final omission may be the most striking of them all and may provide the strongest justification for holding that the shooting script is primary in the order of canonization. Serious and vexing question about the nature of the Buffyverse are answered here to some extent. Among the topics are the nature of the Slayer line and the selection of a slayer when her predecessor dies.

When Buffy died briefly ("I was only gone for a minute" from "What's My Line, Part Two") at the end of Season One ("Prophecy Girl"), a new Slayer, Kendra, was called. When Kendra was killed by Drusilla in "Becoming, Part One," Faith was called. The existence of two Slayers at the same time was unique in the case of Buffy/Kendra. The question that arises from this new situation is whether the Slayer line has forked, in essence creating two lines, or has the line continued with Kendra and her successor, Faith, leaving Buffy as an abandoned side channel. The crux of this question is whether or not another Slayer would be called if Buffy were to die. This issue was made more obvious, and seemingly settled, when Buffy died a second time, this time in season five's "The Gift." As a new slayer was not called to replace her, it seems clear that her ability to pass on the gift was a one time thing.

This runs counter to the shooting script of "Chosen," authored by Whedon. Here, Whedon offers a different answer to this question, answering it in an odd way, and one that seems to have a contradictory implication for the Buffyverse. I know of no speculation in the Slayer Succession question in which the death of both Slayers would be required to activate a new one. Whedon's suggested solution, here, is extraordinary in that respect. However, there is a problematic consequent. If it is the case that both Buffy and Faith would have to die in order for a new Slayer to be called, this casts some doubt on the call of Faith. After all, only Kendra's death was requisite for Faith's calling and no new Slayer was called after Buffy's death in "The Gift."

How should this passage be addressed, then? What import does this passage and its interpretation have on my suggestion that the shooting scripts have canonical priority over the episodes? I will treat these in reverse order.

The fields of text criticism (lower criticism) and source and redaction redaction criticism (higher criticism) have taken as almost an axiom of reconstruction of ancient texts from various fragments that one should give privilege to the more difficult reading. Certainly, the inclusion of this passage, rather than its omission, creates the more difficult reading. This is clearly not conclusive or determinant on its own, but it does serve as a caution for the scholar who seeks to disregard the shooting script in favor of the episode as a way of avoiding difficulties of this sort.

So, how do we address this difficult passage? My suggestion is this. Buffy is not infallible. The character does not really comprehend "the rule." She grasps the underlying structure — the Shadow Men and their descendents, the Watchers, and the First and its minions are instantiations of an oppressive power that must be overthrown by a shared power. She does not necessarily grasp the arcane rules. This seems quite consistent with Buffy's character as developed throughout the seven seasons. Buffy is never portrayed as the one who immerses herself in detail. So, it is not overly difficult to imagine that she simply gets "the rule" wrong.

Throughout the foregoing analysis of the divergent varieties of the text, I have suggested that the shooting script is to be preferred for canonical priority over the episode. The shooting script provides the richer and more nuanced text of the Buffyverse. The "Chosen" scene is but a single example of a broader tendency, that of excising meaning for space. That so much important text is consigned to the cutting room floor for the sake of time and the meeting of onerous and episode-independent constraints is reason to prefer the shooting script as the most complete version of the artistic vision expressed in *Buffy*, even in the face of the DVD collection.

Finally, the artistic vision and artistic intent seem to be present more fully in the shooting script. Thus, we can safely conclude that the *Buffy* canon, though widely, and perhaps, wildly, diverse, is rooted in the shooting script. As a result, the critic of *Buffy*, the text, ought start with the canonically primary shooting script in the critical and/or interpretive enterprise.

# Canon Fodder Revisited
## Buffy *Meets the Bard*

### Brent Linsley

In the tradition of literary studies, the text is the crucial issue underlying every argument made within the field of analysis. Only with the text itself can one create an argument or shed light on key issues that illuminate human development and understanding. Although this is a statement with which few would likely disagree, we should examine it further to reach the heart of the problem of the text found in the subset of popular culture studies dealing with the analysis of television.

Even in declaring a "tradition of literary studies," one concedes a set of procedures commonly agreed upon through time, establishing "tradition." From the beginning of this phrase, and hence the beginning of this essay, and presumably from the beginning of academic inquiry into the analysis of the subject of literature, the canonical issue is forefront. Tradition itself is a type of canon, albeit a canon of method and practice as opposed to the canon of text, or even of Literature, and Canon is most certainly little more than an established tradition. Still, the sets of tradition within literary and philosophical fields comprise the basis for all study in the humanities. Thus the text itself is the heart of academic inquiry in the analytical arts, whatever shape and form that text takes. *Buffy the Vampire Slayer* provides a suitable basis for discussion regarding the variances of these texts in the different formats of their existence.

One thing the scholar of Shakespeare knows quite well: different versions of texts exist. Further, there are competing versions of a text, notably between the quarto and folio editions, neither of which Shakespeare himself had a hand in publishing. What is more troubling for the Bard's band of merry scholars is that none of the existing versions of the text survive in Shakespeare's hand; in fact, only six signatures, all on legal documents, survive. Some have argued that even these signatures are invalid, written by law clerks, though normally their purpose in discrediting these signatures is to paint Shakespeare as illiterate in order to then advance an argument of authorial variance. There are also a few pages of the play *Sir Thomas More* that some believe to be in Shakespeare's hand as part of a collaboration in his later career, an argument that continues to gain support in Shakespearean textual studies. Controversies have arisen surrounding the authorship of Shakespeare's plays as a direct result of these issues, varying from the seemingly plausible to the downright ridiculous. While the conundrum confronting television scholars is not so blatant, the issues of authorship and textual primacy closely resemble, in their own ways, the troubles confronting the field of Shakespearean studies over the past few centuries.

Within television studies, the shape and form of the text can come in several different varieties, the three most commonly used being the shooting script, the episode as aired, and the DVD (and, in the near future, Blu-Ray) release. All three of these formats have significant strengths and weaknesses, and each television studies scholar has the duty to evaluate these strengths and weaknesses in order to establish a canonical priority in academic use. As television studies becomes more and more accepted and practiced within the academy, establishing a hierarchy of the text is necessary to standardize the field of study and formulate a common language of scholarship.

The first format to analyze is that of the episode as aired. Although there are perhaps the most advantages to this particular format, its impracticalities render it nearly useless to the scholar. With this version of the text, the format of the television episode is used to its greatest benefit. In a normal hour-long television episode, the content is broken into several parts: a teaser, the opening credits, then normally four acts, followed by the closing credits. Here these act breaks are used for a specific purpose: while the breaks themselves allow for the commercial advertisements that financially keep the show on the air, the evolution of the structure of the television episode demands that these commercial breaks be points of tension that develop and move a plot along in a very orderly, organized fashion. With the intermittent commercial breaks, the tension created by each act is used to its fullest extent through the delay of each subsequent act. The tension created is much like that of turning a page or reading through an act break in a drama. Often times, when the program resumes, a slight recap or a repeating shot is used to re-establish the dramatic tension and remind the audience of what is at stake in a given scene. These act breaks, in other formats, are somewhat less effective, especially in the DVD.

Of course, the major problem of this particular argument is that the experience of watching or studying an episode in this version of the text is fixed in time. Although transcripts of the episodes as they air are available, those transcripts fail to address every aspect of the episode, most notably in the visual arena. As television is primarily a visual medium, this deficiency detracts from the substantive content of the series text. The episodes are aired originally only once, and often times their syndicated versions are cut substantially to make room for extra advertisements. The syndicated versions will also often cut episodes in different places, so that the buildup of tension is radically different. There is nothing to prevent a scholar from looking at these versions of the text comparatively (except perhaps for time itself), and an investigation into the changes caused by such manipulations of the episode could prove quite interesting, especially in light of the consumerist society that creates such perversions. The problem is simply one of availability.

The DVD version of the text offers a solution to this conundrum. Although in Shakespeare there is no such thing as a canonical performance, what scholar wouldn't want to take a trip through time to examine how the play was first run on the stage? Even without this opportunity, several scholars choose to study the reviews and journal entries that deal with the specifics of these performances and their evolutions throughout time.

With the DVD versions of the text, we don't have to time travel. Time has been preserved for us. With very little different from the originally aired content (except in some cases where a series has been digitally altered, or the music has been changed to accommodate issues of media legality), the DVD option often contains not only the episode but also extras, such as commentaries, deleted scenes, and sometimes even the shooting scripts themselves. The awkward cuts of the syndicated versions are gone. The only major hindrance to looking at this version of the text is that there are no breaks whatsoever. The tension built up within each act is too easily allayed and, and re-establishing shots become somewhat repetitive and even misleading in rare cases.

This being said, the argument for the shooting script and its use within academic study is a bit more complex and deserves more attention before we can comfortably dismiss it. Here we find the television episode in what is likely its most diverse format from what is commonly accepted as television. Most of the basic elements of the television episode are present in this format, although signified by words instead of visual imagery and sound. While the postmodern mind is more adaptive toward the more sensory elements displayed on screen and through speakers, the words used in a shooting script are often *action* oriented, and visual and auditory cues will usually be printed in uppercase lettering. The shooting script can also somewhat deviate from a more standardized format, though not by much. As speeches and scenes are allowed to be somewhat longer and more complex, there is often more development in this particular text than in any of the other versions available.

One other important note to consider in the evaluation of the differences between shooting script and episode is the collaborative nature of the proj-

ect. If we turn to the season seven episode "Chosen," which the previous article examined (and to which I myself will turn momentarily), we find that
Joss Whedon both writes and directs this episode. Here we do not have a
competing philosophical vision of the series, where a writer may have a
slightly different interpretation of the *Buffy* message. This is an extremely
important factor to consider in evaluating the differences between episode and
shooting script. A director who is not a writer (or at least not the writer of
that episode) may have a different interpretation of the script than intended
by the original writer. In the case where this does occur, the question of textual primacy is crucial.

I would argue that, given the nature of contemporary society and the
format of television and the process of creating a television episode, the textual primacy must go to the episode over the shooting script. Television is a
collaborative medium. No one person can fulfill every role necessary for the
completion of a single episode. As a mirror of our increasingly globalized
society, this is a point conceded at the beginning of work on an episode or a
series. The episode becomes the product of a community of people; even in
the writers' room there is normally collaboration in the conception of
episodes. This communal development is one that continues, some would
say, even into the viewership and scholarship of the episode or series, wherein
the discourses surrounding a text create a community of knowledge. This
concept of community is one that pervades out culture and cannot be ignored.

As noted in the previous article, these differences can at least seem quite
substantial. Recall the discussion of the "Choices" speech from "Chosen,"
addressed at length in the previous essay. While the passages certainly seem
at variance, I argue that the differences are not necessarily as extensive as has
been suggested. I argue that the changes made, where significant departures
do exist, are changes that support the reading of the episode over the shooting script, when and where those changes are not simply alterations that must
be made to form a cohesive whole for the episode and its place within the
mythological and philosophical context of the series. In the latter case, obviously, the change would also indicate the reading of the episode over the
shooting script as the more complete text.

In the first major omission from the shooting script to the aired/DVD
text, the major philosophical overtone of the series is truly at conflict. Buffy's
lines concerning her lack of a choice echo to the other potentials in the final
version of the speech. That she never had a choice is not a minor point; rather
it is the pivotal philosophical and theoretical moment of the series. The fact
that Buffy had no choice in becoming a slayer, that she, in fact, expresses several times over the course of the series that she does not even want the responsibility, is hammered home in this final episode's shooting script, but for the

watcher of Buffy through its development, this line is extraneous. Nothing is gained by its inclusion in the final version, except for the casual viewer who may not be aware of Buffy's struggles. In this sense, cutting the line seems to be a matter for the saving of time; after all, Whedon could have cut from several places in this episode, yet he chooses to make cuts in this particular speech.

Of course, there is a huge difference created by the missing line, one that has major significance and points yet again to the crux of the philosophical and theoretical framework of the series. That Buffy had no choice in becoming a slayer symbolizes the burden placed upon her by the Shadow Men and their metaphysical rape of the first Slayer. The line which follows, "I accept that," while a clear contradiction of earlier passages regarding her struggle with the topic, works against the feminist framework of the series. Accepting her circumstances seems somewhat complacent in a moment where her power is being used to fight the very forces (man's evil against humanity) that resulted in her gaining this power in the first place. On the theoretical level, the fact that Buffy fights against the evil and the patriarchal construct is the furthest thing from passivity regarding her circumstances. The whole message behind the series calls on women to use the power given to them without simply "accepting" their circumstances. This particular omission reflects and amplifies this.

The situation is much more complex than this, though. As the omission continues, the next sentence cut is, "I'm not asking you to accept anything." The initial reaction might be to read this line as though Buffy acknowledges that her acceptance of circumstances might be somewhat passive, and that further generations of women merely "accepting" their oppression would run counter to the fight against the evils of the patriarchal construct. While this would seem to address the previous issue, coupled with the next sentence, it poses a serious problem. Buffy continues, in the shooting script, "I'm asking you to make your own choice." At the end of the speech is a similar line, wherein Buffy announces that this is "the part where [the potentials] make a choice." One could make the argument that this repetition is the cause for such an omission, and that the statement at the end of the speech adds emphasis to the issue of the choice; however, the actual situation is far different, and reading the omission in light of the scenario discussed yields a much different, much more disturbing result.

The simple truth is that these potentials do not have much of a choice, if in fact any choice exists. Although Buffy insists that they do have the ability to choose, her decision to have Willow use the power of the scythe to give all the potentials the power of the slayer usurps any pretext of a choice on the part of the potentials. Once Willow performs the spell, they will have the power, no matter what decisions they might make. As expressed in the previous article, with power comes responsibility. By forcing this responsibility onto every potential alive, Buffy's decision over the fates of the women surrounding her varies little in theory (although perhaps significantly in technique) from the decision made by the Shadowmen to create the first Slayer generations ago, and the decisions to keep the power of the Slayer in line by the Watchers. This creates a very negative interpretation of Buffy's decision, as it subjects the potentials to a new source of oppression: she no longer *asks* them to make a choice; she informs them that they must. Any consideration of the autonomy of these girls is merely superficial. As they still do not have control over their own physical bodies (as Buffy's decision usurps any control they might naturally have), Buffy becomes a source of oppression to replace the Shadowmen and the Watchers. If we view Buffy as signifying an earlier generation of feminism and the potentials a later generation seeking female liberation, this conflict could come to represent the dissent within various sects of feminist thought and action. The change to the episode's final project seems to avoid this conflict within the scope of this episode and give the fight over Sunnydale a more positive context without running the risk of villainizing Buffy, but the elimination of the request made by Buffy (that the potentials make a choice) subverts the overall message. If we are, as the preceding article suggests, to seek the more difficult reading, I have to argue that the speech, as presented in the episode, presents that case.

Turning to the substitution of "this" for "it," the broadening of the scope sheds light on Buffy's motivation for action in regards to this decision. As noted above, Buffy often expresses throughout the series her desire to leave the responsibilities of the slayer line. By saying that she is going to "finish this" as opposed to "finish it," she moves beyond the scope of the First Evil to her situation and responsibility as Slayer. As "it" would refer to the First Evil, the change could serve as a mere corrective; as the First Evil has no corporeal form and cannot be defeated through the fight, Buffy's conflict is more with the army assembled by the First instead of the First itself. By saying "this" within the episode, the conflict becomes a conflict against the order of the patriarchy and her own role as Slayer. As we learn in the fifth season of *Angel*, Buffy indeed takes time off from Slayer duties. In a radical interpretation, by viewing this omission along with the final exclusion from the shooting script text, one could argue that Buffy's mission is a suicidal one, where "this" becomes the entire drama of human life, a conflict that seems to grow consistently from the end of the fifth season of *Buffy* through the series finale.

Though perhaps less important on the surface than the previously discussed alterations from the shooting script to the episode, Buffy's acknowledgement (or lack thereof) of those helping her does have an impact on the speech and the episode. The presence of the lines in the shooting script some-what echo the tradition of the catalogue in ancient epics. Its presence might therefore add to the epic conflict against the patriarchal hierarchy. Its omission transforms the speech, the episode, and the series. *Buffy* becomes a struggle of the individual against the oppressive order, undercutting somewhat the more universal aspect of women's struggles to empower themselves and to use that power effectively. What is missing in the omission is Buffy's acknowledgement that she sometimes needs help. Again, the omission of this need might point once more to the struggles within the structure of feminism in the quest for individual autonomy. By not acknowledging the assistance she receives as well as the assistance she needs, her power is emphasized, and the process of her individual empowerment with which the series is concerned becomes more significant.

The final omission is perhaps less significant than it may seem on the surface, although the inclusion in the shooting script is quite interesting. When Buffy states that both she and Faith would have to die for a new Slayer to be called, she speaks in apparent error. As Faith was called after the death of Kendra, Buffy's death should play no role in the calling of a new slayer. After her death at the end of season five, we see no evidence of a new slayer's calling, although this does not necessarily exclude the possibility that, within the Buffyverse, a slayer was called who never appeared. Still, the statement offered in the shooting script would suggest that only one true slayer *should* exist. This statement can be read as an ideological continuation of the patriarchal hierarchy established by the Shadowmen and Watchers' Council. Deleting it before filming would be a corrective measure to preserve the feminist framework, not to mention the potential problem with continuation.

But perhaps the best argument in support of using the episode (DVD or otherwise) over the shooting script can be seen where the speech is taken up again, and we see the second half in each context. The visual cue for the shooting script is quite lacking: "And we lay in a *series of images* to be *intercut* with the living room scene. Some of Buffy's speech we see, some we just hear over the images."

And that's it.

Nothing specific. No young girl suddenly hitting a softball out of the park at a little league game. No young woman leaning against lockers in a swoon over the first breath of power. No girl on the floor suddenly realizing their strength with great heaves. No girl standing up at the table during a family dinner. No young woman standing up to the (obviously male) hand about to strike. No specifics on slayer potentials coming into power in preparation for the fight against the First's army. These are some of the most powerful images of the episode, and possibly the series. The shooting script gives us none of them. Just a "*series of images.*" But isn't that the nature of television itself? A visual medium?

The shortcomings of the shooting script in instances like this are more than somewhat disappointing. While the reading of the texts themselves are perhaps most enlightening when several sources are viewed in conjunction with one another, the canonical primacy should not be granted to incomplete versions of the text. The visual imagery is simply too important to be ignored. This leaves us with the canonical performance offered by the episode in its final form, most accessible on the DVD format (at least for those with the money to purchase the seasons on DVD or those with an active library card). Although for the scholars of Shakespeare we can offer no such remedy, for the scholars of Buffy, the choice exists.

# Genre and the Impact on Storytelling in *Season Eight*

## LEIGH CLEMONS

Reactions to *Season Eight* of *Buffy the Vampire Slayer* have been mixed, with fans both loving it and hating it simultaneously. Some reviewers feel that the shift from television to comic book has deprived the series of its wit and edge (and some of its ethics), while others acknowledge that the freedom the new format provides allows for ideas previously unimaginable to fly. The series, though still not yet half finished, has already garnered some impressive credentials due to its writing. *Buffy Season Eight* is penned by a coterie of well-known authors, most of them with previous attachments to some aspect of the Whedonverse, in general, and *Buffy*, in particular. March 14, 2007, was the release date of Issue #1, the issue that went on to win the Diamond Gem Award for Comic Book of the Year, under $3.00 and the Diamond Gem Award for Licensed Comic of the Year (Melrose). The series was also nominated for two Eisner Awards: one for Best New Series and another for Best Continuing Series. With all this good press, plus the strong built in fan base, it seems that *Season Eight* is destined to fill its total run of 40 issues, even though predictions are it may take over two years for the series to play out. Since the course of *Season Eight* is still in flux, I focus here on the "closed" story arcs, and, as a result, this essay is focused on the first fifteen issues.

Some fans have begun to express their displeasure over decisions made in the storyline, just as they did in the television series. For example, a letter from one fan debates the ethics of Issue 5, "The Chain," which shows the beginning and end of one of *Buffy*'s doppelgangers and compares the recruitment of her to the post as unethical "brainwashing." Another letter briefly touches on Buffy's decision to fund the Slayer operation by stealing from Swiss bank accounts, and how that decision intersects with the character "Twilight" and his use of the U.S. Army to bring down and destroy the Slayers ("Wolves at the Gate, Part Two"). In many ways, however, this trend is no different than those that arrived when Whedon introduced the Tara/Willow or Buffy/Spike storylines later in the series. What is interesting is that, for the first time, *Buffy* is tackling ethical concerns, not merely sexual pairings. While the latter are important, it is this new territory that promises to make *Season Eight* more than a "jump the shark" into a new genre.

What are comics? Scott McCloud defines comics as "pictoral and other images in a deliberate sequence, intended to convey information and/or produce an aesthetic response in the viewer" (McCloud 9). Comics have been around for ages; some would say they are ancient. They have covered all types of stories: superheroes, villains, Nazis, and just everyday generic folks. Comics also contain all types of aesthetic styles: from the pseudo-realistic work of Tom King to the hyper-abstraction of Mary Fleener. While it has taken some time, comics are finally starting to gain respect as both an art form and a storytelling medium, not as a simple cult genre. Whatever the reasoning, comics have a strong following among a variety of age groups because of their ability to transform the natural into "things and people, real or imagined, moving in space and changing over time, as transformed through somebody's eye and hand" (Wolk 118).

Psychologists call *liminal space*, a place where boundaries dissolve a little and we stand there, on the threshold, getting ourselves ready to move across the limits of what we were into what we are to be." The term has been used primarily by Victor Turner, who calls it "a space of transformation between phases of separation and reincorporation. It represents a period of ambiguity, of marginal and transitional state." Other theorists who have used the term include Arnold van Gennep, Edward Said, Homi Bhabha, and Sharon Zukin.

How is *Season Eight* liminal? Comics are a form of liminal art, consisting of both pictures and words working together in various forms of abstraction to tell a story. "The cartoon is a vacuum into which our identity and awareness are pulled ... an empty shell we inhabit which enables us to travel in another realm. We don't just observe the cartoon, we become it!" (McCloud 36). Yet since we also retain our own senses of self and solidity, we exist in a liminal space when interacting with the world of the comic. *Season Eight* also works as a liminal space through three additional ways: the abstraction of characters through drawing representation, the use of closure to fully involve the reader in the process and make the story work, and the juxtaposition of time and space on the printed page.

Comics operate heavily in the world of the symbol, be it the representation of the characters themselves or movement on the comics world. They work, according to Douglas Wolk, because of their use of "symbolic abstraction" and "interpretive distortion" (Wolk 120, 122). The drawings of Buffy and the other characters, while somewhat realistic, still operate on within the world of the cartoon because they are somewhat abstracted. As Scott McCloud tells us, "By de-emphasizing the appearance of the physical world in favor of the idea of form the cartoon places itself in the world of concepts" (McCloud 41). The comic is then free to further explore how these concepts work aesthetically, whereas more realistically-based forms of representation are bound by their resemblance to reality. "Abstraction through simplification," says McCloud, reinforces the storytelling ability of the cartoon image because "By stripping down an image to its specific meaning an artist can amplify that meaning in a way that realistic art can't" (McCloud 30).

This technique is obvious throughout the series. Even though different artists are responsible for penning the characters, each retains some universal characteristics of facial shape and hair color (or some other defining characteristic, like Xander's eye patch), but not enough so that the drawing is photographic in its look. So far, Willow has managed to look the most like Willow, although all characters are recognizable to some extent. Her first appearance, in "The Long Way Home, Part Two, " leaves no doubt as to who she is (through a mixture of dialogue and character appearance). The more universal the character, however, the greater the number of people who will be able to identify with it. (This is why the generic "smiley face" is a more universal symbol than, say, a painting of a person, famous or otherwise.) So, the decision to keep Buffy's visage more neutral in most drawings helps to broaden her appeal to the viewer, and highlights those moments when she is drawn in a more realistic fashion, which tend to be moments of higher tension.

The second way in which comics work liminally is through what is called "closure." Closure is, according to McCloud, "observing the parts, but perceiving the whole" (McCloud 61). Closure is an everyday occurrence; we use it to help make connections between objects and events. Film and television also use closure, just as they use sequences of static images. The major difference is that, in film and television, the static images are moving at many frames per second, whereas the comic relies on upon individual images to tell its story.

Closure in comics works because of the convention called "the gutter," or the space between enclosed panels. In this space, the mind of the reader makes the necessary connections to tie the two (or more) panels together, in effect creating the story individually in his/her own mind. In the words of McCloud, "to kill a man between panels is to condemn him to a thousand deaths" (McCloud 69). These deaths, or feelings, or other actions, depending upon the nature of the panel, are all the result of the reader's interaction and imagination with the picture/text, not the result of the director's feeding the image and dialogue to the viewer. In Issue 14, Buffy brings the corpse of the Japanese Slayer Aiko back to the Slayer compound through a series of action-to-action shots (more about this in a moment) which focus on Buffy carrying the body through a crowd of young Slayers. The perspective changes with each panel (one head on, one shot from above, one from the high right), so the viewer must fill in the changes in angle. Television shows change angle so quickly that most viewers are unaware of what is happening; the static nature of comics, however, puts much more of the onus on the reader to be an active participant in the storytelling.

Space plus time is an important aspect of the way in which comics work, one that differs from the manner in which television works. While Scott McCloud believes that one could define film much like comics (visual art in sequence), film's frames occupy the same space in a continuous flow, whereas comics occupy successive spaces (McCloud 7). However, both definitions do raise the importance of time to the telling of the story in comics. Comic books use different types of transitions to move along the action. Unlike video, where the action is continuously moving forward, it is possible to see comic book action running both forward and backward, depending upon the layout of the panels.

There are different types of time transitions, according to McCloud, from ones that show the most infinitesimal movements (moment-to-moment) to those that have absolutely no relationship to one another (*non sequitur*) (McCloud 70, 72). Issue 13 ("Wolves at the Gate, Part Two") opens with "fifteen minutes earlier" before Xander arrives to see Dracula. McCloud calls this a scene-to-scene transition, where the action jumps back and forth between two or more people, places, or times. Part Four of the same series ends with a series of scene-to-scene panels held together by Dracula's voice-over narration. At the final panels of Issue 15 Dracula, headed home in his ship, does a voiceover narration, "We have a cold journey ahead of us ... find what warmth you can for now ... and I'll stand watch alone" while the scenes cut from him on his ship to Willow conjuring up the goddess she saw earlier (in "Anywhere But Here") to Buffy and Satsu in bed to Xander disposing of Renee's ashes. Dracula's narrative helps to unify the scenes and give them context by pairing the dialogue pieces with certain frames of the comic.

The layout of the page also affects the presentation of time in the comic. As McCloud points out, in comics, "the past is more than just memories and the future is more than just possibilities. The past and future are real and visible all around us!" (McCloud 104). Layout on the page makes that difference visible. The movement of the eye over the page creates the time span. This movement can be left to right, top to bottom, as in traditional "text," but the comic can also use insets, reverse panels and other formats to break up this traditional way of reading, as in the opening pages of Issue 1. The "background panels" show Buffy and her Slayers facing demons; the inset is an extreme close-up of Buffy's face telling us her inner thoughts ("Their first victims. Gotta get 'em past it.") and her orders to her troops ("Flank 'em. Now."). Once again, we get Buffy's inner monologue, but it does not prevent other action from occurring simultaneously.

An unique form of temporal representation used by the comic is the polyptich. In it, a moving figure is superimposed over a continuous, contiguous background. This device is used to introduce and sustain the concept of time passing within the comic. This technique is used in the comic in Issue 1 to introduce Giant Dawn. The artists use a two-page spread of Dawn, drawn over individual side-by-side panels; then, they overlay Buffy in various positions within each panel. The two are having an argument, so the combination of Buffy's shift in position into each panel and the words help to keep the action moving.

Finally, differences in space and time are communicated by the size of the panels, which can range from the small to double-page spreads. The larger the panel, the greater the impact, so large panels are used sparingly. *Buffy* likes to use large panels to introduce the return of a new character, especially early on. Issue 1 ends with the return of Amy; Issue 2 with Willow, and Issue 3 with Warren. Each character gets a full-page panel to herald his/her entrance and provide more impact. Other important moments get full page spreads, such as Renee's impalement by the Tokyo vampires at the end of Issue 14. While large panels don't challenge the reader to make many connections, they do make a subconscious impact as to the importance of the moment being watched.

The differences in genre between the comic book and the television show also make it possible to get inside a character's (namely Buffy's) head on a far more regular basis, using the thought text boxes. The television show, like all forms of scripted text, had to rely on dialogue to fill in gaps or to make issues explicit. Only in "Once More, With Feeling" did we get songs that manifest characters' inner feelings ("Going through the Motions," "Standing," "Under Your Spell/Standing Reprise"). Issue 1 opened with a Buffy interior monologue under the action of her and three other slayers jumping out of a helicopter, "The thing about changing the world ... once you do it, the world's all different. Everybody calls me 'ma'am' these days. There used to be one Slayer in all the world. Eighteen hundred now ... that we've counted. Almost five hundred working with us, in ten separate squads. There's even three of me" ("The Long Way Home, Part One").

The voice, which serves to give us important exposition, continues under dialogue as the action continues. Buffy's monologue finishes and is then replaced by an interior monologue from Xander "I used to be in construction...," which establishes his role as the operations monitor/Watcher at Buffy's headquarters (similar to the role of the character Operations in *La*

*Femme Nikita*). Most of the early issues starts out with an inside the head monologue (1, 2, 3, 6, 7, 8, 9, 11). A couple of them narrate flashback sequences from the television series (Buffy and Faith's season three knife fight in Issue 7; Faith and Mayor Wilkins in Issue 9), placing them in a new context. These internal monologues help to ground characters in their new, unusual circumstances: Buffy as the leader of 500 young Slayers in Scotland (out of the nearly 2000 activated Slayers), Xander as the head of a high-tech operations outfit, or Faith hanging out at the Cleveland hellmouth. Others just set the tone for the issue.

Another way that *Season Eight* operates liminally is in its treatment of the subject matter it has presented. The mini arcs released later as volumes, such as "The Long Way Home," "No Future for You," and "Wolves at the Gate" reflect short storylines that occurred on the television series, but are much more defined than the more general arcs that drove the 22 episode seasons. The television show used the entire season to develop most of its major arcs centered around the "bad guys," with a few mini arcs thrown in, such as in season five, when Buffy/Spike storyline began, only to be more fully fleshed out in seasons six and seven. On the television show, for example, it would have been highly improbable for the show to take a four episode side-track into Faith's world, as it did in "No Future for You, Parts One–Four." The show, being focused around Buffy, would be more likely to find a way to keep focus on her, using Faith as the subplot. While Buffy does become more involved with the arc as the story moves on (by Part Three she and Faith have had a series face-to-face fight), it is clear that the focus, for the arc, is on Faith. She (and Giles) disappear at the end of Issue 9 (off, supposedly, to perform more off-the-map clandestine activities) and have yet to be heard from again as of Issue 15. Likewise Issue 5, "The Chain," is about a Buffy doppel-ganger, also a trek away from the actions of the main character. Rarely do television shows embark on such episodes, given the wide number of guest stars and high cost, but in the comics, all it requires is the ability to storyboard it, draw it, and work it into an already existing framework.

The ability of the comic to transcend technological cost is an important feature of creating the liminal universe. While the television show was able to produce impressive special effects during its run, it was often limited by technology. Depending upon the style and symbology of the artist, *Season Eight* faces no such restrictions. As a result, the scale of *Season Eight* is grander in many ways than the previous seven television seasons. Certain story lines that would have been difficult, if not impossible, to produce in the television world work nicely within the *Season Eight* comic book world. The castle in Scotland that serves as headquarters for Buffy's crew is immense, and while the television show did some "large" sets (Dracula's castle, for instance), not having to worry about film angles and budgets to build an actual set allows for different detailing and representation. Another example is "Wolves at the Gate," partially set in Tokyo and the surrounding environs. The comic book genre also makes it look less like a bad Godzilla movie when Giant Dawn is trashing the town and fighting Mecha-Giant Dawn in "Wolves at the Gate," Part Four. Yet even comics can use television-type effects when it suits their purposes. One good example of how comics can use scenic cuts in much the same way as television uses different types of shots can be found in what many fans refer to as "the incident" from "Wolves at the Gate," Part One. The sequencing of the panels as Buffy and Satsu discuss their relationship resembles the cuts one might find in a regular television episode: a mixture of close-ups with medium length shots.

Comics also affect how much material can be covered at a time. Unlike a television episode, which is expected to introduce a problem and then "solve" it, at least partially, in 42 minutes, comic books can use multiple issues in series to explore a scenario, then balance those arcs with single issues. For example, Issue 5, "The Chain," was a single issue following the series "The Long Way Home" that dealt with the fate of one of Buffy's alter egos (mentioned at the beginning of Issue 1). Single issues can also introduce new problems that recur, as does "Anywhere But Here," wherein we get the first glimpse of Willow's new witch/demon "goddess" (who reappears briefly in Wolves at the Gate," Part Four). Some fans are less than pleased with the abbreviated format, but see the mini arcs as a way of making up for shortened information being doled out over a longer time span. It certainly is not any worse than many contemporary cable shows, which put out only five or six episodes and then go on hiatus for six months to a year.

In short, the liminality of *Season Eight's* storytelling is its ability to remain true to its basic premises while adapting to the demands and opportunities of the new genre. These tactics create a constantly shifting space that both is and is not the universe of *Buffy* as we know it. How Whedon and his team of writers will continue to use and stretch the genre is still up for grabs, creating a liminal, transitory space of its own.

## WORKS CITED

Scott McCloud. *Understanding Comics: The Invisible Art* (New York: HarperCollins, 1993).

Kevin Melrose. "DC, IDW and Viz win top Diamond Gem Awards," Newsarama.com (8 April 2008).

Douglas Wolk. *Reading Comics: How Graphic Novels Work and What They Mean* (New York: DaCapo, 2007).

# Buffy's Seven-Season Initiation

## David Fritts

*"You can learn a lot about a person by how they deal with a hole."*
— Joss Whedon, on the DVD commentary for *"Lessons"*

According to Joseph L. Henderson in *The Wisdom of the Serpent*, "Seven is the number most commonly associated with initiation, a number seeming to denote the steps or stages of an inner, as opposed to an outer journey" (42). Whether by coincidence, serendipity, or design, the seven-season narrative of *Buffy the Vampire Slayer* traces not only Buffy Summers' heroic progress, but also her personal growth, associating the Slayer with heroes of myth who precede her. In particular, the show exploits the myth of descent and return in its full richness, referencing the traditional heroic underworld journey and invoking the pattern of death and rebirth to mark the process of initiation for its heroine. In fact, borrowing a phrase from Stephen O. Glosecki, I suggest that the seven-season story arc of *Buffy the Vampire Slayer* describes a process of "incremental initiation" (152), by which Buffy becomes more and more a master of her true self.

Many *Buffy* scholars have explored the show's mythic elements. Frances Early writes that *Buffy the Vampire Slayer* offers "a fresh version of the classic quest myth in Western culture" with a "personable and responsible young woman cast as hero." Laurel Bowman has shown that Buffy's story through the first six seasons follows closely the hero's journey as described by Joseph Campbell. Bowman points out that Buffy, unlike any single hero examined by Campbell, has passed through all three stages of the hero's journey. Rhonda Wilcox asserts that Campbell's monomyth, in fact, can be "found many times in the one narration of Buffy" (*Why Buffy Matters* 38). Similarly, Nancy Holder shows how the hero's journey can be seen in the five final episodes as well as in the seven-season narrative (199). Specific associations to the myth of descent and return are made by Bowman (Orpheus) and Zoë-Jane Playden (Inanna and the Harrowing of Hell).

Buffy's journey can be traced from four perspectives on the mythic interpretation of descent (or death) and return: its potential shamanic origin, for which I use the description of Stephen O. Glosecki; its association with Christian myth and ritual as described by Alan Watts; its connection to Jungian psychology as described by Joseph L. Henderson; and the synthesis of mythic traditions as represented in the work of Joseph Campbell. In all of these perspectives, a pattern common to an individual/hero's initiation emerges: 1) separation from the body, 2) a journey through a dream landscape led by a guide, and 3) return to the world with a reward. My goal is not to connect Buffy's experiences to all of these traditions systematically, but to see them as touchstones to help us to appreciate Buffy's initiation.

Glosecki notes that among the images that "shamanic initiation" involves are "images of death and rebirth" (8). Associating the "shamanic descent" with *Beowulf*, Glosecki summarizes the "universal traits." Falling into an ecstatic trance, often "equated with ritualistic death," the shaman sends his soul "in quest for superhuman power" to heal the afflicted. While the body remains in a trance, the soul journeys through "mythic dreamtime." On the dangerous and surreal journey, the soul encounters "preternatural creatures that figure in the mythology of the descender (including the spirits of the dead)." The dreamer may return with a talisman and frequently draws a guardian from the spirits represented by shapeshifters, whose form the traveler can borrow (163–4). Glosecki notes that the "goal of the psychic journey" can be to heal "physical, psychological, or sociological problems" (11). As the power of the shaman becomes more generalized, he acquires a larger significance: "Attacked by monsters, acquainted with other worlds, able to move in mythic time, the shaman becomes a culture hero who has been to hell and back for the secret power that will help his suffering people" (23). Thus, "shamans are considered genuine mythic heroes," following the pattern "retraced by epic heroes like Beowulf, Gilgamesh, or Odysseus" (23–4).

Alan W. Watts describes the Christian, specifically Roman Catholic, myths and rituals associated with death and rebirth in a way that relates to initiation. The individual near death calls for the priest, who comes to perform "the viaticum, the rites of passage between this world and the 'next'" (209–10). At death, "the soul [goes] on its way to the Centre of the Universe" (212). The scales held by Michael check for the balance of sin by contrition. Perfect balance will send the soul immediately to heaven (213). Purgatory provides a means by which further trials can achieve the balance (214), but the soul sent to hell will never receive forgiveness. The permanence of the Christian hell provides an extraordinary level of punishment, unprecedented (220). The descent to hell would not be something from which anyone would return. But Watts describes the journey from earth to heaven in initiatory terms: "'Death' is the point at which 'I' come to an end, and beyond which lies the unknown.... For what is most truly and inwardly myself is ever beyond that small area of knowledge and control which is called the ego" (232).

This psychological understanding of the achievement of apotheosis leads us to Joseph L. Henderson's description of the myths of death and rebirth from the perspective of Jungian psychology in *The Wisdom of the Serpent*. For Henderson death and rebirth are central to the theme of initiation, which "provides the archetypal pattern by which the psyche ... is enabled to make a transition from one stage of development to another" (4). The myths often feature the "Great Goddess," whose death and rebirth represents the cycles of nature or the cosmos. But the "triumph of new life over death" may also extend to the myth of the hero (41). The initiate crosses the threshold from the conscious into the unconscious, requiring submission, though not out of apathy or weakness (42). The psychiatrist, as the guide, shifts the initiate's attention from the outside to the "inner, sacred images" (49). Upon entering the "gates of sleep," the initiate undergoes a change that becomes the test and brings about transition. At this stage, the initiate is answerable only to himself, having replaced his guide with "a visionary animal, plant or talisman" as a "guardian spirit" to be obeyed from then on. In the end, the initiate receives supernormal powers (50). This "incorporation" integrates the masculine and feminine. In psychological terms, rebirth means understanding "how to love life in a new way, with the capacity to suffer meaningfully while the change takes place" (40).

Finally, we return to Joseph Campbell, whose *Hero with a Thousand Faces* integrates the shamanic, psychological, and mythical traditions into a unified "monomyth." In his chapter on "Initiation," Campbell describes "The Road of Trials," illustrated by the myths of Psyche and Inanna, the performance of a Shaman among the Lapps, and the dreams of a patient in analysis. The trial requires crossing the boundary into "a dream landscape" (97). The initiate undertakes a "perilous journey into the darkness by descending ... into the crooked lands of his own spiritual labyrinth," where "he soon finds himself in a landscape of symbolical figures (any one of which may swallow him)." Campbell identifies the process in "modern" terms as "dissolving, transcending or transmuting the infantile image of our personal past" (101). In the end, "the ordeal is a deepening of the problem of the first threshold and the question is still in balance: Can the ego put itself to death?" (108).

Contained with the seven-season story of Buffy's personal and heroic growth are repeated tellings of the death and return narrative. In addition to occasional allusions to specific descent myths, the pattern defined by these four examples permeates the series. Each season moves toward a climactic encounter with evil, for which Buffy travels into the realm of the evil, physically descending in five of the seven seasons. As each season moves toward this climax, Buffy has a significant dream encounter from which she returns with understanding and resolve. The heroic encounters of each season function as initiatory experiences for Buffy, as each encounter forces her to make choices that result in personal growth. As the series unfolds, Buffy's personal growth becomes increasingly defined in opposition to her heroic persona.

Season one of *Buffy* establishes the centrality of the death and return motif to the series when the season climaxes not only with Buffy's symbolic descent but also her literal death and rebirth. Before the climactic episode, Buffy experiences a dream journey in the episode "Nightmares." The nightmare world had been opened and merged with the real world by what Giles characterizes as the "astral projection" of a young boy, Billy, in a coma. Giles notes that "things like that are easy when you live on the Hellmouth." As each character experiences his/her own worst nightmare, Buffy faces two. First, her father tells her that her parents' divorce was because of her. Then she meets the freed Master and is made a vampire. Thus, her nightmares reflect the two aspects of her character — the girl and the slayer — the personal and the heroic.

The final episode of the season requires Buffy to conquer her egocentric fears. After initial reluctance to sacrifice her life, Buffy resolves to face the Master after she experiences Willow's anguish over the deaths of her friends. When Willow says she's not okay and asks, "What are we going to do?" Buffy responds, "What we have to." Her duty as Slayer has taken on a personal dimension, and she acts with her own heroic agency: she chooses rather than passively being chosen. She allows herself to be led down into the Master's lair by the Chosen One, a young boy somewhat reminiscent of Billy, whose epithet identifies him with Buffy. After she is killed by the Master and revived by Xander, she announces, "I feel strong. I feel different." She then marches off to defeat the Master. For Buffy the hero, the experience of death and rebirth has made her a more powerful slayer. For Buffy the initiate, she has chosen to suppress her egocentric fears and to sacrifice herself for her friends, if not the world. As Henderson says, "What is required of the true initiate is courage, humility, and purity of heart, all of these qualities together seeming to stand for the awareness of self as infinitely more valuable than the possessive demands of the ego" (53–4). This tension between the personal and heroic, one of the dominant themes of the show itself, continues to be reflected in its manipulation of the descent myth each season.

Season two offers more psychological, as well as mythic, complexity. It opens with Buffy experiencing personal trauma over her encounter with the Master. Her self-involvement nearly leads to the deaths of Giles, Jenny, Willow, and Cordelia. Before the season-ending encounter with Angelus, Buffy meets and kills him in the dreamlike episode "I Only Have Eyes for You." Sunnydale High is once again under a supernatural spell, where people are possessed by the spirits of a teacher and student whose tragic love affair ended in a murder-suicide in 1955. Buffy experiences what she calls a dream — when she is transported to a 1955 classroom for a few moments. Later, everyone's cafeteria lunch spaghetti turns into snakes. This incident not only recalls an incident from the previous season's "Nightmares" when spiders emerged from a student's textbook, but also uses what Henderson describes as "the symbol of rebirth following death" (36). Henderson continues that "the wisdom of the serpent" is the "knowledge of death and rebirth forever withheld except at those times when some transcendent principle, emerging from the depths, makes it available to consciousness" (37). Giles invokes a Christian perspective of rebirth when he says of James, the young student, "He's experiencing a form of purgatory.... He's doomed to, to kill his Ms. Newman over and over and over again, and ... forgiveness is impossible." When Buffy and Angel become possessed by the spirits, a gender reversal allows the two spirits to be reconciled. Buffy, as the young male student James, kills Angel, as the teacher Ms. Newman. Because Angel survives, they are able to reconcile the two spirits, freeing James from his purgatory. The encounter foreshadows not only the encounter that ends season two, but also the resurrection of Angel and his reconciliation with Buffy in season three, beginning the process of interlacing the seasons, especially in terms of Buffy's growth.

When we arrive at the season-ending, two-part episode of season two, personally Buffy seems to be right where she started the year. She endangers the entire group when she marches off to face Angel alone after he calls her out. He points out that she "falls for it every time." Realizing her mistake, Buffy rushes back to the library to find Kendra dead. As the unprecedented second slayer, Kendra is connected to Buffy (and to Buffy's death in season one)—a connection that is made more clear in future seasons as other slayers, past and present, share identity with Buffy. Thus, Kendra's death might be seen as the death of a part of Buffy. Furthermore, Kendra's death might be interpreted as the death of ego in the way that it jars Buffy from her self-centered view of the situation—much as Willow's words had the previous year.

Before the final battle with Angel, Whistler, who serves as a sort of spirit guide for Buffy, tells her, "In the end you're always by yourself. You're all you've got. That's the point." In describing this scene, Rhonda Wilcox notes that Buffy's "loneliness is not a triumph" ("Who Died" 6). However, if we consider the context, we can see Buffy's actions as possibly embracing her true self. At the point of her near-death, when Angel taunts her, asking "What's left," Buffy replies, "Me." At the same moment, she stops the death blow with her bare hands, regains her strength and confidence, and eventually kills Angel. Much as in the previous season, she has emerged from the darkness with renewed power. But there is limited personal growth in her choice to kill Angel; it would be a stretch to give her too much credit for placing the whole world over her lover. Her self-indulgent running away at the end of the episode also suggests that her growth is yet minimal. As Wilcox says, as Buffy "looks like any teen runaway" (6).

However, over the course of season three Buffy makes great strides and, using a key metaphor for the season, earns her graduation. Buffy begins in personal turmoil again, having taken on a new identity to hide from her true self. Interestingly, the season-opening episode "Anne," to a large extent relates to the Harrowing of Hell, the Christian version of the descent and return myth told in the Gospel of Nicodemus, as has been noted by Zoë-Jane Playden (131). As one of the captives of the demon in charge of the hell-like dimension, she is expected to say, like all the other captives, "I'm no one." However, in that moment, Buffy reclaims her heroic identity, declaring, "I'm Buffy, the Vampire Slayer." Wilcox suggests that she also reconnects to her humanity at that moment, which will be followed by her reconnecting to family and friends in the following episode. Wilcox concludes that the sequence of four episodes linking seasons two and three show that "the choice to fight alone, while heroic, is also presented as wrong" ("Who Died" 7). Buffy's personal identity crisis, however, will not be resolved for two more episodes, until she is able to describe to Giles what really happened when she killed Angel. Giles has convinced Buffy that the details of what happened are required for a binding spell. After revealing that Angel had been cured too late, she says, "I told him that I loved him and I kissed him and I killed him."

Buffy's initiatory descent occurs when season three concludes with another two-part episode that mirrors the end of season two. Much more completely than in the previous seasons' climaxes, "Graduation Day" integrates the dream journey and death of ego with the climactic battle with evil. Buffy sets out to kill Faith to bring back her slayer blood as a cure for the poisoned Angel, enacting almost literally the role of the shaman. Notably a hostile shaman may practice "disease-shooting — attack magic attributing illness to injection, often of an animate point 'shot' from afar" (Glosecki 120). Angel's infection had been caused by Faith's shooting him with an arrow from a rooftop. Subsequently, as in season two, Buffy is brought to the edge of death by Angel. After Buffy has failed to bring back Faith's blood, she encourages Angel to drink hers. While comatose in adjoining rooms, the two slayers meet in a dream set in Faith's apartment, where their fight had occurred. Donald Keller provides a thorough discussion of this dream, concluding that Buffy "acts as though the dream was an actual communication with Faith." She uses the information that she receives, that the mayor will retain his "human weakness" when he becomes a demon, to lure him to his death (168). In addition, her victory over the ascended mayor will be facilitated by a talisman brought from her encounter with Faith, Faith's blood on Faith's knife. When Buffy emerges from her death/dream, she does not march out to immediately and single-handedly battle the mayor. Instead, she devises a plan, which involves all of the students of Sunnydale High and others. Buffy has killed her ego (or at least put her in a coma), and demonstrates a balanced sense of self both by applying her intellect and sharing the burden of the fight — and to some extent, for the first time, her power. Sharing power becomes one of the hallmarks of Buffy's personal growth. As the series unfolds over the next four seasons, she increasingly separates her self from her slayer power.

In season four, Buffy takes another big step toward understanding her true self when she experiences the power of the First Slayer. We open the season in the familiar pattern, with Buffy experiencing self-doubt as a new college student. But once Buffy defeats Sunday, the campus vampire leader, she regains her confidence and, in particular, demonstrates her independence from Giles. But by season's end she will reconcile her relationship with Giles. When we reach the final battle, Buffy descends with Giles, Willow, and Xander into the appropriately named Initiative to battle Adam. When her three companions perform the ritual that channels the power of the First Slayer, she is possessed completely by the spirit, and arguably stops being Buffy altogether for a time — if not a death of ego, at least a clear separation from her body. As she reaches in and pulls out Adam's power source, she intones, "You could never hope to grasp the source of our power." Her use of "our" is ambiguous, but significant in that she doesn't say "I." The final episode of the season, "Restless," displaces the dream travel until after the battle — or at least the current battle — emphasizing the interlacing of season four with subsequent events. As in season two's "Nightmares," each of the four experiences in a dream their particular fear. In her dream Buffy encounters the First Slayer and says, "You're not the source of me." It would seem that the First Slayer, or the Slayer line, is the mysterious source of her power as she suggests to Adam, but not the source of Buffy.

Season five represents an apparent fulfillment of Buffy's journey. In the season's opening episode, Buffy is not experiencing personal doubt, but concern about not understanding her power. After defeating Dracula, Buffy echoes her words to Adam, saying to Giles, "He [Dracula] understood my power better than I do." This awareness leads her to ask for Giles' help again to train and educate her. Also, of course, in this opening episode, Buffy is provided a new alter ego, a sister made from her. As Dawn's mythically-enticing name implies, she is not the dark side of Buffy to be suppressed, but the part of her that needs nurturing and growth. In the final episode Buffy says of Dawn, "She's me."

In "Intervention" Buffy is led on the vision quest by Giles, explicitly enacting a rite of passage seemingly reminiscent of shamanic tradition. Giles surrenders his guardianship temporarily, and a mountain lion appears to lead Buffy to a fireside where she meets a guide in the form of the First Slayer, who assures her that she is "full of love" and implies that she does not have to lose her humanity to be the Slayer. The guide tells her, "Love is pain, and the Slayer forges strength from pain.... It is your nature. Love will bring you to your gift," which, she learns, is death.

The culmination of season five could very easily have been the end of Buffy's journey — whether we consider it her heroic journey or simply her life's journey. Buffy faces the female God Glory, who represents the opposite of what Buffy strives to be. Her self-involvement greatly exceeds anything we've seen in Buffy. Her shared consciousness with the human male, Ben, parodies the integration of male and female. It resembles what Alan W. Watts describes as reconciliation "in seeming" where "the equivalent of reconciliation is oscillation" (209). The two consciousnesses are never one, but struggle with one another.

Before the final battle with Glory, Buffy falls into a trance, initiated when Glory has carried Dawn away, despite all of Buffy's efforts. As time for the season-ending battle approaches, Buffy, in her trance, visits events of her past. Willow enters the dream, to act as the psychiatrist and help Buffy resolve the issue that has paralyzed her. Willow witnesses the moment when the First Slayer tells Buffy that death is her gift. Buffy repeatedly returns to a moment of doubt, which she regards as having led to her having "killed Dawn." Willow understands that Buffy is paralyzed by guilt and calls upon her sense of duty. When Buffy asks, "Where are you going?" Willow says "Where you're needed. Are you coming?" As in season one, Willow's words bring out the slayer's resolve. Buffy immediately awakens from this dream resolved to protect Dawn at any cost. While her concern for Dawn appears at first to interfere with the primary objective of saving the world, this personal motive proves to be the very reason that she is able to succeed.

In talking to Giles before the battle, Buffy refers to her season two battle with Angel, describing her current state in terms that recall Whistler's words that "In the end you're always by yourself. You're all you've got. That's the point." Buffy tells Giles, "I loved him so much. But I knew ... what was right. I don't have that any more. I don't understand. I don't know how to live in this world if these are the choices. If everything just gets stripped away. I don't see the point." Like Inanna, who is stripped of layers of clothing as she descends through each gate of the underworld, the initiate, says Campbell, "must put aside his pride, his virtue, beauty and life" (108). Buffy adds, "If Dawn dies, I'm done with it. I'm quitting."

In the final battle Buffy relies heavily on an even larger supporting cast than in her fight with Adam. Spike and Anya join Giles, Willow, and Xander, all contributing significantly to the defeat of Glory. Though she beats Glory into submission, Buffy ultimately wins, not through combat, but through sacrifice. She understands how death is her gift when she chooses to sacrifice herself to save Dawn and the world. She has embraced that part of herself represented symbolically and literally by Dawn. Buffy apparently has achieved Campbell's "ultimate boon." And, of course, as we know from her season six revelation, she is in heaven.

But this is Buffy's seven-season initiation, so what's next? Season six begins, as do the previous four seasons, with Buffy's difficult reintegration into her community after the heroic death/victory of the previous season. Because the death was real and final in season five, the reintegration is even more difficult. In fact, it takes the entire 22 episodes. Bowman describes season six in mythic terms that account for the season's ennui by the fact that the season represents the part of the monomyth usually not depicted, the hero's reintegration.

Perhaps symbolic of season six is the one episode most clearly connected to classical descent myth: "Once More with Feeling." Wilcox and Bowman have noted that this episode's associations with classical versions of the descent myth involving the rescue of one carried off to the Underworld. In fact, Bowman has identified Buffy with Demeter, Orpheus and Eurydice. However, no one is actually carried off to the Underworld, neither Dawn, who is wearing Sweet's amulet, nor Xander who used it to summon the demon. And Buffy doesn't rescue anyone. Despite the heroic build up of "Walk through the Fire," the result is perfectly expressed in the final song: "The battle's done / And we kind of won."

When we reach the end of the three-part finale, it seems appropriate then that Buffy has very little effect in "defeating" Dark Willow; it is Giles and Xander who manage that. This is not all that different from the ends of the previous three seasons, except that Buffy isn't even in the vicinity of the final confrontation. While season six ends with Buffy unusually "fray adjacent," in another way of looking at things, she is exactly where she was at the end of season five: with Dawn. Furthermore, in terms of the theme of this essay, she is exactly where I want her to be: in a hole. Many have noted how this season is framed by Buffy climbing out of the ground at the beginning and end, first physically reborn and the second time, spiritually. The second rebirth points to the culmination of season six's initiation. Buffy and Dawn have fought back to back, even though they are not in the main battle. Buffy embraces her role as mother/mentor to Dawn, not merely protector. She embraces the world and expresses her desire to show it to Dawn. For Buffy, in traditional heroic terms, not much happens in season six. But in terms of her continuing personal growth, a great deal occurs.

And best of all, Buffy's rebirth sets up season seven — which works its way to the final battle by repeatedly recapitulating the pattern of descent and return, culminating in Buffy's first literal descent into the Sunnydale Hellmouth. This theme is repeatedly invoked throughout the early episodes: "From beneath you, it devours."

Season seven opens with a classic heroic descent and return plot in which Buffy rescues Dawn and two other students from the labyrinthine basement of the high school. Dawn and Kit have been literally swallowed through a restroom floor, falling into the basement, where they encounter a third student. Willow has had a vision of the Hellmouth's coming to life, the earth with teeth, consistent with Henderson's assertion that "initiation to the underworld is often symbolized by the swallowing monster" (43). The three students wander helplessly, harassed by three dead people. They are unable to find a way out because as one of the "manifest spirits" says, "This place is like a maze." So Dawn calls Buffy, who immediately responds. When Buffy enters the restroom, she jumps into the hole without a moment's hesitation, prompting Joss Whedon to comment, laughingly, on the commentary that "you can tell a lot about a person by how they deal with a hole." As Buffy fights her way to the three teens, she encounters Spike, who provides the information that the spirits are controlled by a talisman. She calls Xander, who will find and destroy the talisman. When Xander enters the restroom, his careful avoidance of the hole that Buffy has leapt into draws our attention to the contrast.

In the meantime, Buffy tells Dawn, "All we have to do is hold them at bay." As she stands in the basement wielding a handbag containing two bricks, holding off the three spirits who keep coming back at her, there is a sense that we have picked up where season six left off. However, Dawn is not standing back to back in the fight with Buffy. In examining the connections between this first episode and the subsequent events in season seven, especially the final episode, Elizabeth Rambo points out that the episode contains "false clues." The episode had begun with Buffy training Dawn in vampire fighting, suggesting that Dawn would become a member of the Scooby team. But now Buffy seems to have reverted to her role as protector. As in previous seasons, Buffy backslides a bit on the growth experienced in the previous season. And even as the season nears the climactic battle with the First, Buffy will try to have Xander take Dawn away to keep her out of the fight.

The descent themes established in "Lessons" are carried forward in the season in two significant ways. First, the image of the labyrinth recurs throughout the season. Visually the labyrinth is represented in the decorative design on the Seal of Danzalthar. The image of the high school basement as a mysteriously changing labyrinth also recurs. In "Same Time, Same Place" as Buffy and Xander go looking for help in figuring out what happened to the flayed body, Xander says that they can't find their way around even with blueprints because "it's like the walls move or something." According to Henderson, traversing the labyrinth brings about "that particular loss of ego-consciousness necessary for any fundamental change to take place" (50). When Jonathon and Andrew try to find the Seal of Danzalthar, Jonathan says, "Everything is shifting around. Have we circled all around?" Dawn had also referred to going in circles in the basement. The image of the spiral labyrinth suggested by going in circles will be picked up by the design on the floor of the cave where the shadow men place the box with the demon in it. Of the spiral labyrinth *The Woman's Dictionary of Symbols and Sacred Objects* says, "The spiral was connected to the idea of death and rebirth: entering the mysterious earth womb, penetrating to its core, and passing out again by the same route" (14).

In addition, we return to basements (and other underground places) repeatedly during season seven. For example, after Spike provides useful information about the manifest spirits in "Lessons," Buffy seeks him out for information twice more, like the classical hero visiting the underworld: about the flayed body in "Same Time Same Place" and about Cassie in "Help." Buffy talks Spike into leaving the high school basement, but he will eventually take up residence in Buffy's basement. Another basement, at 634 Hoffman Terrace, will be where he buries the bodies of his victims while under the control of the First. And, of course, the Hellmouth in the high school basement will continue to be the focus of evil and several of the season's most important events.

Buffy's next underworld rescue occurs at the end of "Showtime" when she rescues Spike from the cave in which he has been held and tortured by the First. This rescue suggests Buffy's growth in personal awareness as defined by her relationship with men. Spike had earlier tried to get Buffy to kill him, but she doesn't because she has seen his penance. Spike tells Buffy that she needs the pain and hate of men who hurt her to do her job. Buffy says she doesn't "hate like that. Not you, not myself. Not anymore." So when the Bringers kidnap Spike, her insistence on rescuing him reflects her growing acceptance or herself, not the ulterior motives suggested by her — that he has useful insight about the First — or others — Buffy's continuing love for him.

In "Get It Done" Buffy travels into the past and makes an unequivocal rejection of power that dehumanizes her. The episode opens with a dream in which she is walking the house like a worried mother, looking in on the potentials. Buffy's journey to the other world is facilitated by the shadow casters found in the bag from Robin Wood's Slayer mother. As Dawn reads the origin myth of the First Slayer, the spinning shadow casters open a portal that Buffy immediately jumps through — reminding us of her precipitous leap into the basement in "Lessons." Buffy falls into a bright desert land-scape—the one we have seen before in "Restless"—and walks to the three shadow men, who say they have been waiting for her. They begin circling her and tell her that they cannot give her knowledge, only power. She escapes the shadow men's attempt to give her more demon power by breaking their staff, then sarcastically asks them to tell her something she doesn't know. One gives her a vision of countless turok-han inside the Hellmouth. After her return, she says to Willow, "Thanks for bringing me back again," linking this incident with Buffy's death at the end of season five.

This repeated pattern of imagery and incident sets up the final episodes when Buffy makes a series of five descents. The first is a disaster when she reacts to Caleb's calling her out as if she is the Buffy of season two. Despite being poised on the verge of understanding, Buffy seems to "go back to the beginning." She also rejects Giles, telling him to "help the girls who still need a teacher." She foolishly endangers the potentials, and costs Xander an eye. Henderson reminds us of the initial failure of the initiate represented by Gil-gamesh and Gawain (43). After a period of separation and brooding, she returns to the vineyard alone. She has deduced, with Spike's information, that Caleb is protecting the vineyard, not the Hellmouth. This time, she doesn't try to fight Caleb, but frustrates him by evading him until he reveals a trap door that she jumps through immediately. Below, she finds the scythe. When she hears that the potentials and Faith are in trouble, she rushes off. Her descent into the sewer where the potentials are trapped is dramatic. They hear a sound; then a beam of light appears, and Buffy drops through from the ceiling. She next descends into a tomb, this time seeking knowledge, consulting the Guardian, who provides her with knowledge of the scythe that will lead to her understanding of how to use it. Here she finally defeats Caleb.

As the final episode begins, Buffy tells Angel that she's not "finished becoming whoever the hell [she's] going to turn out to be." Her recognition that she has a lot to learn is actually a profound expression of self possession. Or as James South says in his essay on season seven, "Power is really just potentiality." When she tells Spike, "*We're* going to win," I think we can understand that she recognizes the "bloody brilliant" plan to defeat the First is to share her power with all of the potentials, by giving them the choice. She falls in battle, and once again is on the precipice of death, taunted by the First. As she has done before, she rises up with renewed power. But there is more. She is fighting with not only Dawn, but Faith—and all of her sister slayers. She may not be "finished becoming," but I believe her smile at the end of the series represents her achievement, not only of the ultimate boon, but of her own personal balance.

# WORKS CITED

Bowman, Laurel. "*Buffy the Vampire Slayer*: The Greek Hero Revisited." http://web.uvic.ca/~lbowman/buffy/buffythehero.html, September 30, 2003.

Campbell, Joseph. *The Hero with a Thousand Faces*. 2nd ed. Bollingen Series XVII. Princeton, NJ: Princeton University Press, 1973.

Early, Frances. "Staking Her Claim: Buffy the Vampire Slayer as Transgressive Woman Warrior." *Slayage: The Online International Journal of Buffy Studies* 6 <http://slayageonline.com/essays/slayage6/Early.htm>, November 19, 2007.

Glosecki, Stephen O. *Shamanism and Old English Poetry*. New York: Garland, 1989.

Henderson, Joseph L., and Maud Oakes. *The Wisdom of the Serpent: The Myths of Death, Rebirth, and Resurrection*. Princeton, NJ: Princeton University Press, 1990.

Holder, Nancy. "Slayers of the Last Arc." *Seven Seasons of Buffy*. Ed. Glenn Yeffeth. Dallas, TX: Benbella, 2003. 195–205.

Keller, Donald. "Spirit Guides and Shadow Selves: From the Dream Life of Buffy (and Faith). In *Fighting the Forces: What's at Stake in* Buffy the Vampire Slayer. Eds. Rhonda V. Wilcox and David Lavery. New York: Rowman, 2002. 165–77.

Playden, Zoë-Jane. "What You Are, What's to Come: Feminisms, Citizenship, and the Divine." In *Reading the Vampire Slayer: An Unofficial Critical Companion to* Buffy *and* Angel. Ed., Roz Kaveney. New York: Tauris Parke, 2003. 120–47.

Rambo, Elizabeth. "'Lessons' for Season Seven of Buffy the Vampire Slayer." *Slayage: The Online International Journal of Buffy Studies* 11–12 *http://slayageonline. com/essays/slayage11_12/Rambo.htm*, November 19, 2007.

South, James. "On the Philosophical Consistency of Season Seven: or 'It's Not About Right, Not About Wrong....'" *Slayage: The Online International Journal of Buffy Studies* 13–14 < http://slayageonline.com/essays/slayage13_14/South.htm>, November 19, 2007.

Walker, Barbara. *The Woman's Dictionary of Symbols and Sacred Objects*. San Francisco: Harper, 1988.

Watts, Alan W. *Myth and Ritual in Christianity*. Boston: Beacon, 1968.

Wilcox, Rhonda. "'Who Died and Made Her Boss?': Patterns of Mortality in *Buffy*." In *Fighting the Forces: What's at Stake in* Buffy the Vampire Slayer. Eds. Rhonda V. Wilcox and David Lavery. New York: Rowman, 2002. 3–17.

_____. *Why Buffy Matters: The Art of* Buffy the Vampire Slayer. New York: I.B. Taurus, 2005.

# It's All about Power

KEVIN K. DURAND

*"It's about power. Who's got it ... who knows how to use it."*
*— "Lessons"*

The final season of *Buffy the Vampire Slayer* opens with the protagonist both setting the scene for the upcoming season, but also summarizing all that has come before. The Buffyverse is about power — the power of the slayer, one girl in all the world, the power of good and evil, of friendship and community. If there is any doubt that "it's about power," those doubts are dispelled as the first episode of season seven ends. Having opened with those words in the mouth of the protagonist, it closes with the same words in the mouth of the new "big bad." The First Evil, lecturing Spike, concludes his soliloquy in the form of the Master, "It's not about right. It's not about wrong." And then, in the form Buffy, "It's about power."

The Buffyverse presents viewers with two conceptions of power. At times, it seems as if the fight is one of fire with fire and power overcoming power, a dualistic cosmic battle. However, the Buffyverse presents a radical repudiation of one in favor of the other. The first power, the one that is sought after by the good guys and bad guys alike, is the power to overcome obstacles, to coerce others to do one's bidding, or to destroy a power bent on evil. In all of these cases, the power is a straightforwardly patriarchal one. It is characterized by a top-down command structure, by one leader being in charge while the others follow, with a highly individualized system of personal power. In the cases of the Master, Angelus, the Watchers Council, or the Initiative, the power is the same. It's not about right or wrong, but rather, it's about power.

The second type is fundamentally different, and it poses both a critique and a threat to the previous easy, dominant view. This is shared power, and its goal is the empowerment of all. A vision of shared power is threatening to the patriarchal conception of power because it subverts the very structure of the patriarchy itself. This shared power attempts to enable others to fully realize their potential, even if it does not immediately garner overt authority for oneself. This more communitarian notion of power stands in contrast to the highly individualistic patriarchal version because it is counterintuitive

45

at very important times and in critical ways. It tends to be vulnerable rather than overtly strong and depends on the group working together rather than on the actions of an individual superhero or heroine. This conception of power, a contribution of the feminist movement to the philosophical conversation about power and its appropriate uses, is the model of power that makes *Buffy* unique. While it has been argued that *Buffy* fails as a feminist vision, the series is a truly feminist text; one that critiques and rejects the dominant patriarchal conceptions of power for a conception of empowerment. As Buffy says in "Bring on the Night," "There's only one thing on this earth more powerful than evil. And that's us" ("Bring on the Night"). The Buffyverse is no less than a radical repudiation of the patriarchal power structure that is so often simply assumed as the standard operating condition of the universe. This is not merely a matter of season seven's cataclysm, although it is relevant. This is a series-wide theme.

This repudiation of patriarchy is first seen as the Scoobies triumph over the serial big bads. The Master, The Mayor, Adam, Glory — all of these are overcome, not by a Slayer alone, but by a Slayer and her friends. In the Buffyverse, we encounter a true representation of shared power, of partnered power. Further, the "bad guys" are not the only paradigms of patriarchy in the Buffyverse that are overcome. The "good guys" that operate in this way, such as the Watchers Council and the Initiative, both fall as well. Indeed, no patriarchally organized power structure survives.

To fully appreciate the radical vision of the Buffyverse, it is perhaps best to look first at another popular vampire slayer chronicle, Laurell K. Hamilton's tales of the vampire hunter, Anita Blake. Gordon Melton, in *The Vampire Book: The Encyclopedia of the Undead*, describes Anita as a "Bad Girl," a woman "who is able to keep up with the best of the superheroes, but is at the same time completely feminine and attractive to her male contemporaries" (Melton 320). However, in Hamilton's hands, Anita believes that she must disguise her femininity in order to compete in a typically male-dominated profession and world. For example, at a zombie raising, with Dolph and a new young female officer, Anita thinks to herself, "The girl just stared. I could almost smell her fear. She was entitled to it. Why did it bother me so much? Because she and I were the only women here, and we had to be better than the men. Braver, quicker, whatever. It was a rule for playing with the big boys" (*The Laughing Corpse*, 116).

This reflects Anita's attitude throughout the series. Her view of herself is one of being physically inferior and superfluous — an interference to be coddled and protected due, not to her size, but to her gender. It is not simply a matter of being short. When confronted with short males, her reaction is generally that they, too, are discounted, though not as much as she, because however short they may be, they are still men. Willie McCoy, though small in both stature and power, retains a measure of power that she does not have. At the other end of the spectrum, we find her reacting to women who do not share her small stature in a way that supports our view here. When working with women who are, to use her word, "Amazonian," she notes that it is their womanhood, not their size, that affects the way her colleagues view their competency.

A scene from a later novel in the series is instructive (and shows that Hamilton's portrayal doesn't develop beyond the one presented at the series' advent). In *Cerulean Sins*, Anita and her allies set up a trap for a pair of guys tailing them. They decide to stage a mock accident and surround the tails in the confusion. Trying to pick non-threatening members of the group, Bobby Lee picks Claudia. Claudia is "all of six feet six and serious muscle." Anita wonders at the selection, pointing out to Bobby Lee that Claudia is bigger, stronger, and more muscled than he is, "You know Bobby-boy if I had to choose between arm-wrestling you, or Claudia, I'd pick you." Bobby Lee does not get the point. After much discussion, with what Anita refers to as "very clear, small words," Claudia finally tells Anita, "Give it up, just give it up. They're men, they can't help it" (*Cerulean Sins*, 231–3). While Anita may see Claudia for who she is—a supremely competent warrior—the view of everyone else is skewed. Anita recognizes that she, herself, struggles against those perceptions. In fact, every single encounter she has with law enforcement, with the exception of Dolph, opens with the officers discounting Anita, wondering what a small, female civilian could possibly have to offer to the "big boys."

How Anita deals with the patriarchy is different in some pronounced ways from Buffy's approach. Anita begins the series as an animator, raising zombies for an unscrupulous boss with a head for business. She spends time on the side as an expert on the preternatural for the police and moonlights as "The Executioner," scourge of renegade vampires. Throughout the course of the texts, Anita gains power in a variety of ways. As she gains new powers and has new responsibilities thrust upon her, she makes noises about being a consensus leader. However, when faced with difficulties, she inevitably turns to the cold, practicalities of "I have the power, I will enforce my will." While she may be outsized, outnumbered, and at times, outmaneuvered, she leans on her guns and her guile, and later, her sexuality, to overcome her adversaries, and she eliminates those who would threaten her. Anita is a picture of the projection of force—to protect those in her charge and to exact vengeance upon those who harm them.

Two episodes help illustrate the arc of the Anita legend. In *Guilty Pleasures*, Jean-Claude, toys with her, maneuvering his "little animator" into a power play with Nikolaos. Anita is seen by Jean-Claude and Nikolaos as a pawn in their power struggle to reign as master of the city. Anita, through her obstinate refusal to back down from a fight, surprises Nikolaos and kills her. In doing so, she elevates Jean-Claude to the position of master of the city, a position that she must then help him keep.

This brush with power, and the power gained by becoming Jean-Claude's human servant (unwilling though she is), causes Anita's own latent powers as a necromancer to begin to flower. It is these powers that bring her into contact with her own past when she is brought into a police investigation of some suspicious disappearances in *The Laughing Corpse*. There, Anita comes face to face with Senora Salvador. The Senora lived in a bad part of town, but it was a part of town in which there was little crime. Anita reflects, "Gang activity stopped at Senora Salvador's neighborhood. Even teenagers with automatic pistols fear things you can't stop with bullets no matter how good a shot you are. [...] The gangs leave the Senora's turf alone. No violence. It is a place of permanent truce" (*The Laughing Corpse*, 36).

It is important that the word here is "truce;" it is a permanent truce, not permanent peace. There is no peace. There is merely a recognition on the part of the gang members of a power greater than their own. In her bailiwick, the Senora is the supreme power, but she is not the apex of all power. A greater power always exists. The arc of the Hamilton's Anita-verse is that with each successive big bad, another is waiting. As Anita moves up the list, powers that once scared her come to respect her as she surpasses them, but her power is localized and individual. Even when joined with the Triumvirate, her power is her own. Jean-Claude and Richard, her "partners" in the Triumvirate can tap it but only if she allows it. On the contrary, she can drain their power whether they have shielded themselves against her or not. She has become the female patriarch of a bailiwick that, while larger than the Senora's, is dynamically the same. The Senora makes Anita an offer that she does not believe Anita can refuse. She offers to teach Anita to develop and control her burgeoning powers. Anita cannot be controlled in this way, however, so, Salvador sends zombies to kill her. The denouement of the conflict occurs in the cemetery when Anita's control over a raised zombie wins out over the Senora's and the Senora is devoured, literally, by Anita's growing power.

These encounters are typical of Anita's world, and she gains power and responsibilities with each passing victory. Each is a turf battle. Oftentimes, the most obviously powerful does not necessarily win, but it is still a matter of force against force with the cleverest proponent of that power winning and growing more powerful still. It is only in overcoming odds to triumph again and again that she begins to recognize that she is more than Jean-Claude's "little animator." As each successive triumph brings a bit more recognition of her abilities and greater consolidation of her power, she gradually expands the circle of those under her protection. But it is a protectorate, not a partnership; it is a patriarchy, not shared empowerment.

Willingly or unwillingly, wittingly or unwittingly, Anita builds her protectorate into an empire that rivals the very power of the Vampire Council itself. She has become powerful in a way that the Vampire Council understands; indeed, in a way that is fairly easy to grasp. She has become a female patriarch. While she encourages those under her command to strike out on their own, to develop their own strengths, she is not hesitant to make it quite clear to them that to cross her is to bring her wrath, and their demise, down upon their heads. Her mantel of protection is broad, and her vengeance is hot. There are exacting positions for each person to fill and those that get on best with Anita are those who recognize where their place in the power structure is.

This is exactly the picture that one gets of all of the organizations, both those of the Big Bads and those of the "good guys" in the Buffyverse as well. Indeed, at times, it is even the course that Buffy herself chooses. In season seven, faced with the impending apocalypse of the First, her first course of action is to place herself as general in command of an army of slayers-in-training. However, it is instructive to compare other groups, particularly those who see themselves on the side of truth, justice, and good within the Buffyverse and the ways in which they pursue their aims. In this comparison, a striking similarity emerges.

Certain entities within the series are presented as being on the side of "good," yet when compared to those on the side of "evil" are strikingly similar in behavior. After Buffy discovers what she believes to be the purpose behind the Initiative and that Riley is one of them, she joins the group, assuming that since they, too, are fighting the forces of darkness, they must share a common goal. Their methods appear to be much more effective than Buffy's one dusted vampire at a time approach, but while she may want to work with, rather than against, the Initiative, those in power see her as a potential threat.

The Watchers Council is another group that, while on the surface and even within their own minds, appear to be working on the side of "good," their behavior seems to suggest otherwise. Having waged a war against the forces of darkness since the earliest times, the Council seems to be obsessed with maintaining that position — the opposition to the vampires, the demons, and the forces of darkness. Indeed, the status quo of the conflict seems to be their goal, even when it seems to be in direct contrast with that for which they claim to be fighting.

Quentin Travers reminds Buffy in the episode "Helpless" that "the Council fights evil. The Slayer is the instrument by which we fight. The Council remains, the Slayers change. It's been that way since the beginning." To the Council, the ultimate watcher exercises "clear and impartial judgment" in all decisions. Giles's "father's love for the child" is useless to the cause, since affection for a slayer is pointless since "one slayer dies. The next one is called."

Obviously the Slayer is imbued with certain superhumanesque powers; but, so are all the Slayers. What makes Buffy different? Kendra claims that "the slayer must work in secret. For security." She continues later on to explain that "The things you do and have, I was taught distract from my calling. Friends. School. Even family. [...] Emotions are weakness, Buffy. You shouldn't entertain them." Faith also leads a very solitary life, telling Buffy when she offers to help Faith kill Kakistos that "You can mind your own business. I can handle this." Mrs. Post reinforces this belief when she tries to console Faith, telling her that "A true fighter needs nothing else," meaning nothing other than herself. The First Slayer asserts that "I have no speech. No name. I live in the action of death. The blood-cry, the penetrating wound. I am destruction. Absolute. Alone." When Buffy informs her that she is not alone, the First Slayer tells her that "The Slayer does not walk in the world. [...] No ... friends ... just the kill ... we are ... *alone.*" She finally tells the First Slayer that "You just have to get over the whole primal power thing. You're not the source of me."

We can examine the institutions and characters in the Buffyverse by investigating their relationship to power. Here, there seems to be a difference between the "good" guys and the "bad" guys. The "good" guys will not say, at least out loud, that "there is no right, there is no wrong, there is only power." The "bad" guys will and do. However, the "good" guys *act* as if they hold this belief. The Initiative cares for preservation of its power, of its way of prosecuting the war against the forces of darkness. Even when its very existence is threatened, they refuse the help of the group that can actually affect a solution, hindering the Scoobies to the point that the solution is supplied nearly too late. In similar fashion, the Watchers Council tries again and again to impose its will on their slayers—from drugging Buffy, to controlling Kendra from the time she was a young girl till she was called, to attempting to kill Faith. Time after time, even when faced with the destruction of the world that they are powerless to stop, they cling to the little power they have remaining—trying to refuse provide aid against Glory unless Buffy submits to their will. Travers informs Buffy, "Glory is stronger than you. She's a more powerful instrument, if you will. But we can help you. We have information that will help. Pass the review and we give it to you without reservation. Fail the review, either through incompetence or by resisting our recommendations...."

Giles interrupts Travers before he can finish, but the implication is there — the only way they plan to provide any information is through Buffy's submission to their power. Their plan is thwarted, however, when Buffy recognizes that their posturing is a desperate attempt to preserve their dominate role over the Slayer, and she calls their bluff.

Even after this, the Council does not understand. As season seven progresses and more girls are murdered, the Council refuses to go to the aid of the slayer, to let Buffy know what is going on and to enlist the aid of the one person who might save lives and, indeed, save the world, again. Travers reassures another council member that "we are still masters of our fate, still captains of our souls," right before the First destroys the Watchers Council Headquarters with the Council inside.

Like the Master, the Mayor, Adam, and Glory, the Initiative and the Watchers are interested more in power than "good." Regardless of high-flown ideals, the Initiative and the Watchers are fundamentally concerned with the acquisition and cultivation of power. In this, the "good" guys and the "bad" guys are ultimately similar. It turns out that every major group within the Buffyverse, save one, is the same kind of thing. Regardless of the side on which they consider themselves to be, their concern is power. The primary difference between the two seems that the "bad" guys admit that the struggle is all about power while the "good" guys do not. However, at the level of actual conduct, both are functionally equivalent — each operates in the accepted patriarchal structure of accumulation of power and top-down exercise of that power. Buffy verbalizes this nicely in season five, "I finally figured out why. Power. I have it. They don't. This bothers them." The "them" there clearly refers to Glory, the Knights of Byzantium, and the Watchers Council — the "bad" guys, to be sure, but the "good" guys as well.

The Anita-verse is strikingly similar; with the following difference. While in the Buffyverse, the Scoobies subvert the patriarchal status quo, there is no such subversion in the Anita-verse. If it is truly "about power," then Anita is a player. By the conclusion of *Cerulean Sins*, one of the later of the Blake novels, Anita has matched forces with Belle Morte, broken two of her own line away from her (something that had never happened before), and succeeded in bringing to reality that which the Vampire Council in France had feared most — a rival power in the new world. It is truly a battle of powers now recognized as equals. But the nature of the power is identical. It matters not whether a man or woman, male vampire or female vampire wields it — the sword of power cuts exactly the same.

Contrast this with the overarching arc of the Buffyverse, an arc that is perhaps best discerned prior to season seven in season four, when the difference between the patriarchal acquisition of power and true empowerment is thrown into stark relief.

In "Doomed," as the Initiative and the Scoobies separately prepare to forestall an apocalypse, the scene switches back and forth between the two groups. One thing that is absolutely clear is that the two groups are different. One of them will fail in their mission. However, isolating precisely what makes this ascription of difference meaningful requires a fairly close reading of the scene. Looking for differences, the first thing one notices is the clinical, sterile military efficiency of the Initiative as it stands in contrast to the mystical, rich, but no less efficient picture of the Scoobies. Next, one notices that this multi-layered tableau revisits a common theme in the Buffyverse— the conflict between the scientific mindset and one that is more in tune with the forces that are not easily explained by scientific experimentation. Whedon has explored this contrast before with the season one conflict between Giles and Jenny Calendar over the "smelly" books and the odorless computer lab. The Initiative constantly tries to impose its will on the world. Having "tamed" nature and natural creatures, science tries to tame the supernatural. The misunderstanding of the forces at play ultimately devastates the organization. The viewer knows this result is inevitable and thus, as one watches the back and forth preparations of the two groups, the differences between them become clearer.

If this were all that were drawn from this rich scene, it would still miss perhaps the most important aspect. As the teams try to come to grips with the strategy for dealing with the Valhall demons and to prevent the end of the world, one is struck by a profound difference. Riley is clearly in charge of the Initiative forces. Graham asks a single question, and Forrest is given permission to speak about the pheromone signature of the demons. Apart from those contributions, Riley does all the talking. The camera pans to each of the "team" members as they silently take notes. At the Scooby headquarters, a different scene plays out. Each member contributes. The requisite roles are then taken—Buffy to the magic shop and to patrol, Xander and Willow to the book archives at the museum, and Giles to the books. The hierarchical (and patriarchal) Initiative may have a female at its head, but it uses words like "teamwork" only to unite the troops in a common goal that is not necessarily beneficial to any of them, save the Initiative itself. The Scoobies are a team, in every sense of the word. They have a powerful slayer, but they share the burden of saving the world.

This conflict between the two worlds becomes obvious in "The I in Team." The three-handed poker game that opens the episode foreshadows the separation that will occur within the gang in "The Yoko Factor." Soon, Buffy will be brought into the Initiative as an adjunct member. Even in a limited role, the two worlds witnessed so far during season four are fundamentally incompatible. In Buffy's first briefing as part of the Initiative, the contradiction between the two worlds becomes exceptionally, and at times, painfully obvious.

After the briefing that Buffy turns into a question and answer session, the assignments are made and the teams branch out. Buffy, sensing that the briefing had not gone as planned, asks Riley, "Questions? An Initiative faux pax?" He responds, "A bit unusual." The flip comment does little to mask what Maggie Walsh has already discerned and what everyone knows. Buffy is dangerous to the Initiative and must be eliminated. The cracks are already present, however. As the teams left the briefing on their assignments, a new order had already been put in place. Riley and Forrest, heretofore inseparable, are with different squads.

The Initiative attempts to assimilate Buffy into their structure. Failing that, they try to kill her. She upsets their status quo, and her difference in approach subverts the patriarchal Initiative, a preview of what will eventually become the ultimate subversion of the structure of patriarchal power itself in season seven. Before turning to season seven, however, the arc of season sour further supports the view that the Buffyverse presents a fundamentally subversive form of power.

The "Yoko Factor" opens with the paradigmatic old white man, Ward, presumably in the Pentagon and some distance from the situation in charge of evaluating the now fully military Initiative. Maggie Walsh is dead, and the HSTs (Hostile Sub-Terrestrials) are beginning to cause trouble. Colonel McNamara dismisses Buffy as "just a girl." This is not the first time the Initiative has underestimated Buffy. Nor is it the first time that the underestimation has been a result of her femininity. In the preceding episode, Forrest says, "I've always been Riley's second-in-command. Instead he picks a girl." Graham responds, "His girl." Forrest, unwilling to leave the matter rejoins, "Whatever. Three guesses what that boy's thinking with." The possibility that perhaps Buffy is best suited of the Initiative to deal with creatures like the Polgara demon does not even seem to enter his mind. Rather, he believes that Riley picks Buffy over him because of the cleavage factor. Forrest, like the rest of the Initiative, is in the patriarchal mindset that power must come in a stereotypically masculine package and must follow traditional notions of hierarchy.

Returning to the "Yoko Factor," the scene shifts. When McNamara says of Buffy, "She's just a girl," the scene cuts to Spike saying, "She's a lot more than that. The Slayer's dangerous is all I'm sayin'." Adam, dismissive in his condescension, says, "Yes, she does make things interesting." Spike will have none of that. He presses the point, "No, see, you're not getting it, Mr. Bits. You're gonna be interestingly dead. Little Miss Tiny's got a habit of bolixing up the plans of every would-be unstoppable badass who steps foot in this town." The conversation ends, however, as Spike comes to the heart of the matter. He sums up his reasons for his numerous failed attempts to kill the current slayer when he has killed others with, "The slayer's got pals." He is dismissive in tone, but he recognizes her friends as the source of her strength.

After overcoming Spike's Yoko Factor, the core of the Scooby gang returns to Giles's apartment in "Primeval." Armed with the knowledge of where and how to destroy Adam, the group devises a plan to merge their powers; they realize that the only way to defeat Adam is to work together and to recognize the others' abilities for the true powers they are. Xander wisecracks that "So — no problem. All we need is a combo Buffy with slayer strength, Giles' multi-lingual know-how and Willow's witchy power," but in actuality, that, along with himself as the heart, is what is needed to win this fight. Sheer physical power is not enough, which is why the Initiative is eventually unsuccessful. True power entails a shared power that ultimately empowers all through it, and this is the beginning of the Scoobies' realization of this.

Within this conflict between the patriarchal Big Bad — Adam — and the Scoobies, the conflict between the two conceptions of power is also clear. It is not only Adam that stands as a patriarchal power figure. Ward and McNamara are presumably on the side of good by trying to harness the power of the demon realm. The Initiative is cast on the side of good, albeit a good that is misguided, out-of-its-depth, and, often, incompetent — a power without a true moral compass. Within the struggle against Adam, the patriarchal Initiative nearly thwarts the Scoobies' solution to the Adam problem with their own unwillingness to relinquish what they mistakenly perceive to be their base of power. The power struggle between the commander and Buffy after the commandos capture the gang is paradigmatic of the struggle of science against magic; but more importantly of the struggle of two powers — the power of the patriarchal hierarchy or the shared power of the Scoobies.

As the series progresses, the Scoobies begin to stand in a much starker contrast to the other occupants of the Buffyverse by presenting a new understanding of power and its use. In season seven, Buffy and the others finds themselves in the ultimate fight against the First Evil. Buffy recognizes the gravity of the situation, and initially, decides that the best course of action is one in which she bends the Slayerettes to her will, attempting to take the lead in a manner reminiscent of the Watchers Council or the Initiative. She tells them "Look, I wish this could be a democracy. I really do. Democracies don't win battles. It's a hard truth, but there has to be a single voice. You need someone to issue orders and be reckless sometimes and not take your feelings into account. You need someone to lead you." When Giles and the others express concern, she informs them that "I'm still in charge here." The group recognizes the tyranny of her actions and calls her on it, ending with Dawn telling her that if this is how she feels, then Buffy has to leave. It is through this time alone that she realizes that her extended slayer shelf life is only through her efforts combined with those of her friends—components that were exposed in the enjoining spell they used to defeat Adam. Giles's extensive knowledge, Willow's spirit made apparent through her sense of magic, and Xander's heart, a vital part that, while not readily apparent to outsiders, binds the group together.

However, the path taken to defeat the First was almost not taken. Buffy was presented another option. Taken to the men who crafted the first slayer and imbued her with the power to fight the forces of darkness, or more properly, with the power to contend with those forces, Buffy has a choice. Becoming frustrated with the cryptic responses she receives, she says, "Look—I got a First to fight. You three have clearly had some time on your hands. Tell me what I need to know. I came to learn." Their response is telling. The Shadow Man says, "We cannot give you knowledge. Only power." This gets to the heart of the matter. They have conceived the fight, from the beginning, as a force against force struggle, a dualistic conflict between equal powers, a battle that plays by all the rules of the patriarchy—grow, acquire power, accumulate power, and use that power to bend others to one's will. This is power without direction, for its own sake, and divorced from the knowledge or the wisdom that would temper that it into something constructive rather than destructive.

Buffy gains an insight here, one that troubles her and causes her to question the traditional views of power with which she has always been presented. It will require that she, and Willow, and Giles, and all the rest of the expanded Scoobies re-imagine the concept of power—not at the level of two forces arrayed against one another for battle, but at the fundamental level of overturning the very structure of the power itself, destroying the patriarchal hierarchy of trickle-down power from its very roots. The irony is that, had she taken the proffered power from the Shadow Men, nothing would have changed. She would have led an overmatched, outgunned, outmaneuvered, outnumbered, and ill-trained army of girls against the very forces of hell. In refusing to play the game by the age-old rules, Buffy has re-envisioned the nature of power for everyone.

In their final triumph, the gang fights together for the ultimate empowerment and subversion of the patriarchal forces. With the help of the whole group, any girl who has the potential to be slayer is made one. Not only does this help in the immediate fight against the forces of the First, but it also suggests a reality in which females everywhere are empowered to fight, not as individuals striving for individual power, but as one force, fighting for the betterment of all.

In this, Buffy and the Scoobies are the only ones truly fighting the good fight — fight against the forces of patriarchy and domination. And in this, the Buffyverse is different from every other superhero saga — including Hamilton's Anita Blake. Whether they cannot or will not, it never occurs to them to try to change the rules of the game. It occurs to Buffy both to try to share herself completely with the world (itself an amazing epiphany that goes against everything else in the world) and to succeed in what others would have thought impossible, thus overcoming the First Evil — the evil of domination and control.

The similarities between Anita and Buffy are striking. Both are women fighting the forces of darkness, averting one apocalypse after another, protecting their friends and taking the fight to the bad guys. But, more importantly, their difference is critical. Anita is a female patriarch. She has accepted the "system" and fights within it. The system shapes her, and she attains great power, but it is *she* who has it. The vision of the empowerment of women we find in Hamilton's creation is no more than a female in the role of heroic despot. On the other hand, within the universe created by Whedon, we have a truly powerful story of the feminist vision of shared power, of an empowerment that elevates all rather than trading subjugation to a villain with subjugation to a benevolent dictator. Anita Blake is an entertaining character, but the tales do little to present anything resembling a new vision of how power might be exercised in the world. Buffy, Willow, Giles, Xander, and all the rest are radical characters; radical because they stand as a threat to the status quo and because they are representative of the true feminist vision of power.

# Buffy Never Goes It Alone
## The Rhetorical Construction of Sisterhood in the Final Season

SUSAN PAYNE-MULLIKEN
*and* VALERIE RENEGAR

In the final season of *Buffy the Vampire Slayer*, Buffy faced her most challenging adversary. In order to emerge victorious, and to subsequently save the world, she needed more resources than she alone could muster. Buffy sought help from the ancient Shadow Men, a group of elders responsible for creating the Slayer lineage. However, when the Shadow Men tried to force their power on her, Buffy rejected them. In the end, an ancient woman named She, a powerful scythe that She helped create, and the abilities of Buffy's friend Willow, a witch, provided Buffy with the resources that she needed to conquer evil. Furthermore, Buffy realized that with these resources, she had the power to change the rules of the Slayer lineage and end the tradition of a single Slayer by empowering all of the potential Slayers simultaneously. The joint effort of the newly empowered Slayers combined with the legacy of ancient women enabled Buffy to defeat her enemies and to save the world. The ideas of cooperative action and self-empowerment embody many of the central tenants of feminist thought. As such, *Buffy the Vampire Slayer* can be understood as an exemplar of contemporary feminism.

In this essay, we argue that popular culture texts, such as *Buffy the Vampire Slayer*, can enhance feminism by making it accessible to a larger audience. While definitions of feminism vary, it can broadly be defined as a social movement that strives for social, economic, and political equality for women and men (Baumgardner & Richards 2000). Sonja K. Foss (1996) suggested that despite differences in definition, there are basic principles with which most feminists agree. One such principle is the belief that people are oppressed by the patriarchy. The patriarchy is "a system of power relations in which men dominate women so that women's interests are subordinated to those of men,

*This essay first appeared in the* Iowa Journal of Communication, 38, 55–79.

and women are seen as inferior to men" (Foss 166). Thus, a prevailing goal of feminism is to change or unseat this patriarchal power structure.

Similarly, the concept of sisterhood has been an integral part of the feminist movement since its beginning. While there are variations in meaning, sisterhood recognizes the common oppression that women face in a patriarchal society, and suggests that strength can be found in unification. Keith E. Melder (1977) discussed the impact of sisterhood on the early women's movement of the 1800s and early 1900s, which is now referred to as the first wave: "Sisterhood strengthened women's collective identity.... From their active, collective enterprises, women gained a sense of power" (48). The strength of sisterhood generated dramatic changes for women's rights. By working together, the women of the first wave were able to accomplish many goals, including winning the right to vote. During the second wave of feminism in the 1960s and 1970s, sisterhood was again a unifying force. According to Ruth Rosen (2000), the concept gained popularity during the second wave via the 1968 slogan "Sisterhood is Powerful." Karlyn Kohrs Campbell (1999) explained that sisterhood was generated through consciousness raising: "meetings of small, leaderless groups in which each person [was] encouraged to express her personal feelings and experiences" where the goal was to make "the personal political: to create awareness (through shared experiences) that what were thought to be personal deficiencies and individual problems [were] common and shared" (128). Sisterhood generated "a widespread optimism about the ability of the women's movement" (Farrell 1998, 71). Gloria Steinem, a leader of the second wave, used the concept of sisterhood as a rallying point by emphasizing "the bonds and the sexual oppression that transcend differences of race, economics, religion, and all other social categories" (Farrell 71). Sisterhood, once again, produced political and social changes for women. Currently, the women's movement is in its third wave. Critics argue that today's feminists are too individualistic, and that the movement is all but dead (Baumgardner & Richards). Those involved directly in the third wave strongly denounce such claims, and argue that the movement is indeed alive and active, and that sisterhood is still an important part of its survival (Baumgardner & Richards). A criticism of the second wave was that it spoke primarily to middle to upper class white women (Baumgardner & Richards). The third wave strives to include more diverse voices, including those of men (Digby 1998) and those of non-white heritage (Hernández & Rehman 2002). Consequently, sisterhood for the third wave truly means the unification of all and the oppression of none.

An examination of *Buffy the Vampire Slayer's* final season reveals the presence of both patriarchal and feminist metaphors. Although metaphor was once viewed merely as a decorative linguistic device, rhetorical scholars have argued that metaphor constructs reality in powerful ways (Burgchardt 2000; Foss 1996; Ricoeur 1993). While feminism is negatively represented in many contemporary media outlets (Faludi 1991), texts such as *Buffy* construct feminism as an empowering critical perspective. The dialectical tension between the patriarchal metaphors and the feminist metaphors in the program rhetorically construct sisterhood as an agent of social change. In order to better understand how feminism is constructed in *Buffy*, we begin with an overview of the series and previous scholarly work that it has generated. A brief discussion of the nature of metaphor and its role in rhetorical criticism is then offered. We then provide examples of patriarchal and feminist metaphors present in the final season of *Buffy*, and discuss the implications of bringing these concepts into conversation with one another. We end the essay by reflecting on the ways that this research enhances the field of communication.

## Buffy the Vampire Slayer

The television series *Buffy the Vampire Slayer* began airing in 1997. The show's creator, Joss Whedon, consciously set out to turn the tables on the typical horror scenario in which a beautiful, blonde girl is always attacked and killed (Wilcox & Lavery 2002). Although Buffy may have a silly name, and may look like the typical blonde victim, she is the Slayer; "In every generation there is a Chosen one. She alone will stand against the vampires, the demons, the forces of darkness. She is the Slayer" (as cited in Wilcox & Lavery xvii). Ancient men, known as the Shadow Men, created the Slayer tradition and lineage, and proclaimed that the Slayer must always be female. If the Slayer dies, a new girl becomes the Chosen one.

Buffy lives in Sunnydale, California. The town looks pleasant on the surface, but in fact sits over the Hellmouth, a demon magnet. While Buffy confronts various forms of evil during each episode, each season of *Buffy the Vampire Slayer* has its own "big bad" villain who dominates throughout the season. The power of the "big bad" always threatens to end the world, but Buffy ultimately overcomes him or her in the season finale. Although the legend of the Slayer states that the Chosen one will stand alone, each Slayer has a Watcher who trains and guides her. Giles, Buffy's Watcher, trained and fought by her side for years. Other than her Watcher, Slayers are discouraged from maintaining friendships and family relationships. Buffy has always eschewed this rule, and has come to rely on a group of close friends nicknamed "the Scoobies" for support.

On May 20, 2003, *Buffy the Vampire Slayer* came to an end. Over the course of seven seasons, the show reached cult status and garnered critical acclaim (Malcom 2003). This analysis is concerned with the seventh, and final, season of *Buffy*. Although feminist metaphors are evident throughout the series, the seventh season employs them in important and distinct ways. The metaphors present in the final season are integral components of the series' overall conclusion.

The series *Buffy the Vampire Slayer* has generated many studies and critiques, hailing from a variety of academic disciplines. *Buffy* has been analyzed in terms of ethics (Kawal 2003; Korsmeyer 2003; Milavec & Kaye 2003; Stroud 2003), religion (Anderson 2003; Held 2003; King 2003; Pasley 2003; Sakal 2003), and philosophy (Aberdein 2003; Daspit 2003; Greene & Yuen 2003; Lawler 2003; Muntersbjorn, 2003; South 2003b). There is even an online journal devoted entirely to *Buffy* studies, called *Slayage: The Online International Journal of Buffy Studies*, which is operated by English professors David Lavery and Rhonda V. Wilcox (Guy 2003). The two have also co-edited a book entitled *Fighting the Forces: What's at Stake in Buffy the Vampire Slayer* (Wilcox & Lavery 2002), which consists of academic *Buffy* studies. Two similar books, *Buffy the Vampire Slayer and Philosophy: Fear and Trembling in Sunnydale* (South 2003a) and *Reading the Vampire Slayer: An Unofficial Critical Companion to Buffy and Angel* (Kaveney 2001), also offer academic *Buffy* essays. The vast amount of academic research that *Buffy the Vampire Slayer* has generated certainly points to the series as a fascinating phenomenon.

Several scholars (Byers 2003; Chandler 2003; Daugherty 2001; Early 2002; Marinucci 2003; Miller 2003; Pender 2002; Playden 2001; Vint 2002) have examined *Buffy* from a feminist perspective. Michele Byers (2003) argued that popular culture artifacts that can be read as offering versions of feminism, such as *Buffy the Vampire Slayer*, should be taken seriously, even if they are not perfect feminist texts. Holly Chandler (2003) suggested that while vampires acted as metaphors for the patriarchy in the early seasons of *Buffy the Vampire Slayer*, Buffy successfully used a combination of physical strength and verbal power to subvert and destabilize traditional masculine connotations of vampire characters, which created fluidity in regards to the vampire-as-patriarchy metaphor in *Buffy*. Anne Millard Daugherty (2001) analyzed four episodes of *Buffy the Vampire Slayer* to support her argument that Buffy is a symbol of female empowerment. In each of these episodes, Buffy and other females face attacks on their empowerment. In each situation, Buffy and her friends resist and overcome the challenges and attacks. Frances Early (2002) argued that *Buffy the Vampire Slayer* depicts a transgressive woman warrior: a female action-adventure hero fulfilling her destiny, while at the same time transcending the typical quest script by offering alternative problem-solving methods. Mimi Marinucci (2003) suggested that the violent acts of vampires (specifically, their goal to suck blood) in *Buffy the Vampire Slayer* are symbolic of rape. She therefore argued that Buffy's fight against vampires represents the struggle against women's oppression.

In another feminist analysis of *Buffy the Vampire Slayer*, Jessica Prata Miller (2003) utilized Carol Gilligan's (1982) research, which suggested that two different approaches to morality exist, the masculine "justice perspective" and the feminine "care perspective." Miller suggested that Buffy is able to employ the "care perspective" without sacrificing her personal autonomy. Patricia Pender (2002) responded to the polarity of many feminist critiques of *Buffy the Vampire Slayer* that attempt to categorize *Buffy* as either "good" or "bad" for feminism. Pender argued that such binary judgments are archaic and miss the mark completely. She opined that Buffy is not either/or; she is both. Zoe-Jane Playden (2001) argued that *Buffy the Vampire Slayer* offers audiences an autonomous woman, one who actively questions and fights the patriarchy, while simultaneously fostering and relying upon her community. Sherryl Vint (2002) analyzed the contradictions between the representation of Buffy (the character) as portrayed in the series (the primary text) and that of the actor who plays Buffy (Sarah Michelle Gellar) as depicted in magazine articles and photos (secondary texts). She concluded by suggesting that such contradictions are not a problem, but are instead an impetus for debate and scholarly engagement. This essay will contribute to the ongoing scholarly discussion regarding *Buffy*, but more importantly, it will reveal how *Buffy* communicates feminist ideas to a young female audience through a popular culture text.

The fan base for *Buffy the Vampire Slayer* is comprised primarily of young women (Early 2002). Several feminists (Baumgardner & Richards 2000; Faludi 1991; hooks 1996; Wong 2003) have acknowledged the effects, both positive and negative, of popular culture on the feminist movement. Kristina S. Wong stated, "Pop culture provides an effective vehicle to carry the self-celebrating concepts of ... feminism" (296). One of the hallmarks of contemporary feminism is that young women and men have been steeped in a feminist backlash that misrepresents feminists with negative, alienating stereotypes (Sowards & Renegar, 2004). The positive portrayal of feminist ideas in popular culture texts, such as *Buffy,* act as a vehicle for new images that can counteract these kinds of negative connotations of feminism. This essay argues that *Buffy* communicates a feminist message to its audience through the use of metaphor.

## The Function of Metaphor

Many rhetorical scholars have theorized about the function of metaphor. It is through their work that the understanding of metaphor has evolved. The work of I. A. Richards (1950) has been deemed a "pioneering job ... [that] cannot be overestimated" (Ricoeur, 1993 76). Richards recognized that metaphor was more than mere ornamentation, and his work set out to "put the theory of metaphor in a more important place than it has enjoyed in traditional Rhetoric" (95). He argued, "Metaphor is the omnipresent principle of language.... We cannot get through three sentences of ordinary fluid discourse without it" (92). Richards stated, "In the simplest formulation, when we use a metaphor we have two thoughts of different things active together and supported by a single word, or phrase, whose meaning is a resultant of their interaction" (93). Richards introduced the concepts "tenor" and "vehicle" to identify the two thoughts being brought together by metaphor. Max Black (1962) elaborated upon Richards' work and developed the interaction theory of metaphor. Black suggested that the tenor and vehicle of a metaphor, although not superficially connected, are in fact related by a "system of associated commonplaces" (40) consisting of shared characteristics between the two. The commonplaces of the two terms, taken together, create the metaphor. The vehicle may impact the perception of the tenor so much that other information pertaining to the tenor is filtered out and alternative interpretations are suppressed. Kenneth Burke (1968) described this type of phenomenon in terms of "terministic screens," which "direct the attention into some channels rather than others" (45). For example, the use of a particular metaphor to describe a person may eventually dominate perceptions of the person and consequently filter out any information to the contrary.

George Lakoff and Mark Johnson (1980) also argued that metaphor is more than just a decorative device. They stated, "Metaphor is pervasive in everyday life, not just in language but in thought and action. Our ordinary conceptual system, in terms of which we both think and act, is fundamentally metaphorical in nature" (3). Lakoff and Johnson's theories of metaphor are similar to those of Black (1962). They identified several different types of metaphors, including structural and orientational. For Lakoff and Johnson, "The essence of metaphor is understanding and experiencing one kind of thing in terms of another" (5). Lakoff and Johnson, like Black, also acknowledged that metaphors highlight certain relationships between two concepts while simultaneously hiding others.

Kenneth Burke (1945) has also theorized about the function of metaphor and in fact considered metaphor to be one of the "four master tropes" (503). For Burke, metaphors offer a perspective on reality. He stated, "Metaphor is a device for seeing something *in terms of* [italics in original] something else. It brings out the thisness of a that, or the thatness of a this" (503). Like many other theorists, metaphors for Burke are much more than mere figures of speech, and may in fact help us to discover "the truth" (503). Rhetorical theorists have provided us with a rich definition of metaphor. There is now a greater understanding of the capabilities, functions, and effects of metaphor; clearly, metaphor is more than a mere ornament. Scholars who adhere to the broader definition of metaphor, as delineated above, have generated the metaphoric approach to rhetorical criticism and have adopted this critical perspective to reveal the social significance and implications of specific metaphors. Consequently, metaphor should be understood as a powerful mechanism for creating new ways of thinking and for constructing alternative realities.

## Metaphors of Patriarchy and Sisterhood

*Buffy the Vampire Slayer* relies heavily on the use of metaphor to convey meaning to its audience. In this essay, we argue that the final season of *Buffy* utilizes metaphor in a way that constructs a positive image of feminist attitudes. Because metaphors help to construct reality, the use of this device to demonstrate feminist concepts in *Buffy* has a crucial impact on its audience.

The metaphors in the final season of *Buffy* can be divided into patriarchal and feminist metaphors.

### Patriarchal Metaphors

In the seventh season of *Buffy the Vampire Slayer*, three characters or groups of characters served as metaphors for the patriarchy. The First, Caleb, and the Shadow Men each functioned to construct a patriarchal presence in the show. The First was "the original evil ... the one that came before everything else" (Noxon, Petrie, & Grossman, 2). As the source of all evil, The First was Buffy's most challenging and threatening adversary. The First could not take corporeal form, and therefore could not physically fight, but it could assume the likeness of any dead person. The First employed powerful agents, both human and vampire, to perform physical tasks in preparation for its upcoming war. This battle was intended to destroy the known world. Success would ultimately allow The First to gain power and to take corporeal form by feeding on the energy of the surviving humans, which would in turn enable the purest form of evil to enter all of the remaining humans. The First knew that the Slayer was a threat to its victory, and systematically set out to destroy its lineage. Early in the seventh season, The First had the members of the governing body of the Slayer line, known as the Watchers Council, brutally murdered. As the Council was meeting to discuss a plan to resist The First, their headquarters were bombed and all of the Council members were killed, and their records, documents, and ancient texts were destroyed (Goddard & Solomon).

The laws of the Slayer lineage required that countless possible Slayers, known as Potentials, must always exist throughout the world. In the event of the current Slayer's death, one Potential would be called to duty, and would immediately gain Slayer strength and power. To ensure the extermination of the Slayer lineage, The First sought to kill all of the Potentials. Eventually, many of the remaining Potentials who feared for their lives migrated to Sunnydale to seek refuge with Buffy. The Slayer and the Potential Slayers, who embody female power, particularly threatened the First.

Caleb, The First's human agent, also functioned as a metaphor for patriarchal control over female power. Caleb's arrival late in the season marked the beginning of the final struggle between Buffy's gang and The First. Caleb was eager to enact The First's plan to destroy the Slayer lineage, since he despised all women and relished the thought of killing them.

Caleb initially appeared to be an attractive young man dressed in the garb of a preacher. As he was driving into Sunnydale for the first time, a frightened girl fleeing from attackers suddenly jumped into his truck in search of safety. The girl was soon identified as Shannon, a new Potential. Caleb initially seemed to console Shannon, and it appeared as though she was safe with him. After a few moments, however, it became obvious to Shannon and to the audience that Caleb was not to be trusted, and was in fact an evil misogynist:

> CALEB: Well, Shannon, you feel like telling me why those freaky joes were after you?
> SHANNON: I'm not sure.
> CALEB: Did you ever give thought that maybe they were chasing you because you're a whore?
> SHANNON: What?
> CALEB: ... You know what you are, Shannon? Dirty [*Dirty Girls*].

Caleb proceeded to injure Shannon and then used her to lure Buffy and her gang into a trap. Buffy realized that Caleb was an agent for The First, but did not immediately understand his strength. Buffy, along with the Scoobies and the Potentials, were overpowered and defeated during their first encounter with Caleb. After several Potentials were killed and one of the Scoobies was blinded in one eye, the group was forced to retreat and develop new strategies for fighting Caleb and The First.

Shortly after meeting Caleb, Buffy learned of a powerful scythe forged in stone that he had been trying to hide from her. With renewed confidence, she decided to confront Caleb alone, in hopes of retrieving this weapon. This time, when Buffy faced Caleb, she held her own. This show of strength infuriated Caleb, who screamed, "You whore!" (Kirshner & Solomon 65).

Buffy stopped in her tracks and retorted, "You know, you really should watch your language. Someone didn't know you, they might think you were a woman-hating jerk" (65). Buffy's statement made Caleb's patriarchal and misogynistic values explicit. Moments later, Buffy discovered the scythe, and was able to pull it from the stone with ease, which angered and frightened Caleb.

Buffy killed Caleb with the scythe in the beginning of the final episode of the series. Before his demise, however, Caleb directed several derogatory comments at Buffy. At one point, he taunted her by yelling, "You ready to finish this, bitch?" and "Stupid girl. You'll never stop me" (Whedon 2–3).

Caleb's sexist language and values, coupled with his obvious delight in overseeing The First's project to destroy the Slayer lineage, function as metaphors for the larger patriarchal structure. Sunnydale is a microcosm of the larger culture, where Caleb and The First represent the deep-seated misogyny that is prevalent in contemporary society. Furthermore, Caleb's choice to represent himself as a preacher alludes to the patriarchal tendencies in many Christian traditions. This aspect of his character further reinforces his metaphoric function as a tool of oppression.

The Shadow Men, the creators of the first Slayer and the first set of Watchers, also function as metaphors for patriarchy. While the series usually depicted a male Watcher for every female Slayer, the origins of this practice were not exposed until the seventh season. During this final season, the patriarchal history of the Slayer tradition was revealed. Buffy realized that in order to defeat The First she needed to gain resources beyond what she currently possessed. In her quest for additional knowledge, Buffy entered a portal during the middle of the season, which took her back in time and introduced her to the Shadow Men (Petrie 2003). Before this meeting, Buffy had no previous knowledge of the Shadow Men, or of the exact origins of the Slayer tradition. When Buffy asked the Shadow Men for knowledge, they replied by stating, "We cannot give you knowledge. Only power" (Petrie 48–49). Moments later, they proceeded to knock Buffy unconscious and chained her up inside a cave. Then the Shadow Men attempted to do to Buffy what they had done to create the very first Slayer: Rape her with what the Shadow Men called "the energy of the demon" (52).

The history of the Slayer lineage revealed that the Shadow Men violated the first Slayer by raping her with demon energy. When Buffy went to them in search of answers, they tried to do the same to her. The demon energy was in the form of mist, which made it difficult for Buffy to battle. The insidious nature of the mist is similar to that of patriarchal values within society, which are also often difficult to confront directly. The Shadow Men clearly function as a metaphor for patriarchy. They embodied force and used it to create and control the first Slayer. In season seven, they tried to use their power to control and dominate Buffy.

The First, Caleb, and The Shadow Men all function as metaphors of patriarchy by embodying misogyny and a desire to control women. Their hatred, as well as the insidious ways in which they extend their influence, serve as reminders that the world is often a dangerous place. Furthermore, the gendered nature of these battles as men against women functions as a metaphor for the ongoing struggle for equality, including an end to domestic violence and sexual assault. The patriarchal metaphors in the final season of *Buffy* are countered by an equally compelling set of feminist metaphors.

## *Feminist Metaphors*

After Buffy spurned the assistance of the Shadow Men, she found the strength to defeat Caleb and The First in the creation of a powerful sisterhood. There are a number of feminist concepts in the series, but this analysis will focus on sisterhood since it is often an integral concept for contemporary feminism (Morgan, 2003). The Scoobies, the Potentials, and She all functioned as metaphors for sisterhood in the final season of *Buffy the Vampire Slayer*.

*Buffy the Vampire Slayer* consistently conveyed a "strength in numbers" ideology. Although the legend of the Slayer called for the Chosen One to act alone in the fight against evil, Buffy rejected such restrictions. Throughout the series, she relied on the Scoobies for support. While it was solely Buffy's destiny to protect the world from evil, she and her gang realized that their chances of winning were significantly increased by combining their powers and skills. Although each of the Scoobies contributed in the fight against evil in his or her own way, several of them, like Buffy, possessed superpowers. Indeed, four Scoobies with superpowers played integral roles in the defeat of The First in the final season. Willow was one of the world's most powerful witches. Faith was also a Slayer who was indirectly summoned as a result of Buffy's brief death in an earlier season. In addition, both Spike and Angel were vampires (all vampires possessed super strength) with souls (akin to a conscience). In the end, these four, along with the other Scoobies, gave Buffy the resources that she needed to defeat The First.

Over the course of seven seasons, several Scoobies came and went. Three of the original Scoobies, however — Giles, Willow, and Xander — remained with Buffy until the end. The importance of this core group was underscored in the final episode (Whedon, 2003). The entire group of Scoobies and Potentials had arrived at Sunnydale High School to open the Hellmouth to take on The First's army. As each member of the large group separated to take their designated positions for battle, there was a significant moment in which Buffy and the three original Scoobies were left alone together. The directions in the script read, "There is a moment, all of them looking at each other, and we realize it's the original four: Buffy, Giles, Willow, and Xander. The camera slowly circles around them as they realize it, too, [and] look at each other with unspoken feeling" (Whedon 37–38).

The four of them each had different jobs for the battle, and would soon be separated. This made the moment especially significant. Facing uncertainty, they all realized that it might be their last time alive together. After seven years of fighting side by side, this was an especially important scene that emphasized the strong bonds between Buffy and the original Scoobies. Before going their separate ways, the four shared some casual banter about their plans for the next day. Not only did their conversation act to lighten the mood, it also demonstrated the confidence that the four had in each another. By discussing plans for the next day, they were communicating the faith that they had in one another as a team, that they could indeed pull together and win.

In *Buffy the Vampire Slayer*, success came from the bond of sisterhood between Buffy and the Scoobies. Although the Scoobies were both men and women, they function as a recurring metaphor for sisterhood throughout the series, and especially in the final battle of the series. Sisterhood connotes shared interest, unification, and derived strength and is not necessarily gender exclusive. The Scoobies metaphorically represented all of these aspects of sisterhood in *Buffy's* final season. Additionally, because Buffy's group consisted of both female and male members, a new expanded definition of sisterhood is being promulgated.

The sisterhood metaphor was also evident in season seven by the addition of the Potentials. Buffy and the Scoobies first learned of the Potentials midway through the seventh season (Noxon, Petrie, & Grossman, 2002). Giles, who had been traveling, arrived at Buffy's house with three unfamiliar girls. Buffy and the Scoobies were understandably confused. Dawn, Buffy's younger sister, asked, "They're all Slayers?" (21), to which Giles replied, "Potential Slayers. Waiting for one to be called. There were many more like them, all over the world. Now there's only a handful, and they're all on their way to Sunnydale" (21). Giles then explained that The First was trying to wipe out the entire Slayer line. As more Slayers began to arrive in Sunnydale, Buffy made it clear that she did not merely plan to protect them. She intended to train them in order to join the fight. Although the young women did not yet have Slayer strength, as Potentials they possessed the Slayer instinct. Initially, the Potentials were scared, confused, and somewhat skeptical of their ability to defeat The First. They also had their doubts about Buffy's chances.

Buffy realized that in order for the group to work as a team, the Potentials had to develop confidence and learn to trust in her and in themselves. Shortly after the arrival of the Potentials, Buffy, Willow and Xander devised a plan to solidify their confidence (Fury & Grossman, 2002). Buffy lured an enemy to a vacant construction site and proceeded to battle him in front of all of the Potentials and several of the Scoobies. As Buffy declared, "Welcome to Thunderdome" (55), the girls began to realize that this battle was for their benefit. They watched as Buffy struggled and finally slayed her adversary. The Potentials stared down on her in awe, as Buffy, "bloody, bruised, and winded" (59), looked up at them and stated, "I don't know what's coming next. But I do know, it's all gonna be just like this. Hard. Painful. But in the end, it's gonna be us. If we all do our part, believe it, we'll be the ones left standing" (60).

In the episodes that followed, Buffy and the Scoobies continued to train the Potentials. Over time, the girls began to gain the experience and confidence necessary to fight the powers of evil successfully. Setbacks did occur, however. Uncertainty and doubt resurfaced when several of the Potentials were killed by Caleb and other agents of The First. However, in the final episode, "Chosen" (Whedon, 2003), all of the Potentials came together and participated in Buffy's plan to defeat The First.

The episode "Chosen" (Whedon, 2003), features one of the most obvious metaphors for sisterhood. Rather than follow Slayer tradition, Buffy devised a plan that allowed all of the Potentials to become Slayers simultaneously. This plan defied the Shadow Men and their ancient rules, which had allowed for only one Slayer to exist at any one time. By investing all of the Potentials with the power of the Slayer, Buffy elevated the power of her allies. The women were empowered individually, and the group was united by the process of becoming ready to combat The First. In this way, the Potentials constituted a prominent metaphor for sisterhood in the final season of *Buffy the Vampire Slayer*. Sisterhood refers to unification, strength in numbers, and shared interest. The Potentials, like the Scoobies, acted as a metaphor for sisterhood by adding their numbers and strength to Buffy's battle. Additionally, Buffy and the Potentials united to create a new sisterhood of Slayers.

The remaining metaphor for sisterhood in the final season of *Buffy the Vampire Slayer* was located in the character She. She appeared late in the season, and provided Buffy with the final resource necessary to beat The First: a mystical scythe made "for her alone to wield" (Greenberg & Contner, 2003, 58). Buffy discovered the scythe before meeting She, and had many questions about its origins and power. The Scoobies' research of the scythe led Buffy to a tomb where she first encountered the mysterious woman identified only as "She." Buffy was initially hesitant to approach She, but soon discovered that She had the answers that Buffy sought:

She serves as a metaphor for sisterhood. As the only remaining member of an ancient group of women, the Guardians, She secretly watched over the Slayer. She ultimately provided Buffy with the knowledge that she needed to defeat The First. She was particularly significant as standing for the bonds of sisterhood that exist between the older and newer generations of women. The scythe was created by women (She and her group of female Guardians), without the knowledge or approval of men (the Shadow Men and the Watchers), for a woman (the Slayer). Buffy ended up using it to kill Caleb and many of The First's vampire minions. She then had Willow use it to empower countless Potentials in the effort to defeat The First. She and the scythe represented female history, knowledge, and power, all components of sisterhood.

In the end, each of these metaphors for sisterhood combined to contribute to the victory over The First. Each of the Scoobies helped in their own way, culminating with Willow's spell. The Potentials agreed to become empowered, thus providing Buffy with an army of Slayers. She gave Buffy the knowledge, power, and confidence necessary to beat The First. Buffy's realization of her groups' strength, and the subsequent empowerment of all of the Potentials, serve as metaphors for sisterhood. Taken together, these metaphors encapsulate the idea of sisterhood as an avenue of resistance to patriarchal control. Buffy and her friends embodied this struggle as they faced off against The First.

## Implications and Conclusions

One of the basic principles of feminism is the belief that people are oppressed by the patriarchy. Therefore, a shared goal of the movement is to change or critique this patriarchal power structure. An analysis of the final season of *Buffy the Vampire Slayer* revealed several metaphors for the patriarchy that interact with feminist metaphors for sisterhood. Buffy and her friends were threatened by the people and ideas represented by the patriarchal metaphors, and eventually succeeded in defeating or defying them by creating sisterhood and acting in feminist ways. The metaphors present in *Buffy the Vampire Slayer's* final season depict feminism as a plausible and effective response to the patriarchy. When Buffy is threatened by the evil patriarchal characters The First and Caleb, she reaches out to the Shadow Men, her supposed allies, and finds even more oppression, control, and violence. Realizing that all three sets of characters are damaging to her wellbeing, she turns to alternative sources of strength, the Scoobies, the Potentials, and She, all metaphors for sisterhood. Ultimately, Buffy and her "sisters" are able to defeat The First and Caleb and defy the Shadow Men by utilizing feminist approaches to power.

The interaction between the patriarchal metaphors and the feminist metaphors communicates several ideas to the audience. First, the patriarchal metaphors represented via the three sets of characters always depict the evil or antiquated approach to life. Never do the patriarchal characters embody a desirable viewpoint. The message that is communicated to the audience is clearly one of disapproval and/or disdain for patriarchal values. Conversely, the feminist approaches to problem solving are clearly depicted as the moral and successful methods. Buffy and her friends join together, make group decisions, share power and knowledge, and ultimately prevail. The audience is given a positive view of feminist values as an alternative approach to life, as well as a sense of hope that patriarchal oppression can be overcome.

The expansion of the definition of sisterhood is another idea that is conveyed by the metaphors in *Buffy the Vampire Slayer*. While the term "sisterhood" has traditionally referred only to the bonds between women, Buffy and her friends demonstrate this concept of sisterhood within a group of mixed gender. Although all of the Potentials, She, and many of the Scoobies are female, the men in the group are never excluded, but also never attempt to dominate. Buffy is clearly the leader, but it is acknowledged within this particular sisterhood that each and every member of the group, regardless of sex or status, is equally important for the overall survival of the group. They all work as a team, share the same ideological goals, and honor the bonds of friendship. *Buffy* not only communicates to its audience the possibilities available through sisterhood, but also broadens its very definition.

The importance of female history is also communicated via metaphor in *Buffy the Vampire Slayer*. The character, She, provides Buffy with the crucial knowledge and power necessary to prevail in battle. It is evident that without She's information, Buffy may not have had the final resources necessary to defeat The First. To form a successful sisterhood, women must be aware of their history, and must initiate a dialogue between generations. The importance of this connection is communicated to the audience via Buffy's relationship with She.

In the final episode of *Buffy the Vampire Slayer*, Buffy creates a new type of sisterhood between herself and the Potentials. Instead of keeping her power and uniqueness to herself, she chooses to share it by empowering the others. Although it is evident that Buffy needed the Potentials to become Slayers in order to defeat The First, her act was not a selfish act. By sharing, not only did she further ensure the group's survival, she also elevated the worth of the Potentials and further unified her group. Buffy's act can serve as a model for the empowerment of women by women. She demonstrates the significance and strength that comes with a sharing of power and talent. At the same time, Buffy and the Potentials defied the Shadow Men and the legend of the Slayer, which allowed for only one Slayer at a time. In the final season of *Buffy*, Buffy and the Potentials rejected such restrictions and formed a new sisterhood of Slayers.

Ultimately, the final season of *Buffy the Vampire Slayer* uses metaphor to condemn patriarchal values, while at the same time presenting feminist strategies as viable alternatives. Audience members are exposed to the destructive nature of patriarchal oppression and dominance. Feminist approaches to life, particularly those demonstrating the benefits of sisterhood, instead offer hope. Expanded definitions of sisterhood are explored, and value is placed on the connections between generations and the sharing of talents and power. Significantly, Buffy and her allies do encounter difficulties, which demonstrate that sisterhood is not always easy. However, the feminist approach to life is valued and portrayed as the more desirable worldview.

*Buffy the Vampire Slayer* is an example of a text that serves to construct feminism in positive and empowering ways. This essay has explored the relationship between patriarchal and feminist metaphors in constructing a feminist popular culture text. In the final season of *Buffy the Vampire Slayer*, metaphor played a critical role in the overall plot, and metaphors for the patriarchy contributed to the development of feminist metaphors. The dynamic between the patriarchal and feminist metaphors in *Buffy the Vampire Slayer's* seventh season demonstrates to the audience that adversity can be defeated. It also suggests that patriarchal knowledge and methods, represented via the Shadow Men, although usually the dominant paradigm in society, can be rejected and replaced with new sources of power. People, particularly girls and women, can find strength, knowledge, and power via feminist approaches to life, as Buffy did. Buffy and her friends also offer new perspectives on what it looks like to be a feminist. They defy the stereotypes, and make feminism young, attractive, and cool.

*Buffy the Vampire Slayer's* seventh, and final, season incorporated many metaphors, which can be viewed as representations for feminist concepts. When one subscribes to the belief that metaphors affect our view of reality (Foss, 1996), it becomes apparent that the analysis of the metaphors present in popular culture texts is important. The examination of metaphors that construct feminist concepts is especially significant to the movement, as these metaphors most definitely contribute to an audience's conception of feminism.

Feminism has suffered in recent years, and many young women today do not consider themselves feminists even when they share feminist ideals (Baumgardner & Richards, 2000). We believe that in order for the movement to survive and to continue to gain advancements for women, covert examples of feminism should be examined for the positive effects that they may produce. *Buffy the Vampire Slayer* does not overtly claim to be a feminist text, but a close analysis of its metaphors reveal that it is indeed championing ideas that are important to the feminist movement. The girls and young women who compose the core audience are exposed to the positive portrayal of feminist concepts embedded in *Buffy* via metaphor. Because social reality is constructed through metaphor, fans of *Buffy*, both female and male, are being introduced to perspectives regarding feminism that they do not receive in other media outlets. Because a popular culture television series, such as *Buffy*, can reach an audience of young women and offer them a positive representation of feminism through the use of metaphor, such a text should be recognized as an important tool for the movement's future. Amidst the climate of the backlash, the use of metaphor to communicate feminist ideology may be more persuasive than overt feminist messages.

*Buffy the Vampire Slayer* is just one of several popular culture texts which offer its audience a positive, albeit not perfect and somewhat covert, representation of feminism. Future studies must identify other popular culture texts to discover similar tools for feminism. Such studies act to contribute to feminist scholarship, metaphoric criticism, and communication studies simultaneously.

As several other scholars (Byers, 2003; Daugherty, 2001; Pender, 2002) who have studied *Buffy the Vampire Slayer* have pointed out, the series is not a perfect feminist text. The characters are played by actors who all adhere to Hollywood standards of beauty. They are all thin, have perfect bodies, and wear the latest fashions. We admit that this aspect of the series is somewhat problematic in promoting a feminist agenda. The creators may be trying to dismantle stereotypes about feminist appearances, or they may just be succumbing to Hollywood pressures. However, since *Buffy the Vampire Slayer* does not overtly claim to be a feminist text, we think that such criticisms pale when compared to the positive feminist ideals that the series conveys to its audience. The metaphors in the seventh season alone covertly communicated feminist values to millions of viewers ("Buffy finale," 2003). While the perfect appearance of the actors is certainly a limitation that should be mentioned, we, like Michele Byers (2003), Anne Millard Daugherty (2001), and Patricia Pender (2002), feel that to dismiss the series because of such an imperfection is to reject the feminist contributions that it does make. Through the use of metaphor, *Buffy the Vampire Slayer* is significant for communicating a positive portrayal of feminism to its viewers.

## WORKS CITED

Aberdein, A. "Balderdash and Chicanery: Science and Beyond." In J. B. South (Ed.), *Buffy the Vampire Slayer and Philosophy: Fear and Trembling in Sunnydale* (pp. 79–90). Chicago: Open Court, 2003.

Anderson, W. L. (2003). "Prophecy Girl and the Powers That Be: The Philosophy of Religion in the Buffyverse." In J. B. South (Ed.), *Buffy the Vampire Slayer and Philosophy: Fear and Trembling in Sunnydale* (pp. 212–226). Chicago: Open Court, 2003.

Baumgardner, J., Richards, A. *Manifesta: Young Women, Feminism, and the Future.* New York: Farrar, Straus and Giroux, 2000.

Benoit, W. L. "Framing Through Temporal Metaphor: The 'Bridges' of Bob Dole and Bill Clinton in Their 1996 Acceptance Addresses." *Communication Studies, 52,* (2001) 70–84.

Black, M. *Models and Metaphors: Studies in Language and Philosophy.* Ithaca, NY: Cornell University Press, 1962.

"Buffy" Finale Stakes Strong Ratings for UPN, 2003. Zap2it.com. Retrieved February 27, 2004, from http://tv.zap2it.com/tveditorial/utils/tve_article_print.

Burgchardt, C. R. "Metaphoric Criticism." In C. R Burgchardt (Ed.), *Readings in Rhetorical Criticism*, 2nd ed, p. 337. State College, PA: Strata, 2000.

Burke, K. *A Grammar of Motives.* New York: Prentice-Hall, 1945.

Burke, K. *Language as Symbolic Action: Essays on Life, Literature, and Method.* Berkeley and Los Angeles: University of California Press, 1968.

Byers, M. "Buffy the Vampire Slayer: The Next Generation of Television." In R. Dicker & A. Piepmeier (Eds.), *Catching a Wave: Reclaiming Feminism for the 21st Century*, Boston: Northeastern University Press, 2003, pp. 171–187.

Campbell, K. K. "The Rhetoric of Women's Liberation: An Oxymoron." *Communication Studies, 50,* (1999), 125–137.

Chandler, H. "Slaying the Patriarchy: Transfusions of the Vampire Metaphor in Buffy the Vampire Slayer." *Slayage: The Online International Journal of Buffy Studies, 9* (2003). Retrieved October, 17, 2003, from http://www.slayage.tv/essays/slayage9/Chandler.htm.

Daspit, T. "Buffy Goes to College, Adam Murders to Dissect: Education and Knowledge in Postmodernity." In J. B. South (Ed.), *Buffy the Vampire Slayer and Philosophy: Fear and Trembling in Sunnydale.* Chicago: Open Court, 2003, (pp. 117–130).

Daugherty, A. M. "Just a Girl: Buffy as Icon." In R. Kaveney (Ed.), *Reading the Vampire Slayer.* London: Tauris Parke, 2001, (pp. 148–165).

Digby, T. (Ed.). *Men Doing Feminism.* New York: Routledge, 1998.

Early, F. "Staking her Claim: Buffy the Vampire Slayer as Transgressive Woman Warrior." *Slayage: The Online International Journal of Buffy Studies, 6* (2002). Retrieved October 17, 2003, from http://www.slayage.tv/essays/slayage6/Early.htm.

Faludi, S. *Backlash: The Undeclared War against American Women.* New York: Crown, 1991.

Farrell, A. E. *Yours in Sisterhood: Ms. Magazine and the Promise of Popular Feminism.* Chapel Hill, NC: University of North Carolina Press, 1998.

Foss, S. K. *Rhetorical Criticism: Exploration and Practice* (2nd ed.). Prospect Heights, IL: Waveland, 1996.

Fury, D. (Writer), and Grossman, D. (Director). "Showtime" [Television series episode], 2002. In J. Whedon and M. Noxon (Producers), *Buffy the Vampire Slayer*. Script retrieved September 12, 2003, from http://www.buffyscripts.net/.

Gilligan, C. *In a Different Voice: Psychological Theory and Women's Development*. Cambridge, MA: Harvard University Press, 1982.

Goddard, D. (Writer), and Gershman, M. (Director). "Dirty Girls" [Television series episode, 2003]. In J. Whedon and M. Noxon (Producers), *Buffy the Vampire Slayer*. Script retrieved September 12, 2003, from http://www.buffyscripts. net/.

Goddard, D. (Writer), and Solomon, D. (Director). "Never Leave Me" [Television series episode, 2002]. In J. Whedon & M. Noxon (Producers), *Buffy the Vampire Slayer*. Script retrieved September 12, 2003, from http://www.buffyscripts. net/.

Graves, M. "Functions of Key Metaphors in Early Quaker Sermons, 1671–1700." In S. K. Foss (Ed.), *Rhetorical Criticism: Exploration and Practice* 2nd ed. Prospect Heights, IL: Waveland, 1996, pp. 368–387.

Greenberg, D. Z. (Writer), and Contner, J. A. (Director). "Empty Places" [Television series episode, 2003]. In J. Whedon & M. Noxon (Producers), *Buffy the Vampire Slayer*. Script retrieved September 12, 2003, from http://www.buffy scripts.net/.

Greene, R., and Yuen, W. "Morality on Television: The Case of Buffy the Vampire Slayer." In J. B. South (Ed.), *Buffy the Vampire Slayer and Philosophy: Fear and Trembling in Sunnydale*. Chicago: Open Court, 2003, pp. 271–281.

Guy, M. "Middle Tennessee State U. Professor Sinks his Teeth into 'Buffy.'" *University Wire*, March 19, 2003. Retrieved February 21, 2004, from http://80-web. lexis-nexis.com.libproxy.sdsu.edu/universe/printdoc.

Held, J. M. "Justifying the means: Punishment in the Buffyverse." In J. B. South (Ed.), *Buffy the Vampire Slayer and Philosophy: Fear and Trembling in Sunnydale* (p 227–238). Chicago: Open Court, 2003, pp. 227–238.

Henry, D. "The Rhetorical Dynamics of Mario Cuomo's 1984 Keynote Address: Situation, Speaker, Metaphor." *The Southern Speech Communication Journal, 53*, 1988, pp. 105–120.

Hernández, D., and Rehman, B. *Colonize This! Young Women of Color on Today's Feminism*. Seattle, WA: Seal, 2002.

hooks, b. *Reel to Real: Race, Sex, and Class at the Movies*. New York: Routledge, 1996.

Huesca, R. "Honda: The Ultimate Tri." In S. K. Foss (Ed.), *Rhetorical Criticism: Exploration and Practice* 2nd ed. Prospect Heights, IL: Waveland, 1996, pp. 388–391.

Ivie, R. L. "Metaphor and the Rhetorical Invention of Cold War 'Idealists.'" *Communication Monographs, 54*, 1987, pp. 165–182.

Kanengieter-Wildeson, M. "Architectural Metaphor as Subversion: The Portland Building." In S. K. Foss (Ed.), *Rhetorical Criticism: Exploration and Practice* 2nd ed. Prospect Heights, IL: Waveland, 1996, pp. 392–395.

Kaveney, R. (Ed.). *Reading the Vampire Slayer: An Unofficial Critical Companion to Buffy and Angel*. London: Tauris Parke, 2001.

Kawal, J. "Should We Do What Buffy Would Do?" In J. B. South (Ed.), *Buffy the*

*Vampire Slayer and Philosophy: Fear and Trembling in Sunnydale.* Chicago: Open Court, 2003, pp. 149–159.

King, N. "Brownskirts: Fascism, Christianity, and the Eternal Demon." In J. B. South (Ed.), *Buffy the Vampire Slayer and philosophy: Fear and Trembling in Sunnydale.* Chicago: Open Court, 2003, pp. 197–211.

Kirshner, R. R. (Writer), and Solomon, D. (Director). "Touched" [Television series episode, 2003]. In J. Whedon and M. Noxon (Producers), *Buffy the Vampire Slayer.* Script retrieved September 12, 2003, from http://www.buffyscripts.net/.

Korsmeyer, C. "Passion and Action: In and Out of Control." In J. B. South (Ed.), *Buffy the Vampire Slayer and philosophy: Fear and Trembling in Sunnydale.* Chicago: Open Court, 2003, pp. 160–172.

Lakoff, G., and Johnson, M. *Metaphors We Live By.* Chicago: University of Chicago Press, 1980, pp. 160–172.

Lawler, J. "Between Heavens and Hells: The Multidimensional Universe in Kant and Buffy the Vampire Slayer." In J. B. South (Ed.), *Buffy the Vampire Slayer and Philosophy: Fear and Trembling in Sunnydale.* Chicago: Open Court, 2003, pp. 103–116.

Malcom, S. So Long, Slayer. *TV Guide, 51* (20), May 17–23, 2003, 28–32.

Marinucci, M. "Feminism and the Ethics of Violence: Why Buffy Kicks Ass." In J. B. South (Ed.), *Buffy the Vampire Slayer and Philosophy: Fear and Trembling in Sunnydale.* Chicago: Open Court, 2003, pp. 61–75.

Melder, K. E. *Beginnings of Sisterhood: The American Women's Rights Movement 1800–1850.* New York: Schocken, 1977.

Milavec, M. M., and Kaye, S. M. (2003). "Buffy in the Buff: A Slayer's Solution to Aristotle's Love Paradox." In J. B. South (Ed.), *Buffy the Vampire Slayer and Philosophy: Fear and Trembling in Sunnydale.* Chicago: Open Court, 2003, pp. 173–184.

Miller, J. "'The I in Team': Buffy and Feminist Ethics." In J. B. South (Ed.), *Buffy the Vampire Slayer and Philosophy: Fear and Trembling in Sunnydale.* Chicago: Open Court, 2003, pp. 35–48.

Morgan, R. *Sisterhood is Forever: The Women's Anthology for a New Millennium.* New York: Washington Square, 2003.

Muntersbjorn, M. M. "Pluralism, Pragmatism, and Pals: The Slayer Subverts the Science Wars." In J. B. South (Ed.), *Buffy the Vampire Slayer and Philosophy: Fear and Trembling in Sunnydale.* Chicago: Open Court, 2003, pp. 91–102.

Noxon, M., and Petrie, D. (Writers), and Grossman, D. (Director). "Bring on the Night" [Television series episode, 2002]. In J. Whedon & M. Noxon (Producers), *Buffy the Vampire Slayer.* Script retrieved September 12, 2003, from http://www.buffyscripts.net/.

Osborn, M. "Archetypal Metaphor in Rhetoric: The Light-Dark Family." In C.R. Burgchardt (Ed.), *Readings in Rhetorical Criticism* 2nd ed. State College, PA: Strata, 2002, pp. 338–349.

Pasley, J. L. "Old Familiar Vampires: The Politics of the Buffyverse." In J. B. South (Ed.), *Buffy the Vampire Slayer and Philosophy: Fear and Trembling in Sunnydale.* Chicago: Open Court, 2003, pp. 254–267.

Pender, Patricia. "'I'm Buffy, and You're ... History': The Postmodern Politics of Buffy." In R. V. Wilcox & D. Lavery (Eds.), *Fighting the Forces: What's at Stake in Buffy the Vampire Slayer*. Lanham, MD: Rowman & Littlefield, 2002, pp. 35–44.

Perry, S. "Rhetorical Functions of the Infestation Metaphor in Hitler's Rhetoric." *Central States Speech Journal, 24,* 1983, 229–235.

Petrie, D. (Writer/Director). "Get It Done" [Television series episode, 2003]. In J. Whedon & M. Noxon (Producers), *Buffy the Vampire Slayer*. Script retrieved September 12, 2003, from http://www.buffyscripts.net/.

Petrie, D. and Espenson, J. (Writers), and Grabiak, M. (Director). "End of Days" [Television series episode, 2003]. In J. Whedon and M. Noxon (Producers), *Buffy the Vampire Slayer*. Script retrieved September 12, 2003, from http://www.buffyscripts.net/.

Petrie, D. (Writer), and Marck, N. (Director). "Beneath You" [Television series episode, 2002]. In J. Whedon and M. Noxon (Producers), *Buffy the Vampire Slayer*. Script retrieved September 12, 2003, from http://www.buffyscripts.net/.

Playden, Z. J. "'What You Are, What's To Come': Feminism, Citizenship, and the Divine." In R. Kaveney (Ed.), *Reading the Vampire Slayer*. London: Tauris Parke, 2001, pp. 120–147.

Richards, I. A. *The Philosophy of Rhetoric* (2nd ed.). New York: Oxford University Press, 1950.

Ricoeur, Paul. *The Rule of Metaphor: Multi-Disciplinary Studies of the Creation of Meaning in Language*. Toronto: University of Toronto Press, 1993.

Rosen, R. *The World Split Open: How the Modern Women's Movement Changed America*. New York: Penguin, 2000.

Sakal, G. J. "No Big Win: Themes of Sacrifice, Salvation, and Redemption." In J. B. South (Ed.), *Buffy the Vampire Slayer and Philosophy: Fear and Trembling in Sunnydale*. Chicago: Open Court, 2003, pp. 239–253.

South, J. B. (Ed.). *Buffy the Vampire Slayer and Philosophy: Fear and Trembling in Sunnydale*. Chicago: Open Court, 2003a.

South, J. B. "'My God, It's Like a Greek Tragedy'": Willow Rosenberg and Human Irrationality." In J. B. South (Ed.), *Buffy the Vampire Slayer and Philosophy: Fear and Trembling in Sunnydale*. Chicago: Open Court, 2003b, pp.131–145.

Sowards, S. K., and Renegar, V. R. "The Rhetorical Functions of Consciousness-Raising in Third Wave Feminism." *Communication Studies, 55,* 2004, pp. 535–552.

Stroud, S. R. "A Kantian Analysis of Moral Judgment in Buffy the Vampire Slayer." In J. B. South (Ed.), *Buffy the Vampire Slayer and Philosophy: Fear and Trembling in Sunnydale*. Chicago: Open Court, 2003, pp. 185–194.

Vint, S. (2002). "'Killing Us Softly?' A Feminist Search for the 'Real' Buffy." *Slayage: The Online International Journal of Buffy Studies, 5* (2002). Retrieved October 17, 2003, from http://www.slayage.tv/essays/slayage5/vint.htm.

Whedon, J. (Writer/Director). "Lessons" [Television series episode, 2002]. In J. Whedon & M. Noxon (Producers), *Buffy the Vampire Slayer*. Script retrieved September 12, 2003, from http://www.buffyscripts.net/.

Whedon, J. (Writer/Director). "Chosen" [Television series episode, 2003]. In J. Whedon and M. Noxon (Producers), *Buffy the Vampire Slayer.* Script retrieved September 12, 2003, from http://www.buffyscripts.net/.

Wilcox. R. V., and Lavery, D. *Fighting the Forces: What's at Stake in Buffy the Vampire Slayer.* Lanham, MD: Rowman & Littlefield, 2002.

Wong, K.S. "Pranks and Fake Porn: Doing Feminism My Way." In R. Dicker & A. Piepmeier (Eds.), *Catching a Wave: Reclaiming Feminism for the 21st Century.* Boston: Northeastern University, 2003, pp. 294–307.

# PART II. *BUFFY* MEETS THE CLASSICS

# King Lear, Buffy, and Apocalyptic Revisionism

## CLINTON P.E. ATCHLEY

A cursory glance at *King Lear* and *Buffy the Vampire Slayer* would seem to reveal that they have nothing in common. One is a contemporary television series devoted to nubile, ass-kicking vampire slayers while the other is, well, *Shakespeare*, for God's sake. If one thinks about this pairing though, some interesting parallels come to mind.*

Highbrows, who hail Shakespeare as the epitome of artistic and intellectual merit, often castigate television as soporific pablum for the masses, an Eliotian quagmire into which no self-respecting intellectual ventures. As far back as 1961, no less a figure than Newton Minnow, former chair of the Federal Communications Commission, had these (in)famous words regarding the medium of television:

> ...when television is bad, nothing is worse. I invite each of you to sit down in front of your television set when your station goes on the air and stay there, for a day, without a book, without a magazine, without a newspaper, without a profit and loss sheet or a rating book to distract you. Keep your eyes glued to that set until the station signs off. I can assure you that what you will observe is a vast wasteland [Minnow].

Likewise, the theater in Elizabethan England, that bastion of highbrow intellectualism, functioned in much the same way as television does today.

The Renaissance was a period of change. The Black Death of 1348 destroyed not only a third to half the population of England but also the existing social structure. The feudal system with its indentures and limitations was left behind in its death throes. No longer tied to the land, people flocked to the cities where jobs were plentiful, occupations were available, and money could be made. With the invention of the printing press in 1453,

---

*Joss Whedon's affinity for Shakespeare is well attested. He has discussed in several interviews the weekly Shakespeare readings that he held for cast members of both* Buffy the Vampire Slayer *and* Angel.

books could be cheaply made and education began to flourish. The end of the 15c also saw the exploration of new worlds. The Renaissance was, indeed, a rebirth.

With new found wealth come new forms of entertainment. Cheap enough to be accessible for all but the very poor, the theater blossomed as the preeminent medium of choice, frequented by everyone from peasants to low-ranking nobles. The writers of the day were able to make money in the theater. After trying to establish himself as a Poet with a capital *P* and trying to find a patron, Shakespeare turned to the theater for support as many "serious" writers today turn to television. Shakespeare the poet, the artist, sold out in a sense. He wrote 37 plays from 1589 to 1613, a prodigious feat by anyone's standards. Not all of them achieved the grandeur of a *Hamlet* or a *Lear*—some, quite frankly, are dogs—but all were popular and achieved the intended goal of making a groat. While many of Shakespeare's contemporaries only survive in college literature classes as fodder for tragic undergraduate term papers, Shakespeare continues to live and speak to us today. Perhaps *Buffy* will still be drawing blood as well in 400 years.

Aside from the similarities of the cultural milieu, closer scrutiny of *King Lear* and season seven of *Buffy* reveals significant thematic similarities. Not intended as an exhaustive list and in no particular order, these are a few themes relevant to *Lear* and *Buffy*: human suffering, the bestial within humanity, the primacy of passion, the folly of the world, self-discovery, regeneration (with every pun intended), human cruelty toward humans, helplessness, Christian values, pagan values, the perversion of love, the destruction of love, the redemptive power of love, the monstrosity of the Freudian id, contingency, mortality, gradations of service, errors in judgment and their consequences, power and the Machiavellian version of political reality, division and disorder, the education of the young and old, contention between young and old, nothingness, the paradoxes of reasoning in madness and seeing in blindness as well as images of sight and sightlessness, isolation and alienation, and the Apocalypse. While all these themes are tightly interwoven into the fabric of both *King Lear* and *Buffy*, they significantly combine to make the series-ending season seven a complex revision of the Buffyverse of the first six seasons. Due to space constraints, however, I will focus in this paper on just three themes—blindness, isolation, and the Apocalypse—as they correspond in *Lear* and *Buffy*. Physical and moral blindness as well as isolation and alienation accentuate characterization in both texts. Although not generally recognized in *Lear*, the apocalyptic tradition of *Buffy the Vampire Slayer* is well attested; however, the writers of season seven utilize an overarching reliance on *King Lear* to present a different worldview, a different sort of apocalyptic vision, at the end of the last season. Recognizing the parallels between *King*

*Lear* and season seven provides for a richer understanding of the birth of a new order and what it means.

Blindness is a theme that is first introduced in *King Lear* during the all-important act 1, scene 1. King Lear, an old but able king of pagan Britain, prepares to divest himself of his power in favor of his three daughters. Although he has already divided his kingdom among his daughters, he takes this opportunity to stroke his ego by having his daughters publicly act as sycophants and gush their undying love for him. He pits the sisters against one another; and the first to speak, Goneril, the eldest, introduces the theme of sight and sightlessness barely 56 lines into the play when she says, "Sir, I love you more than [words] can wield the matter, / Dearer than eyesight, space, and liberty" (1.1.55–56). Of course, Goneril and Regan, the two older sisters, are hypocritical harridans who will say and do anything to get what they want. Cordelia, the youngest daughter (and possible namesake for Cordelia Chase), is unable to play the game and express herself adequately by Lear's standards. Her problem stems, not from lack of love for Lear, but from the embarrassment of making flowery public speeches. Unlike her sisters who fawn over Lear and indicate that they love him even more than they love their husbands, Cordelia clearly delineates the nature of her love.

For Lear, however, her response is unacceptable, and in his wrath he admonishes her to "avoid my sight" (124). Lear's moral blindness as to which daughter truly loves him becomes the basis of a tragic misunderstanding of appearance versus reality, of *seeing* versus understanding the true intentions behind each daughter's speech. Much of the play will be concerned with true vision, or insight into character, as opposed to surface vision which can only see the outward shows of character. The Earl of Kent, Lear's loyal retainer, tries to intervene on Cordelia's behalf; he cautions the king, "See better, Lear, and let me still remain / The true blank of thine eye" (158–59). Unfortunately, Kent's reward for speaking the truth is banishment from the kingdom. Kent and Cordelia are foils in that both are blunt and honest but tactless in their handling of Lear. Thus in good fairy tale, Cinderella-like fashion, the two evil sisters apparently prevail over the virtuous younger sister, setting up many of the other themes discussed above.

The situation of Gloucester and his two sons represents a subplot which parallels Lear's family problems and the motif of fathers deceived by thankless children. Edmund, the younger bastard son of Gloucester, hates his father and his brother Edgar and schemes to usurp his brother's inheritance. His lies and intrigues poison Gloucester against Edgar. Gloucester, like Lear, is too gullible, too quick to believe the worst about Edgar. Just as Lear blindly accepts at face value Goneril and Regan's claims of love, Gloucester blindly accepts Edmund's insinuations about Edgar. The theme of blindness culminates in a most horrific scene with the literal, physical blinding of Gloucester by the Duke of Cornwall on the flimsiest of pretenses instigated by Edmund. Physical blindness as a symbol of moral or intellectual limitation is a common topos in many texts such as *Oedipus Rex* and Chaucer's "Merchant's Tale." Only after his eyes are put out onstage is Gloucester able to see the truth. Cast out of his own castle to "smell / His way to Dover" (3.7.93–4), Gloucester laments his folly:

> I have no way, and therefore want no eyes;
> I stumbled when I saw. Full oft 'tis seen,
> Our means secure us, and our mere defects
> Prove our commodities. O dear son Edgar,
> The food of thy abused father's wrath!
> Might I but live to see thee in my touch,
> I'ld say I had eyes again [4.1.18–24].

With the breakdown of the nuclear family units and the fragmentation of the kingdom come the increasing isolation and alienation of the protagonists which underscores the fragility of the natural order of things. This breakdown and fragmentation tears apart the most vital aspects of human life. Gone are the things that make life worth living and worth striving to maintain — love, home, fidelity, country. The result is banishment, despair, and madness. Cordelia is the first to suffer as Lear effectively banishes her for speaking the truth; she is has descends into madness as a kind of self-imposed isolation. Edmund flees his brother's persecution first by hiding in a hollow tree, cut off from his home. Edmund must disguise himself as Poor Tom O'Bedlam, feigning madness, a stranger in what has become a strange land. After his blinding, Gloucester is forced to wander through the countryside accompanied only by his son whom he cannot recognize and who cannot reveal himself to his father. Thus the basic primal bonds which hold us together culturally and politically are shattered. Throughout the disintegration of society and the resulting chaos, the antagonists thrive.

Similarly, the last season of *Buffy* utilizes the theme of sight and sightlessness in many of the same ways that *Lear* does but offers some variations. The seventh season of *Buffy* opens with a changing of the guard. Dawn advances to high school where Buffy has a job as a counselor. Giles is in England. Xander is a contractor; Willow is in rehab. Spike is certifiably insane and wrestles with the theological implications of what it means to have a soul. All of the gang are now adults with adult problems. The first episode, "Lessons," introduces the audience to these new circumstances, establishes parameters, and provides foreshadowing for the rest of the season. The episode opens in Istanbul with monks, the Bringers, murdering a girl, a Potential, unbeknownst to us at the time. The first words of the season come, suitably, from Buffy via voice-over narration, "It's about power. Who's got it, who knows how to use it." "Beneath You," the second episode, shows the Bringers killing a girl in Frankfort, and we get our first whisper of the enigmatic phrase, "From beneath you, it devours."

The first three episodes are tied together by the theme of isolation and alienation, which is dramatically represented in Willow's return in "Same Time, Same Place," the third episode. This episode also overtly introduces the theme of sight and sightlessness which will underlie most of the remaining episodes. During her return to Sunnydale, Willow is trapped in a parallel universe. Buffy and Xander cannot see Willow, nor can Willow see them. In another moment of thematic pointing, Buffy kills the demon Gnarl by blinding him, the first of several graphic portrayals of blinding. In a later episode, after cutting off the übervamp's head, she pokes him in the eye with a crossbow bolt ("Showtime").

All of the major characters become isolated or alienated. We see that Spike's isolation, much like Lear's, manifests in his insanity ("Help"). Buffy sums up his predicament when she states, "What do you do when you know that you can't help?" In "Selfless," we relate to Anya's isolation, even as she becomes human again, by getting her back story. When Buffy tries to kill her, Anya says, "You get down on me for cutting myself off." Buffy replies, "In the end the Slayer is always cut off. [...] Human rules don't apply. I'm the law," reestablishing something that we've known all along: it's about power. Ultimately, the fate of the world rests on Buffy's shoulders alone, in isolation. Blindness is again emphasized when Anya tells Xander, "You only see what you want to see," but what Xander sees, he sees with "eyeballs of love."

Giles, too, is isolated. Presumably no longer needed, he is in England, cut off from those he loves; but interestingly, Giles is a Watcher, by definition one who watches, one who sees, supposedly the very incarnation of sight; but he, too, suffers from an inability to see when he sides with Principal Wood against Spike. The episode "Him" has Spike move in with Xander so Xander can keep an eye on him. "Conversations with Dead People" opens with all the characters alone to the tune of "Will I Spend the Night Alone," with all the major characters in isolation. The vampire Holden Webster tells Buffy, "It all adds up to you feeling alone; but Buffy, everybody feels alone. Everybody is until you die." All of this is part of the First's plan to isolate and plant seeds of suspicion, to divide and conquer. In "Sleeper" isolation and alienation causes doubt; Dawn believes that Buffy will betray her. Dawn's paranoia grows in "Potential," but she and Xander share a tender moment as the humans without any special powers. Xander tells Dawn, "I see more than anybody realizes because nobody's watching me." Dawn replies, "Maybe that's your power [...] seeing, knowing." Xander responds, "Maybe it is. Maybe I should get a cape." This exchange foreshadows Caleb's despicable blinding of Xander six episodes later when Caleb tells Xander, "You're the one that sees everything, aren't you? Well, let's see what we can't do about that." Caleb then proceeds to gouge out Xander's left eye in a scene that resonates with Gloucester's blinding scene in *King Lear*. The result, however, is an inversion of what happens in *Lear*. Gloucester "sees better" after his blinding; Xander "sees better" before his blinding. Xander loses sight of the big picture and joins the mutiny against Buffy. In a misguided attempt at humor, he tells Buffy, "I'm trying to see your point, but I guess it's a little too far to the left" ("Empty Places").

In "Never Leave Me," we find out that the Bringers are blind, that they have no eyes. This revelation can only function thematically, for there is no particular reason for the Bringers to be blind except to emphasize this theme and to provide a metaphor for mindless servitude blindly following orders and power. This episode really prepares the audience for bad Spike, "William the Bloody is back," yet it also sets up Spike as savior. Buffy, like Xander, truly sees, "You are a better man. You may not see it, but I do. I believe in you, Spike." Buffy sees the big picture. As she tells Principal Wood, "You try anything again, [Spike'll] kill you. More importantly, I'll let him. I have a mission to win this war, to save the world. I don't have time for vendettas. The mission's what matters" ("Lies My Parents Told Me"). She knows what must be done to avoid defeat; she is the one who must make the tough decisions and make the Potentials into warriors. Buffy is the one who must enter the portal to be transported back to the beginning of time in order to see the future. Making the tough decisions, however, does not endear Buffy to the others. After Faith arrives, a power struggle ensues which results in another kind of inversion of the *Lear* plot. An internecine rivalry among the Potentials results in mutiny and Faith's replacing Buffy as leader. Faith, Willow, and Dawn become Buffy's "evil sisters," and Buffy, like Cordelia, is banished from her house by her sisters and "daughters," the Potentials, for refusing to kowtow to their desires and demands, thus creating a physical isolation to accompany her emotional isolation.

The Apocalypse theme is not as transparent in *Lear* as is the theme of blindness, and it is a theme that is not usually associated with the play. It is first introduced, however, early in act 1, scene 2 when the pagan and superstitious Gloucester discusses with Edmund the mutability of the world:

> These late eclipses in the sun and moon portend no good to us. Though the wisdom of nature can reason it thus and thus, yet nature finds itself scourg'd by the sequent effects. Love cools, friendship falls off, broth-

ers divide: in cities, mutinies; in countries, discord, in palaces, trea-
son; and the bond crack'd 'twixt son and father. This villain of mine
comes under the prediction; there's son against father: the King falls
from bias of nature; there's father against child. We have seen the best
of our time. Machinations, hollowness, treachery, and all ruinous dis-
orders follow us disquietly to our graves [1.2.103–14].

Replace male references with female references and Gloucester could easily
be describing *Buffy* season seven, but Gloucester's lamentation is much more
than an old man's reflections on how the younger generation is going to hell,
literally in Buffy's case. Although *King Lear* is set in a distant pagan past,
Shakespeare places a common Christian topos in Gloucester's mouth; the
"prediction" to which he refers is the end of the world.

Shakespeare had a rich tradition of apocalyptic literature from which to
draw, the most obvious being the bible itself. Gloucester's words echo Luke
21.25 which states, "And there will be signs [of the apocalypse] in sun and
moon and stars." Matthew predicts, "And you will hear of wars and rumors
of wars. [...] For nation will rise against nation, and kingdom against kingdom, and there will be famines and earthquakes in various places. [...] And
then many will fall away, and betray one another, and hate one another. [...]
And because wickedness is multiplied, most men's love will grow cold" (Mat
24.6–12). The whole book of Revelation details this impending event. There
were many other texts that Shakespeare could have known such as the apocryphal *Apocalypse of Thomas* and the Fifteen Signs before Doomsday ascribed
to St. Jerome as well as numerous sermons and homilies devoted to the subject which informed thinking and attitudes throughout the Middle Ages and
Renaissance. During this period, the question was not *if* the apocalypse would
happen but *when* it would happen.

Though alluded to in act 1, this apocalyptic theme becomes more apparent at the end of act 5 during a crucial exchange between Kent, Edgar, and
Albany. After the battles have been fought, after good has seemingly triumphed over evil, Shakespeare gives us one last tragic heart wrench. Cordelia
has been murdered offstage, and the old beaten Lear, who has suffered,
descended into madness during the play, and regained his senses, enters carrying the dead body of his only faithful daughter. This is a moment of tremendous pathos for the audience and the characters onstage. Lear howls his
outrage, his grief, his denial:

> O, [you] are men of stones!
> Had I your tongues and eyes, I'ld use them so
> That heaven's vault should crack. She's gone for ever!
> I know when one is dead, and when one lives;
> She's dead as earth. Lend me a looking-glass,

If that her breath will mist or stain the stone,
Why then she lives [5.3.258–64].

Immediately following this outpouring of emotion comes the significant exchange. Kent states, "Is this the promis'd end?" Edgar: "Or image of that horror?" Albany: "Fall, and cease!" (5.3.264–65). This quick bit of dialogue is easily lost in presentation onstage because of the intense emotion of the scene and the focus on Lear, but the questioning and the word choice is significant. None of the characters are quite sure of the meaning of what they see. They are, of course, shocked and deeply moved and resort to cosmological religious interpretations to make sense of it. "Is this the promis'd end?" can only refer to the Apocalypse promised in Matthew, Luke, and Revelation; but the characters are also aware that it may be a fiction or the "image of that horror." Either way it is the end of the world as they know it; a new order will have to arise. What that order will be is unknown at the end of the play. The three highest ranking survivors— the Duke of Albany; the Earl of Kent; and Edgar, Duke of Gloucester by his father's recent death — are uncertain of the future. Ultimately, Lear again goes mad, his heart breaks, and he dies in front of his subjects, leaving them to sort out the chaos, to try to make sense of what they have witnessed.

Albany, as Lear's son-in-law, would seem to be next in line for the kingship, but he tries to foist it onto Kent and Edgar: "Friends of my soul, you twain / Rule in this realm, and the gor'd state sustain" (5.3.320–21). Kent refuses cryptically, "I have a journey, sir, shortly to go: / My master calls me, I must not say no" (5.3.322–23). Edgar, the youngest and least experienced in leadership, has the last words of the play which are usually reserved for the most important character left standing at the end of Shakespeare's tragedies and the one who usually restores order from chaos. Edgar's final words, however, are anything but comforting:

The weight of this sad time we must obey,
Speak what we feel, not what we ought to say:
The oldest hath borne most; we that are young
Shall never see so much, nor live so long [5.3.324–27].

Thus the play ends in the confusion of knowing that everything has changed. What the future holds can only be played out as the young people seek to carve their way in a brave new world. This is exactly the same response found at the end of *Buffy* season seven.

*Buffy the Vampire Slayer* has a long and venerable history of apocalypses, so much so that in season four Riley Finn balks at trying to come up with the plural of *apocalypse*. When Giles first declares in season seven, "I'm afraid we have a slight apocalypse," our reaction is much the same as Spike's and

Buffy's, "I'm done waiting. They want an apocalypse, we'll give them one" ("Bring on the Night"). Apocalypse? Pah, been there, done that. Our first indication that season seven's might be the apocalypse to end all apocalypses comes when Anya states, "Buffy seems to think this apocalypse is going to actually be, you know, apocalyptic" ("Storyteller"). Buffy reinforces this idea when she states, "Any apocalypse I avert without dying, those are the easy ones" ("Lies My Parents Told Me"). The tension builds throughout the final episodes as we get the sense that the First is unlike anything Buffy has ever encountered. Incorporeal, able to prey on people's insecurities, able to shape shift — how can Buffy fight it? Finally, Buffy hatches the plan to empower all women everywhere to become Slayers if they wish. With the help of Willow's magic tapping into the connectedness of all things, "Everything is part of the earth, everything's connected" ("Beneath You"), she realizes the Potentials' potential and turns them all into Slayers, elevating Willow to godhead in the process. After Sunnydale has sunken into oblivion, the survivors of the final battle survey the pit, Albany's "gorg'd state," that once was Sunnydale. Just as in *King Lear,* the survivors question what has happened and what the future will hold. Giles says, "I don't understand. What did this?" Buffy answers simply, "Spike." After some preliminary discussion, the final exchange of the episode, the season, and the series is significantly among the women. Willow begins a series of questions, "What do you think we should do, Buffy?" Faith adds, "Yeah, you're not the one and only chosen anymore. You just gotta live like a person. How does that feel?" Dawn repeats a variation of Willow's initial question, "Yeah, Buffy, what are we going to do now?" The closing head shot of Buffy shows her smiling.

So, is this the promised end? Well, yes and no. For the characters of the show, the ending represents another day at the world-saving office. True, Sunnydale has been wiped off the face of the earth, but good has triumphed over evil, again [yawn], and "order" has been restored. However, as in *King Lear* the old order has disappeared to be replaced with — what? The same uncertainty and apprehension that grip Edgar, Albany, and Kent envelop those who remain except for Buffy. Anya, who has learned more than anyone else what it truly means to be human, is dead, victim of the promised end that a major character would suffer the obligatory death. Spike has melted with his soul into some hell dimension only to reincarnate in another parallel television universe on *Angel.* No longer will the concept of one world, one slayer prevail. By empowering all the trainees and elevating them to slayerhood, Buffy has changed the rules, the natural order, "my power will be your power" ("Chosen"); she has unleashed a new power into the world, one whose effectiveness remains to be proven in a new medium as "season eight" takes place in comic books. Finally, at the meta-level this is the promised end —

the end of the story arc, the end of the season, the end of the series, the end that Joss Whedon had promised, made incalculably richer by his use of *King Lear* and Shakespearean themes.

## WORKS CITED

*Buffy the Vampire Slayer: The Complete Seventh Season on DVD*. Twentieth Century–Fox Home Entertainment, 2004.

Evans, G. Blakemore, ed. *The Riverside Shakespeare*, 2nd ed. Boston: Houghton Mifflin, 1974.

Minnow, Newton. Address, National Association of Broadcasters, 9 May 1961, http://janda.org/b20/news%20articles/vastwastland.htm.

# Grimm Realities
## Buffy *and the Uses of Folklore*

### Elizabeth Bridges

In reference to *Buffy* creator Joss Whedon, Wesleyan film professor Jeanine Basinger has characterized her former student as "the village storyteller." Detailing what she posits as his intuitive understanding of the human need for familiar narratives that are nevertheless continually reinvented to reflect their audiences' shared culture and everyday experience, she suggests that Whedon would have taken essentially the same career path regardless of the culture or time in which he might have been born (Basinger). Indeed, the staying power of *Buffy, Angel,* and *Firefly* should begin to attest to the timeless quality of Whedon's stories and characters, particularly in an era when cultural productions can easily drown in the constant and ever-increasing wash of media, aided by the notoriously short attention spans of contemporary audiences. However, as often cited in critical assessments of his work, Whedon's ability to tap into deeply shared cultural memory and experience at least partly accounts for both the immediate popularity of his work, but more importantly as time goes on, its staying power with audiences and the continued academic interest that it has generated. Contrary to the notion that TV viewers prefer the nonsequential, "one-off" stories that characterized most television series before *Buffy,* Whedon's complex, multilayered, truly episodic approach to television continues to appeal to the literary sensibilities and overall cultural literacy of audiences. Yet, although Whedon's clever use of pop culture and historical film references have often been highlighted favorably in critical assessments of his work, his adept use of intertextuality neither begins nor ends with the age of mechanical reproduction. As the present analysis will show, Whedon's best-known series, *Buffy the Vampire Slayer,* relied heavily on a mesh of literary and pre-literary texts that tie the Slayer's adventures to a long and rich folkloric tradition.

Many readers will attest a certain familiarity with a number of widely known fairy tales of European origin. However, the fairy tales that have made their way to the contemporary Anglo-American cultural imaginary are largely the sanitized versions made popular by Disney. It is widely known, of course,

that the darker origins of these tales were inherited from oral traditions originating in central and Eastern Europe. Most famously collected in the early
nineteenth century by German folklorist brothers Jakob and Wilhelm Grimm,
and much like vampire lore itself, many of these stories such as "Hänsel and
Gretel," "Little Red Riding Hood," "Snow White," "Sleeping Beauty," and
"Rumpelstilzkin," have existed in varying forms since pre–Christian times.
Like *Buffy* does for audiences today, fairy tales often served to dramatize the
real, life-and-death struggles of their original pre-literate European audiences. These tales placed everyday problems in supernatural settings, allowing for a sense of mastery over the unseen, uncontrollable forces that
influenced daily life. Although such superstitious times are long past, contemporary audiences still face many of the same uncontrollable forces encountered by our ancestors—from the abstract threats of war and terrorism to the
very real prospect of life-threatening illness and ultimately of course, our
shared mortality. It is thus unsurprising that *Buffy* evokes such a deep level
of audience reaction and longstanding interest.

Folkloric themes and motifs connect the series in a direct line to stories
and ideas that have been part of Western culture since preliterate times. In
fact, several *Buffy* episodes, namely "Killed by Death," "Gingerbread," and
"Hush," deal very specifically in European folklore traditions as a way to
underscore the connection of the series to our world. Meanwhile, this use of
folklore enhances the realism of the series by offering viewers a mythological framework shared with the show's characters. Beyond the vampire and
related Christian lore that pervades the entire series and gives the Buffyverse
its rulebook, these episodes further probe the primordial origins of fear itself.

## *"Killed by Death" and the German Literary Tradition*

The Season Two episode "Killed by Death" opens with Buffy suffering
from the flu. Further diminished by a nasty run-in with Angelus, she col-
lapses and is brought to the hospital by the Scoobies. Buffy has traumatic associations with hospitals, as revealed when the audience learns that the Slayer
was in the hospital room when her cousin and childhood friend Celia died
at a very young age. In a delirium of high fever, Buffy catches a glimpse of a
hideous demon passing by the door of her room as it stalks Ryan, a little
patient in the same wing, and she later overhears two orderlies discussing the
death of a little girl. When she explains these occurrences to the Scoobies,
they dismiss it as a figment of her imagination brought on by her fear of the
hospital and her desire to have something tangible to fight. As Buffy begins
to recover from the illness and her suspicions persist, her friends focus their
investigation on Dr. Backer, who Buffy believes is practicing experiments on

the patients of the children's ward. He does seem sinister, but when he is brutally killed by an invisible assailant, they have to assume a supernatural enemy. The group determines that this demon is Der Kindestod, German for "child's death," a hideous creature visible only to sick children, who literally sucks the life out of little ones. His presence on a children's ward is, of course, doubly hideous, because as Cordelia so bluntly states, "a children's ward is like an all-you-can-eat kind of thing." Buffy must therefore reinfect herself with the illness so she can see the demon to fight it and save the young patients on the ward. The virus weakens her, but she is the Slayer, so Der Kindestod has met his match.

Of the many assorted demons and creatures of the night featured in *Buffy*, undoubtedly one of the very few that evokes true, visceral horror is Der Kindestod. This level of horror is due not only to his particularly hideous appearance, but also to his choice of victims and the way in which he kills them. Our instinctive revulsion at this character and his *modus operendi* are also strongly connected to common childhood fears, the same kind that are dramatized in fairy tales. In this episode, common childhood fears of fairy tale monsters are connected to the very real and sinister nature of illness and death in the youngest and most vulnerable among us, namely children.

Buffy's own vulnerability is brought into relief in this episode through the experience of illness and the revisiting of her own childhood trauma. She is thereby reduced to a childlike state, which is highlighted in several ways throughout the episode. First, Buffy's Slayer powers are diminished due to her illness, and they are further reduced through the medicine that sedates her when she becomes agitated upon entering the hospital. Buffy's mother Joyce and her Watcher Giles connect via a brief exchange about Buffy's well-being, which provides a glimpse of the traditional mother/father parental authority that is rarely evident in the series, again placing Buffy in the position of child. Buffy's natural, no-makeup look in this episode also lends her a more childlike appearance, and her loose pajama pants and tank top de-emphasize her grown-up physique. Thus, through her illness, uncharacteristic submission to authority, and appearance, she is reduced to a vulnerable state that is contrary to our normal perception of this character.

Through this highly atypical vulnerability, Buffy is placed on the same level as the children in the ward. In an exchange with Ryan, Buffy first refers to herself as a grown-up but then adds the qualification, "I'm not that grown up." She further establishes a connection to the little boy, saying, "We both know there are real monsters." Through this parallel with the boy, the audience is reminded that Buffy — age seventeen at this point in the series — is still a child in many ways herself, though a child with extremely adult responsibilities.

At first, it seems that the "real monster" is Dr. Backer, but later, the key to the true monster's identity appears on the cover of a dusty book snapped shut by a frustrated Cordelia. The red leather volume, containing woodcut images of numerous demons that attack in a variety of disgusting ways, features the profile of Der Kindestod in gold foil on the cover. The book appears antique, possibly European in origin, and the demon's profile emphasizes his hooked nose, tusklike teeth, and his brimmed hat. The book leaves the distinct impression of a volume of folklore, which in *Buffy* terms, serves as a guidebook because as Buffy told Ryan, "We know there are real monsters." The glimpse of the demon in the doorway during Buffy's delirium and the sinister profile on the cover of the antique book serve as initial clues in a series of revelations about the hideous nature of Der Kindestod. When Cordelia relays information about the demon to Buffy via telephone, all Cordy can manage is a simple "eww" as Giles shows her the passage that describes Der Kindestod's feeding method. She simply hands the phone to Giles so he can explain. Indeed, the "eww" seems warranted when it is revealed that the demon sits on top of its young victims, pinning them down and draining the life from them. Giles adds that this experience is horribly traumatic for the child, and Buffy immediately flashes back to what is clearly the death of her cousin Celia, the little girl thrashing and screaming and staring up in horror at something evidently invisible to young Buffy. Therefore, the Slayer has unknowingly encountered this demon before, and she wishes more than ever to defeat it.

Buffy and Willow deduce that to see the demon in order to fight it, she must be sick with a fever. The fact that she can see it at all again underscores the recurring theme in the episode, the idea that the Slayer is still a child herself. By drinking a few diluted drops from Dr. Backer's handy stash of virus samples, she becomes immediately feverish, and Der Kindestod becomes visible. In a conventional horror cinema "reveal," the small, tantalizing glimpses of the monster culminate in a full-body shot of Der Kindestod. He wears tattered clothes suggestive of a nineteenth-century men's suit and a tattered undertaker's hat. His appearance therefore underscores the Grimms'-era folklore connection already alluded to with the appearance of the antique volume from Giles' library. As the monster descends to the hospital basement, where the children from the ward have attempted to hide, the mise-en-scène takes on a more surreal, Expressionist character, with lighting angles that emphasize the long, distorted shadows of the demon as he advances along the dripping wet cinderblock walls of the labyrinthine corridors beneath Sunnydale General. The shadows accentuate Der Kindestod's already menacing appearance by lengthening his clawed hands and his beaked visage in shadowy double on the wall. This particular shot mirrors some of the more haunting images of the title monster in F.W. Murnau's 1922 vampire opus *Nosferatu*, which also rooted much of its narrative power in overt connections to European folklore and the Romantic literary tradition.

In the final fight sequence of "Killed by Death," the monster reveals his true hideous nature as he perches on top of little Ryan, pinning him down inescapably. In a point-of-view shot that forces the viewer into the same position as the victim, the looming monster's horrid face claustrophobically fills the entire frame. Still more horrifying, the creature's eyes— up to this point inhumanly white, little-orphan-Annie-from-hell blanks— now transform into disturbing mouthlike appendages, which open and extend downward from the demon's eye sockets towards the boy's face. Initially, the mouths are an eyeline match for where Ryan's— and by proxy the viewer's— eyes would be. However, in an over-the-shoulder shot, it is revealed that they attach to the terrified child's forehead as the demon begins to suck the life out of him. Luckily, Buffy intervenes, but not before she too finds herself dangerously face-to-face with Der Kindestod. In a quick resolution reminiscent of the single act that often brings triumph in a fairy tale (the magical kiss, magic word, shoving the witch into the oven) Buffy deftly breaks the demon's neck, and he is defeated. The children can now live happily ever after.

Having already established that the monster in this episode is horrifying on a visceral level that is atypical even for the Buffyverse, a closer examination of the monster reveals that he evokes horror not only in the form of physical revulsion, but also at a more psychological level. Der Kindestod, while invented for Buffy, traces its origins to a long tradition of folk and subsequent literary fairy tales, stories written by authors who incorporate motifs typical of those from oral folk traditions. His correspondence to elements of a prominent German literary fairy tale, *Der Sandmann* by early 19th-century author E.T.A. Hoffmann, reveals this connection clearly. The novella features a brief retelling of a hideous bedtime story as related to the protagonist Nathanael by his childhood nanny. The Sand-man, an inhuman, beaked creature that lives on the moon, is said to come down to Earth at night and kidnap little children who don't go to bed on time, taking them back to its nest, where its young can feed on the eyes of the kidnapped children. Nathanael describes the creature as, "a fearful incubus" that terrified him throughout his childhood (Hoffmann 185). Later, Nathanael associates the nanny's horrifying story with a real figure of equal menace, Coppelius, who is described as, "a large, broad-shouldered man, with an immensely big head, a face the colour of yellow ochre ... and a prominent Roman nose hanging over his upper lip" (Hoffmann 186). This description goes on and corresponds in several ways to the appearance of Der Kindestod. Furthermore, Coppelius is known for his hatred of and cruelty to children (Hoffmann 187).

It is later revealed that Coppelius is responsible for the sudden and tragic death of the boy's father. This traumatic death of a loved one, and Nathanael's association of it with the Sandman tale, follow the protagonist through the main narrative of the novella, which deals with his efforts to overcome this trauma in his adult life. Again, the correspondence to elements of childhood trauma addressed in this episode is notable. Besides the reference to the Sandman feeding the eyes of its victims to its young, eyes or lack thereof are a motif throughout this story, an association that also extends to Der Kindestod's appearance and feeding method.

Freud later addressed this story in his essay on "the Uncanny," wherein he attempts to explain (as I tell my students) "what creeps us out and why." In predictable fashion, the long and short of his argument in relation to the Sand-man story is the notion that the fear of losing one's eyes corresponds to the castration complex (Freud 140). Nevertheless, perhaps if one assumes that sometimes eyes really are just eyes, elements of Freud's essay can still be brought to bear on the *Buffy* episode in question. After all, it appears to the viewer that the creature will go for the child's eyes, which only underscores the audience's visceral reaction. It is, after all, a basic, involuntary animal instinct to protect one's eyes. Yet, without entirely dismissing a sexual interpretation of the nature of Der Kindestod's attack, it is also worth pointing out that his method strongly resembles that of the incubus, as referred to by Nathanael above. The incubus is a demonic creature from medieval lore, believed to sexually assault women in their sleep, also sucking out the life force. The positioning of Der Kindestod over the child, pinning him down helplessly, strongly parallels the composition in depictions of incubi assaults and certainly has an unsavory sexual connotation. Indeed, it certainly cannot be denied that Der Kindestod violates the children, so this connection to incubus lore suggests that applying a sexual interpretation *a la* Freud may not be entirely without merit. The undeniably perverse aspect of this monster's method of killing adds a layer to the revulsion that the audience already feels for this character.

In addition to the imminent physical threat posed by Der Kindestod, another menacing aspect of this character is the more general vulnerability and isolation of children as evident in folktales and in the aforementioned literary fairy tales as well. In these stories, children are isolated, left to the harsh reality of a violent situation with no parents to protect them. Der Kindestod contributes to this element of the fairy tale formula as he seeks to further isolate the children on the hospital ward — where are the parents of these sick children, anyway? — by killing off their one protector, Dr. Backer, who was making progress on helping the children recover. The fairy tale pattern of children left abandoned to be victimized by evil forces is a pattern that is certainly evident here, and it adds to the sense of urgency Buffy feels to help the children triumph, intensified by her need to triumph over the childhood trauma that has left its imprint on her burgeoning grown-up psyche.

As is the case with fairy tales generally, adults can relate to the childhood fears addressed in this episode, but on another level, the hideous nature of Der Kindestod speaks specifically to adult fears as well. The illness or death of a child is the worst nightmare of any parent or family member, and the hideous and senseless deaths at the hands of Der Kindestod dramatize this horrifying experience. The triumph of Buffy over this monster offers a brief sense of mastery and hope in the face of a basic human fear that has not changed over the centuries. As Bruno Bettelheim claims in *The Uses of Enchantment,* fairy tales have always served the function of offering children a sense of mastery in the face of dark, unseen forces over which they have no control (8). Likewise, the entire *Buffy* series serves this function for its audiences, but this episode in particular connects our heroine in a very specific way to a centuries-old tradition of storytelling as a way to cope with these darker parts of the human experience.

## "Gingerbread" or "Fairy tales are real"

As in "Killed by Death," the narrative in the season three episode "Gingerbread" centers on the vulnerability of children, with the focus at the beginning of the episode on a little boy and girl who appear to have been killed viciously while innocently playing on a merry-go-round. The grisly double murder is discovered by Buffy's mother Joyce, who has suddenly taken an interest in her daughter's nighttime occupation, accompanying Buffy on Slayer patrol in the city park. The gruesome nature of the crime is dramatized in a series of full-frame crime scene stills, aestheticized in artistic black and white, emphasizing the children's blondness and playing on the audience's presumed ethnocentric associations of fair hair with innocence. Their vulnerability and isolation are underscored by wide-angle, overhead shots that emphasize the starkly exposed playground, a horrible sense of isolation juxtaposed with a location normally considered a site of play and innocence. In contrast to the uncharacteristic focus on Buffy's childhood in "Killed by Death," Buffy and Joyce initially exhibit a parent/child role reversal in the crime scene sequence, when Buffy hugs Joyce and unconvincingly tries to comfort her mother, saying, "I'm so sorry you had to see this, but I promise everything's going to be okay."

The Scoobies begin their investigation of the incident with a strange symbol found on the victims' hands. Giles asserts that this evidence points to ritual murder or occult sacrifice, which of course suggests human involvement. As rumors fly and the suspicion of human occult ritual becomes the leading theory around Sunnydale, the narrative starts to parallel the dynamics of the real-life "West Memphis Three" case of the early 1990s. The events of this case were presented in the 1996 HBO documentary, *Paradise Lost*, which called into question the investigation of a grisly child murder case with Satanic ritualistic overtones. The thesis of the documentary was that the townspeople of this small, rural, Mississippi delta community succumbed to hysteria in assuming that three local misfit teens committed the murders, and that the subsequent investigation unfolded in a biased and faulty manner. This documentary circulated widely on DVD during the early seasons of *Buffy*, and it was particularly popular among the teen goth set, who saw themselves in the young defendants of the case. The "Satanic panic," a modern incarnation of the witch hunts of previous centuries, was common to small, fundamentalist Christian U.S. communities in the 1980s and 1990s, when displays of gothic fashion sense could fuel accusations ranging from sexual perversion to vampirism and Satanism, undoubtedly leading to the harassment of untold numbers of young people. The West Memphis Three provided a capstone to this phenomenon and illustrated its extreme, a botched investigation that apparently resulted in wrongful imprisonment and, in the case of one defendant, placement on death row.

This type of local hysteria is dramatized in "Gingerbread," an episode featuring the recurring witch character Amy, herself looking more "goth" than in previous episodes. Her friend Michael, appearing in this episode only, embodies the ultimate male goth stereotype: dyed hair, pale skin, black lipstick and nail polish, black clothing, and indeterminate sexual orientation. Willow aligns herself with these two characters, who share her interest in witchcraft. This association leads to a brief misdirection that suggests their possible implication in the murder, but ironically, their conjuring is revealed to be part of a birthday gift for Buffy. This momentary alignment of the audience with the hysterical residents of Sunnydale dissolves in identification with the picked-on youngsters after their innocence is quickly established. In the school hallway, a much larger "jock" pins Michael against a locker, voicing the bumbling small-town sentiment, "Everyone knows he's into that voodoo witchcraft." ... "People like him ... gotta learn a lesson." In the same scene, Cordelia, reverting to her original role as Sunnydale's "mean girl," declares, "Everyone knows that witches killed those kids, and Amy is a witch, and Michael is whatever the boy of 'witch' is, plus being the poster child for 'yuck.'" She goes on to describe them as "freaks and losers." At this point, the audience is aligned squarely with the outsiders, as is almost always the case in *Buffy* generally.

This episode continues the fairy tale motif of children — or more precisely, teenagers — left isolated and vulnerable to monstrous forces beyond their control. Despite the minimal role of parental authority in the series, Buffy's mother Joyce makes frequent appearances. Meanwhile, references to and appearances by the other Scoobies' parents are virtually nonexistent. The exception that proves this rule is the appearance of Sheila Rosenberg in this episode. The mother of Buffy's best friend Willow, Sheila is cast as the absentminded and career-driven professor, whose academic interests eclipse her ability to spend time with, much less relate to her daughter. When Buffy expresses her exasperation that her mom wanted to go with her on patrol the previous night, Willow remarks, "Wow, your mom would take the time to do that with you?" Later, Sheila does take an uncharacteristic interest in her daughter, sitting her down to have a "talk." The composition of this scene parallels that of the parental "drug talk" scene prevalent in public service announcements from the Nancy Reagan "Just Say No" era. Ironically countering the kind of real connection advocated by such ads, when questioning her daughter about her possible involvement in witchcraft, Sheila immediately depersonalizes the interaction, citing "a recent paper about the rise of mysticism among teenagers." Willow finds the whole discussion suspicious, stating, "The last time we had a conversation over three minutes it was about the patriarchal bias of the Mister Rogers show." However, the conversation ends in an unprecedented show of traditional parental authority, intercut in parallel scenes in which both Willow and Buffy are grounded by their mothers and forbidden to associate with one another.

Such instances of parental authority take on a more sinister character as the parents form an organized response to the apparent murder of the two children. Hosted by the Mayor at City Hall, Buffy's mother leads a candlelight vigil, complete with signs bearing the children's likenesses and the words "Never again." In her speech, she declares that, "It's time for the grown-ups to take Sunnydale back." At this point, it is clear that parental authority has gone awry, and more malevolent forces are at work, as the images of adults mindlessly parroting the slogan give way to a police locker search at Sunnydale High. This scene plays like the iconic school drug bust, but the Ziploc bags of herbs turned up in Principal Snyder's are intended for use in witchcraft, drawing further parallels between the "witch hunt" motif and Reagan-era anti-drug rhetoric and iconography.

The "drug bust" scene leads to still another staple of Reagan-era parental hysteria, namely a nod to the book banning campaigns waged during the 1980s and 1990s. Upon seeing Giles' panic as his research library is plundered, Snyder plays on a quote from *Apocalypse Now*, when he says, "I love the smell of desperate librarian in the morning," an especially appropriate reference, given the fact that the book confiscation will soon culminate in a Nazi-style book-burning. Snyder also refers to another facet of Sunnydale's wave of growing parental hysteria, the formation of a "powerful new group" known as MOO (Mothers Opposed to the Occult), headed by none other than Buffy's mother. This acronym points to the wave of similarly named 1980s parental groups like MADD and the PMRC, both of which were criticized as purvey-ors of hysteria and infringement on civil rights. Buffy confronts her mother about the unfortunately named group, but Joyce stares blankly and insists, "MOO just wants to weed out the offensive materials." After Buffy leaves, the slain children appear to Joyce, encouraging her in creepy monotone to "get rid of the bad girls." Shown in pale makeup and accompanied by eerie music resembling a discordant lullaby, they resemble the "demon child" char-acters in movies like *The Omen* (1976), and *The Shining* (1980).

It finally occurs to the Scooby gang that nothing is known about the background of the murdered children, not even their names or the names of their parents. Conducting an Internet search while grounded in her room at home, Willow helps the group trace the origins of the "murdered children" story, finding that an identical event seems to have occurred every fifty years, reaching back to 1649 and originating with the murder of siblings Hans and Greta Strauss near the Black Forest. Giles posits a plausible explanation: "There is a fringe theory held by a few folklorists that some regional stories have actual, very literal antecedents." In other words, as Oz simply states, "Fairy tales are real." Consenting to a demonic explanation after all, Giles explains, "Some demons thrive by feed[ing] us our darkest fear and turn peaceful communities into vigilantes." The group then draws the essential connection between fairy tales, children running home to tell their parents about the mean old witch, and the resultant persecution of women suspected of witchcraft, the literal "witch hunts" upon which the colloquialism is based. Just then, Michael stumbles in looking beaten up and reports that a witch trial is about to take place at City Hall.

Flanked by an angry mob armed with torches, the "bad girls," Buffy, Amy, and Willow, have all been tied to stakes, to be burned simultaneously with the offending occult books. In order to escape the bonds, Amy displays her actual powers of witchcraft by turning herself into a rat and runs away. Again, in a swift, fairy-tale resolution, Giles casts a spell revealing the true demonic nature of the two children. Meanwhile, Buffy wakes up from chlo-roform-induced unconsciousness just in time to bend over, snap the stake, and stab the hulking demon with its oversized business end. The spell bro-ken, the adult population wakes up as well, and Sunnydale is restored to its usual state of (relative) normalcy.

Aided by the isolation of children that is characteristic in fairy tales generally, and "Hänsel and Gretel" in particular, this episode uses this fairy tale motif to highlight the vulnerability of young people to the whims of adult hysteria. The "Gingerbread" that lures Hänsel and Gretel in the original tale is transformed into the children themselves, whose deceptive appearance lures adults to destructive behavior and an attempt to dispatch the suspected "witches," not by shoving them into the oven, but by fire nonetheless. As was the case in "Killed by Death," this episode dramatizes a real life struggle of young people isolated from their parents, reduced to an age group or a social problem rather than approached as individuals. Unlike Der Kindestod, who symbolized the illness that isolates the children in their mortal struggle, in this case, the parents themselves have enacted that isolation, missing the real source of danger to themselves, their children, and society. Overtly tying real life instances of parental hysteria — the West Memphis Three case, the "Just Say No" era, and the scapegoating of misfits — to the self-absorbed parents in "Hänsel and Gretel," this episode ties the Grimms' story not only to "real" events within the *Buffy*verse, but also to real events outside in our own 'verse, via the common denominator of shared cultural heritage.

## "Hush," the Gentlemen, and Real Fairy Tales

Needing almost no introduction, "Hush," the "silent episode" from season four is one of the most acclaimed in the series. Its overt connection to folklore also requires very little in the way of background. The nursery rhyme appearing in Buffy's dream sequence at the beginning of "Hush" reveals much about the subsequent folklore tie-in. Disturbingly reminiscent of the little rhymes like "Mirror, Mirror" that often serve as refrains, as well as mnemonic devices for the purposes of oral transmission, in the Grimms' and other fairy tales, in "Hush," the verse is accompanied by eerie music box tones and delivered by a small, blonde girl with a blank stare and a sing-songy voice that starkly contrasts the grisly content of the rhyme: "Can't even shout,/ Can't even cry./ The Gentlemen are coming by,/ Lookin' in windows, lookin' in doors./ They need to take seven,/ And they might take yours./ Can't call to mom,/ Can't say a word./ You're gonna die screaming,/ But you won't be heard." This rhyme contains the main points of the invented fairy tale of "The Gentlemen," who are said to come to a town, steal the voices of the citizenry, then proceed to cut out the hearts of seven unlucky residents. "No sword" can kill these nasty intruders. Only "hearing the princess scream" can put their deadly exploits to an end.

Having shown this episode to my own classes, the reaction almost always includes the question, "Is that a real fairy tale?" In fact, many elements of this tale and its accompanying rhyme are so "authentic," that this reaction is not implausible. Indeed, plenty of children's folk rhymes deal overtly in death, juxtaposed by a happy melody and a cute rhyme. For instance, "the Gentlemen" rhyme has a tune similar to that of "Ring around the Rosy," which itself contains references to symptoms of and death by the Plague ("they all fall down"), or the lullaby "Rockabye, Baby," which ends ominously with the cradle falling from a tree, "baby and all." The text of the traditional bedtime prayer, "Now I lay me down to sleep" is another children's rhyme that also juxtaposes overt themes of death with a catchy rhyming verse. Indeed, my students' reaction to "Hush" mirrors that of Giles, who, after repeating the text of the Gentlemen rhyme, remarks to Buffy on the telephone, "It sounds vaguely familiar." The tune, the rhyme and its meter, and the subject matter all cue memories of these disturbing childrens' rhymes common in the English-speaking countries.

The Gentlemen, as it turns out, are "real" fairy tale figures in the *Buffy*-verse, in the same sense as "Hänsel and Gretel" and "Der Kindestod" are posited as real figures in the previously discussed episodes. My students also perceived the tale as "real" in our world because, between the rhyme and the bloody details of the Gentlemen's exploits, the tale shows marked similarity to some of the apocryphal Grimms' tales they had read in my course. In fact, the Grimms' original fairy tales often rival any modern horror movie in their graphic descriptions of death and dismemberment. In "Sex and Violence: The Hard Core of Fairy Tales," folklorist Maria Tatar remarks,

> For many adults, reading through an unexpurgated edition of the Grimms' collection of tales can be an eye-opening experience. Even those who know that Snow White's stepmother arranges the murder of her stepdaughter, that doves peck out the eyes of Cinderella's stepsisters, that Briar Rose's suitors bleed to death on the hedge surrounding her castle, or that a mad rage drives Rumpelstiltskin to tear himself in two will find themselves hardly prepared for the graphic descriptions of murder [and] mutilation ... that fill the pages of these bedtime stories for children [Tatar 364].

The grisly violence perpetrated by the Gentlemen, as it turns out, is very comparable some of the incidents in these tales. For this reason, the audience nods inwardly when, upon viewing a sketch made by Giles' friend Olivia of a Gentleman's face seen out the window the night before, Giles rushes over to a shelf and pulls out a stately looking red leather volume with the generic title *Fairy Tales* embossed in gold on the cover.

The characters' ensuing battle to find their voices and conquer the Gentlemen mirrors their inner battles to process and express unacknowledged feelings about their loved ones over the course of this episode. Buffy wrestles with her feelings for Riley. Willow struggles with her remaining feelings for Oz while confronted with the unexpected possibility of a relationship with Tara. Anya must come to terms with her unruly human emotions in the context of her love for Xander. Giles looks to redefine his role as Buffy's Watcher as he sees his charge mature. All of these inner battles play out silently against a backdrop in which "hearts" can literally be lost.

As Bettelheim points out, the level of violence in fairy tales corresponds to "the most serious inner struggles which growing up entails" and when read in a wider context, they offer "solutions to pressing difficulties" (8). In Joss Whedon's use of folklore in its violent extremes, tempered by a certain level of fantasy offered by the popular genres from which he draws, *Buffy* offers its audiences the same sense of mastery over uncontrollable forces—both internal and external—that have always kept fairy tales popular and timeless. It is for this reason that the description of Joss Whedon as a "village storyteller" will surely continue to fit as he continues to reinvent familiar narratives that show us ourselves and the grim but ultimately surmountable nature of everyday human struggles.

## WORKS CITED

Basinger, Jeanine. "Joss Whedon, Film Major: A+ All the Way." SC3: Slayage Conference on the Whedonverses. Henderson State University, Arkadelphia, AR. 8 June 2008.

Bettelheim, Bruno. *The Uses of Enchantment: The Meaning and Importance of Fairy Tales.* New York: Knopf, 1976.

Freud, Sigmund. *The Uncanny.* David McClintock, trans. New York: Penguin, 2003.

"Gingerbread." *Buffy the Vampire Slayer.* 4:10. 1999. DVD. WB Television Network, 2003.

Hoffmann, E.T.A. "The Sand-Man." *The Best Tales of Hoffmann.* E.F. Bleiler, trans. and ed. New York: Dover, 1979. 183–214.

Holder, Nancy, Jeff Mariotte, and Maryelizabeth Hart. *Buffy the Vampire Slayer: The Watcher's Guide 2.* New York: Pocket, 2000.

"Hush." *Buffy the Vampire Slayer.* 4:10. 1999. DVD. WB Television Network, 2003.

"Killed by Death." *Buffy the Vampire Slayer.* 4:10. 1998. DVD. WB Television Network, 2002.

Tatar, Maria. "Sex and Violence: The Hard Core of Fairy Tales." *The Classic Fairy Tales.* Maria Tatar, ed. New York: W.W. Norton, 1999.

# The Failed Quest for
# "Anti-Self-Consciousness"

DENISE TISCHLER MILLSTEIN

Geoffrey H. Hartman explains the theory of anti-self-consciousness thus: art is often employed as a means to transcend life's oppressive material existence in the absence of religion, which previously made such transcendence possible. However, a problem arises because art only increases self-awareness, creating a vicious self-perpetuating and self-devouring cycle whereby "every increase in consciousness is accompanied by an increase in self-consciousness" (47). As Wordsworth once wrote, this analysis can easily become a passion that "murders to dissect." An inherent paradox lies at the heart of this search. While the quest to break out of stereotypically acute Romantic subjectivity finds particular expression in Edgar Allan Poe's "The Fall of the House of Usher," the theory can also be applied to characters in Joss Whedon's canon. Like Usher, Angel and Spike are morbidly self-aware artists, whose art, painting and poetry respectively, rather than bringing them satisfactory, healthy release, only intensifies their self-consciousness. Buffy herself is not traditionally conceived of as an artist, although one could argue that her ability to kill borders on art. In "Once More, With Feeling," Buffy takes on the more common artistic role of singer and dancer. Each of these artists seem to indicate that attempting to overcome materiality through art is destined to fail.

The narrator of Poe's "The Fall of the House of Usher" receives a letter from Roderick Usher in which he writes of "a mental disorder which oppressed him [...] with a view of attempting, by the cheerfulness of my society, some alleviation of his malady" (232). With the arrival of the narrator, Usher hopes that he will feel release from a certain nervous agitation, which has been plaguing him for some time. This "morbid acuteness of the senses" (235) has physical manifestations such that, according to Charles E. May, "he finds all but the most bland food intolerable, can wear garments of only certain textures, finds the odors of flowers oppressive, cannot bear anything but the faintest light, and cannot listen to anything but some peculiar sounds from stringed instruments" (105). In short, all sensory input, all sensations that remind Usher of his physical, material body have become oppressive to him. The only activities Usher actively participates in are the appreciation and perpetuation of art. However, Roderick Usher employs his art not as a means to explore and expand his mind, but to deny it. Usher uses his art — his paintings, music, and poetry — in an attempt to hide from knowledge of himself. Thus, his quest is essentially one of "anti-self-consciousness."

The artist, seeking to forget his materiality, realizes that this self-consciousness, the thing he most wants to transcend, "cannot be overcome" (Hartman 49). As a consequence, the artist often separates himself from life, even in the midst of life. He exists rather in a kind of life-in-death, like Coleridge's Ancient Mariner. Usher does this perhaps unwittingly by way of his sense-based malady, which he blames on a family predisposition. As May says, Usher has cut himself off "from any stimulus from the external world" (105). Lousie J. Kaplan also mentions Usher's self-imposed exile from the material world, arguing that Usher has "deliberately isolated himself from the world of earthly delights [...] in order to create visionary abstraction" (59). Hartman suggests that as the Romantic artist's abstract knowledge of himself increases, so does his solitude. Acute consciousness then alienates the artist from life and "imposes the burden of a self which religion or death or a return to the state of nature might dissolve" (51). The burden of self might be alleviated by a simple return to nature; however, this is impossible because nature itself, the physical world, only furthers contemplation of materiality. The artists' return then is rather "via knowledge, to naivete," (48) to an "organized innocence," as William Blake maintained.

Usher's story has been called one "about the ultimate romantic artist" (May 107). Like many Romantics, Usher engages in several different genres of art: he paints, improvises on guitar, and writes poetry. A close examination of the artistic impressions produced by Roderick Usher, specifically his poem that Poe imbeds in the tale, "The Haunted Palace," might prove useful before exploring Whedon's characters.

"The Haunted Palace," according to G. R. Thompson, "is an integral part of the tale; it has an imagistic, symbolic, thematic, and structural function, and these functions cannot be separated without damage to the story's overall meaning" (314–15). In a letter to a friend, Griswold, Poe indicates that he published the poem "The Haunted Palace" independently first, then "embodied the poem in a tale called 'The House of Usher'" (316). Thus, "the poem had something to do with the genesis of the story'" (reprt. in Thompson 316). However, the exact meaning of the poem is debatable. Thompson offers the most widely accepted interpretation of the ballad, saying that it contains a transparent allegory "with a single conceit [...] the castellated palace and the human head" (315). Poe once wrote that "by the palace he meant 'to imply a mind haunted by phantoms—a disordered brain'" (reprt. in Thompson 316). In the poem, the palace is completed with images of eyes as windows and pearls and rubies as teeth, lips, and doors. In a short critical leap then, the palace/head equation of the poem stands in for the disordered mind of Usher himself, making the poem overall, Poe's lament "to the tottering of Roderick's mind, his loss of connection to the life of reason" (Kaplan 58). But what has caused this collapse?

Romantic artists often express a desire to return to innocence, even while in the grip of insanity. Roderick Usher has lost his innocence, and fallen into mental collapse probably due to his relationship with his sister Madeline. As most readers quickly realize, the specter of incest between Usher and Madeline is "omnipresent from the beginning" (Kaplan 60). Yet, Usher knows that incest is wrong. His attempts to rid himself of all earthly passions could be an effort to repudiate his incestuous longing for his sister. Usher's strategy is doomed to fail because, as Hartman says, self-consciousness cannot be overcome, especially by an artist. Usher's art can only momentarily disguise or conceal his forbidden desires. It cannot permanently obscure them. In the end, the source of Usher's passions cannot remain buried; it is revealed when Madeline returns from her premature grave to seek revenge. It is easy to understand then why Usher eventually loses his mind. Kaplan insists, "when the effort to banish passion through asceticism fails, as eventually it must, there is either a fulfillment of forbidden sexual desire or something worse — the madness of total emotional surrender [...] and a loss of identity" (62). The latter is the only choice left Usher. It is through the poem "The Haunted Palace" that Usher as an author himself both reveals and denies his true aims, even though the poem does not explicitly discuss incest. As a poet, Usher is trapped by his desire to transcend materiality and at the same time, the larger story of the tale implies that his problems stem from a physical longing for sexual union with his twin.

Spike has similar, though more complicated troubles in the *Buffy* series, especially in his relationship with his mother and his mother/lover Drusilla as seen in the episode "Lies My Parents Told Me" in season seven. Both of these relationships are not without their incestual overtones. Before Spike even becomes a vampire, he lives with his mother and the intimacy they share is much more akin to that of husband and wife than mother and son, even if this exists solely on the level of the subconscious. While his mother insists, "You need a woman in your life," Spike's reply, "I *have* a woman in my life" indicates that their bond already fulfills his need for a suitable mate. Spike's feelings for Drusilla, on the other hand, always involve the active double consciousness that she is both his sire and the object of his lust. She is the cause of his rebirth into the world of the vampire; in a very real way then, Drusilla is Spike's second mother. When meeting Spike's mother for the first time, Drusilla introduces herself with, "I'm the woman who gave birth to your son." And yet, as the series makes clear time and again, they share a barely-contained, active sexual relationship. It is partially under Drusilla's influence that Spike finally murders his mother, but not before she has actually accused Spike of incestual feelings for her. Once a vampire, Spike's mother chides him, "All you ever wanted was to be back inside." She taunts him further: "You finally got you wish, didn't you? Sank your teeth into me in an eternal kiss." The vampire's "kiss" or bite has long been seen as a kind of sexual penetration.

The guilt that Spike feels over his conscious and subconscious impulse towards incest and murdering his mother lies buried deep within him, like Madeline in the Usher family crypt. However, The First has discerned the source of Spike's guilt. In fact, she/it uses a traditional English folksong his mother used to sing to him, "Early One Morning," to "trigger" him into committing brutal crimes that he literally buries in the basement of one of his victims. The basement here is not unlike the Usher subterranean crypt, and could be used to represent Spike's subconscious as well. After years of not feeding on humans, Spike is killing again and hiding the evidence. In this case, art in the form of the song The First employs, reinforces rather than expunges guilt. He has only to think of the song to have the trigger engage. Spike is forced to face his guilt when Buffy and the rest of the Scoobies attempt to "deprogram" him. Of course, this fails until Principal Robin Wood deliberately tricks Spike into attacking him, not coincidently for Spike's murder of another mother, Wood's, the slayer from whom Spike stole his signature leather coat. When Spike tells his mother, "I'm sorry," in a memory or vision of her from the past, he effectively releases himself from the guilt of their relationship and the song no longer serves as a trigger.

Moreover, Spike also considered himself a poet when he was mortal, like Usher. Spike's albeit dreadful Romantic verse was employed as means to achieve sexual fulfillment with the young mortal woman, Cecily Underwood. It is after her stern public rebuke that Spike finds himself cornered in an alley by Drusilla in the first place. And who can blame her harsh rejection in "Fool for Love" from season five of *Buffy* to such poetry as: "My heart expands, it's grown ebulgent/inspired by your beauty effulgent"? In this episode we also learn the origin of two of Spike's names. He is known as "William the Bloody," we are told by a female socialite at a salon, due to his "bloody awful poetry." A male guest at the same party indicates that "I'd rather have a railroad spike through my head than listen to that awful stuff." Whatever the reception of his art, Spike's commitment to poetry continues over the years, we later find out in the final episode of *Angel*, "Not Fade Away," when Spike recites his poetry at a Coffee House to some acclaim.

Unlike Spike, Roderick Usher is also a visual artist. His work as a painter is in some ways even more demonstrative of his quest for "anti-self-consciousness" than his poetry. The narrator, attempting to describe Usher's effusive style, offers, "if ever mortal painted an idea, that mortal was Roderick Usher" (Poe 237). As he tries to describe Usher's paintings specifically, he can only say that they "grew, touch by touch, into vagueness" (Poe 236). Indeed, Usher's depictions are so immaterial and vague that they demand a more intense scrutiny. Matthew C. Brennan compares Usher's style to that of painter J. M. W. Turner's, which is equally "vague, obscure, mysterious, and redundant." Brennan argues that these qualities, also found in Usher's paintings, evoke the characteristics of the sublime as specified in Edmund Burke's *The Sublime and the Beautiful* (1756). Usher's paintings rely almost exclusively on sublime imagery such as "vastness, obscurity, and blinding light" (605), which may be seen to visually represent "sublime consciousness," or an awareness of the immaterial world. This knowledge is such that it essentially dissolves "external reality" (606). The sublime consciousness that Usher recreates in his paintings obliterates perspective, and disintegrates boundaries to such an extent that he "expressionistically distort[s] reality" ("Turnerian Topography" 605). Usher's reality, like the one reproduced in his paintings, is no longer "real" and material, but has become distorted, unreal, and immaterial.

Brennan also attempts to diagnose Usher's mental disorder, claiming that he "exhibits traits related to schizophrenia." More specifically, he is a schizophrenic nightmare sufferer "experiencing the terror of psychic disintegration" (*The Gothic Psyche* 141), which is exactly the experience that his vague paintings reproduce in the viewer. And, like the nightmare sufferer "who fails to keep images of annihilation and disintegration out of his dreams, Roderick fails to keep them out of his painting" (140). Brennan blames this degeneration on Roderick's incestuous relationship with his twin, which being unresolved, results in "a complete psychic breakdown" (142). Ultimately then, Usher's paintings fail to offer him a way to transcend materiality. Instead, the quest for transcendence itself ends in insanity, diagnosed by Brennan as schizophrenia.

Again, this pattern is repeated several times in both *Buffy the Vampire Slayer* and *Angel* series as we have already seen in the case of Spike. The impulse towards incest which compels both Spike and Usher deeper into their own consciousness applies equally well to the example of Angel. Angel, too, commits incest with his "mother" Darla, only to stake her. This pattern changes slightly when Wolfram & Hart bring Darla back from Hell. Angel's sire and former lover invades his thoughts and dreams so that he cannot escape her, awake or asleep. In fact, as his dreams about Darla become more regular, Angel becomes reluctant to stay conscious at all, preferring the distorted reality of his dreams, which embody the sublime characteristics of vastness, obscurity, and distorted reality, a reality in which Darla is still alive. His dreams become more real than life within the Hyperion Hotel. And yet, his dreams are not always peaceful ones, becoming increasingly replaced by nightmares. Angel's guilt at having killed Darla is acknowledged by Wesley in "Dear Boy" from season two of *Angel*. Wesley supposes that Angel's nightmares could be caused by "guilt over killing your sire." Cordelia adds, with her absent-minded candor, "Who loves guilt like you love guilt?" Rather than becoming a full-blown schizophrenic like Usher, Angel seems to suffer the repetitive nightmares of someone suffering from Obsessive-Compulsive Disorder (OCD).

At times, Angel shows other signs of OCD that connect more directly with his artistic expressions. This is seen dramatically in "Darla" from season two of *Angel*. Wesley visits Angel's room in the hotel, where he has all but imprisoned himself. Wesley asks, "So you're sure there's nothing on you mind? That is to say, nothing you'd like to perhaps ... share?" When Angel stoically replies, "No," Wesley enters the room, revealing for the first time that it is covered with literally hundreds of sketches of Darla. He sarcastically pushes: "Really?" Angel here is not too unlike Usher, repeatedly painting depictions of the family vault where Madeline's body lays. Because Angel's thoughts are returning to Darla compulsively, he is literally unable to think of anything else. Thus, it stands to reason that he should be unable to sketch anything else as well. His art, like Usher's reveals the one thing preventing his transcendence. This is anticipated when Angel becomes obsessed with Buffy in season two of *Buffy*. In "Passion," after turning into Angelus for the first time on screen, he breaks into Buffy's room one night to sketch her while she sleeps, leaving the picture on her pillow as a means to threaten and terrify her.

There is, however, one extenuating circumstance in Angel's specific case, the gypsy curse. This curse, uttered by a father in memory of his daughter whom Angel had murdered, makes it impossible for Angel to forget his sins. With the restoration of his soul, Angel also receives a conscience that obsessively tortures him with excessive feelings of guilt. Like Usher and Byron's Alpine anti-hero Manfred, Angel is trapped in "knowing" what he has done. Perhaps this is one reason why Angel tries in vain to prevent Darla's becoming a vampire again in season two. For certainly, sketching his thoughts does not allow Angel the opportunity to escape this pain; rather, it only makes his morbid self-awareness more intense, like Usher before him. This echoes Hartman's refrain that self-consciousness can never be overcome.

G. R. Thompson applies a similar theory to Poe's tale, "The Paradoxical

Law of Terror," replacing feelings of guilt with the fear of being afraid. Thompson observes that "the consciousness of one's own fear, rather than alleviating it by rational confrontation, serves merely to increase it" (323). This mental quicksand enmires both the narrator and Usher. In the final scene, the narrator reads "The Mad Trist," clearly demonstrating The Paradoxical Law of Terror at work. As Thompson predicts, "Usher's terror of impending madness will rapidly accelerate it, as will the narrator's more generalized terror, if the latter becomes more conscious of his own fear of Usher's terror. Which is precisely what happens" (330). Yet, the narrator reads the romance in the first place to distract Usher's attention from his heightened self-consciousness as well to deflect his own, but "the reading proves less than therapeutic" (333). The tale merely heightens the fears of both Usher and the narrator. Because they are so aware of their own terror, both characters cannot escape the influence of their heightened consciousness on each other or themselves. This revelation can by now hardly be surprising, for as Hartman notes, "every increase of consciousness is accompanied by an increase in self-consciousness" (47), whether that consciousness is infused with forbidden and taboo sexual longing, torturous feelings of guilt, or in this case, terror. This awareness encloses the artist in a web of self or subjectivity, much as Usher and the narrator are enclosed.

Of course in this case, the art trapping Usher in his heightened awareness of himself is not his own. Poe reproduces "The Mad Trist" for the reader, creating a story within the story, a metafiction. This phenomenon, attributing his art to his characters, is pervasive in Poe's canon. He is an artist who frequently plagiarizes himself as well as others. As Kaplan explains, "in the life of Edger Allan Poe, artistic creation served as [...] a kind of fetish device that enabled him to conceal and yet still reveal the unbearable secrets and phantoms that haunted his mind" (54). Sir Launcelot Canning's text also influences events in Usher's story. That is, the fictional author Canning is just as involved in commenting on the action in "The Fall of the House of Usher" as he is in narrating his own "Mad Trist." As May explains, "sounds described in the fiction are echoed in Roderick and the narrator's own fictional world. The shriek of the dragon [...] is echoed by a shriek in [...] 'the house of Usher'" (107), increasing Usher's and the narrator's self-awareness of their own fear. But Poe applies yet another layer of self-consciousness. Even the romance within the interpolated tale discusses the heightened consciousness of yet another character, the champion in "The Mad Trist," Ethelred. When the good sir knight self-consciously "feel[s] the rain upon his shoulders, and fear[s] the rising tempest" (243), this reflects Usher's and the narrator's awareness of the tempest in their world. Ethelred's fear*less*ness at facing the dragon, however, serves to increase the fear*ful*ness of Usher and the narrator, who are about to confront Madeline. Therefore, the character in the romance and the characters in the tale operate in a mire of subjectivity which none cannot escape; each of them further encloses the other and themselves.

In another moment of metafiction, the episode "Once More, With Feeling" in which Xander has purposefully summoned the singing/tapdancing demon Sweet, who causes the town of Sunnnydale to burst into spontaneous song and dance, we get an exploration of Buffy's nightmare. As the demon explains his purpose, we hear the anti-self-consciousness refrain. Sweet says that he aids people in exploring their pain in song and dance. While at first this might seem refreshing, the artistic impressions expressed become more increasingly intense, and the feedback cycle ends in death, literally in spontaneous combustion.

Buffy's terror is actually the waking world. Having been removed from Heaven, pulled out suddenly by Willow's increasingly powerful magic, Buffy finds the world a terrifying place. In order to keep her grief quiet so as not to produce feelings of guilt in her friends, Buffy has been hiding this information from those around her, in the process shutting herself out from life even in the midst of life, like Angel and Usher. Instead, she prefers to keep the pain bottled inside of her, cutting her off from the support of her friends. This truth comes out in the metadrama the demon has created, most notably in Buffy's climatic solo "Something to Sing About." Buffy laments, "There was no pain. No fear, no doubt. / Till they pulled me out ... of Heaven." She continues, "I live in Hell 'cause I've been expelled ... from Heaven." Buffy is only saved from bursting into flames by Spike, who reminds her that the world has never been a perfect place. Spike sings, "Life isn't bliss. / Life is just this— it's living.... The pain that you feel, / You only can heal from living." He warns Buffy against cutting herself off from life in order to escape the pain of the material world. The immaterial existence of art likewise does nothing to stop the cycle of guilt. Willow similarly seeks to suppress her own guilt in the episode "Tabula Rosa." In attempting to erase Tara's memory of their argument over her addiction to magic, Willow casts a spell, which makes everyone forget who they are. Willow's art, her magical powers, does not offer anything but a temporary transcendence, and Tara leaves her.

The unbearable specters that haunt Poe's tale include what Brennan calls "the dark side of the Romantic quest for unity" (146). The artist seeks, through the dark side of human consciousness, here Usher's descent into madness, to discover an "organized innocence" (Hartman 49). This innocence is supposed to help the artist transcend materiality and "the consequences of being mere body by retreating into the art work itself" (May 102), thus ridding him of his oppressive self-consciousness. In other words, art is supposed to release the artist from his morbid self-consciousness, allowing him to create an anti-self that can transcend materiality and function for him as a kind of religiously inspired myth, without the need for metaphysical convictions. Usher ultimately fails in his attempt to create an anti-self that transcends self-consciousness. In fact, all his attempts to deny his own awareness through art fail and rather only intensify his subjectivity. Usher simply cannot deny his materiality, thus he cannot return to innocence, in part because he cannot deny his sexual longing for Madeline.

This concept also applies to Buffy's continued cycle of grief and guilt from being pulled out of Heaven. After the truth comes out in "Once More, With Feeling," Buffy begins a disturbing sadomasochistic sexual relationship with Spike. Rather than turning away from the physical world as Usher does, it appears that Buffy rather rushes into it, turning to violent sex as a way to push away her feelings of grief and betrayal. This, of course, increases her guilt at allowing herself to be sexually brutalized by her soulless, vampiric lover. What's more, the pain that Buffy and Spike inflict on each other sexually, can also be read ironically as evidence of Buffy's continued denial of her oppressive physicality after she has returned from the grave. The logic is that the pain of the sexual act reminds her of her body to such an extent that she will temporarily forget the simple, healthy pleasure of being at peace in Heaven. The memory of peace is what essentially makes her existential angst all the more acute. In these examples, whether it be incest or sadomasochism, sexual taboo lies at the heart of physical and emotional torment.

And yet, it can be argued that Buffy actually experiences more success at forgetting her material body than any of the other characters we have examined. One need only to recall that in the episode "Gone" from season six, Buffy enjoys being invisible a little too much, before learning that the ultimate effect is total physical disintegration. The art that temporarily frees Buffy comes from a source outside herself, though, in the form of the invisibility ray created by the evil triumvirate of Jonathon, Andrew, and Warren. While she is invisible, Buffy at last experiences some relief from her oppressive physical body, even though it has not really evaporated, she does not have to see or be reminded of it. Part of the reason Buffy feels such relief if that she has momentarily achieved an escape from her materiality, the ultimate goal of Romantic artists; she has gained transcendence from the material world. Buffy, is at last free of her body. Of course, the break can only be temporary, if Buffy does not wish to completely disintegrate like the traffic pylon found by Xander and Willow. The central irony of it all is that one of the first things Buffy does when she is invisible is visit Spike, to again be reminded of her body through violent sex.

In Whedon's *Buffy the Vampire Slayer* and *Angel* series, we find the same basic quest to forget acute awareness of self-consciousness that can be traced in Poe's "The Fall of the House of Usher." Just as Usher cannot successfully complete this quest, the same holds true for Spike, Angel, and Buffy herself. All of theses characters must learn in the end that art, rather than delivering release from painful self-awareness, only increases it.

## Works Cited

Brennan, Matthew C. *The Gothic Psyche: Disintegration and Growth in Nineteenth Century English Literature.* Columbia, SC: Camden House, 1997.

_____. "Turnerian Topography: The Paintings of Roderick Usher."*Studies in Short Fiction.* 27 (1990): 605–608.

"Darla." *Angel, Season Two on DVD.* Writ. Tim Minear. Dir. Tim Minear. WB. 14 November 2000. DVD. Twentieth Century–Fox Home Entertainment, 2003.

"Dear Boy." *Angel, Season Two on DVD.* Writ. David Greenwalt. Dir. David Greenwalt. WB. 24 October 2000. DVD. Twentieth Century–Fox Home Entertainment, 2003.

Engel, Leonard W. "The Journey from Reason to Madness: Edgar Allan Poe's 'The Fall of the House of Usher.'" *Essays in Arts and Sciences.* 14 (1985): 23–31.

"Fool For Love." *Buffy the Vampire Slayer, The Complete Fifth Season on DVD.* Writ. Douglas Petrie. Dir. Nick Marck WB. 14 November 2000. DVD. Twentieth Century–Fox Home Entertainment, 2003.

"Gone." *Buffy the Vampire Slayer, The Complete Sixth Season on DVD.* Writ. David Fury. Dir. David Fury. UPN. 8 January 2002. DVD. Twentieth Century–Fox Home Entertainment, 2004.

Hartman, Geoffrey H. "Romanticism and 'Anti-Self Consciousness.'" *Romanticism and Consciousness.* Ed. Harold Bloom. New York: Norton, 1970. 149–172.

Kaplan, Louise J. "The Perverse Strategy in 'The Fall of the House of Usher." *New Essays on Poe's Major Tales.* Ed. Kenneth Silverman. New York: Cambridge University Press, 1993. 47–64.

"Lies My Parents Told Me." *Buffy the Vampire Slayer, The Complete Seventh Season on DVD.* Wirt. David Fury and Drew Goddard. Dir. David Fury. UPN. 25 March 2003. DVD. Twentieth Century–Fox Home Entertainment, 2004.

May, Charles E. *Edgar Allan Poe: A Study of the Short Fiction.* New York: Twayne, 1991.

"Not Fade Away." *Angel, Season Five on DVD.* Writ. Jeffrey Bell and Joss Whedon. Dir. Jeffrey Bell. WB. 19 May 2004. DVD. Twentieth Century–Fox Home Entertainment, 2004.

"Once More, With Feeling." *Buffy the Vampire Slayer, The Complete Sixth Season on DVD.* Writ. Joss Whedon. Dir. Joss Whedon. UPN. 6 November 2001. DVD. Twentieth Century–Fox Home Entertainment, 2004.

"Passion." *Buffy the Vampire Slayer, The Complete Second Season on DVD.* Writ. David Tyron King. Dir. Michael Gershman. WB. 24 February 1998. DVD. Twentieth Century–Fox Home Entertainment, 2002.

Poe, Edgar Allan. *The Complete Tales and Poems of Edgar Allan Poe.* New York: Vintage, 1975.

"Tabula Rosa." *Buffy the Vampire Slayer, The Complete Sixth Season on DVD.* Writ. Rebecca Kirshner. Dir. David Grossman. UPN. 13 November 2001. DVD. Twentieth Century–Fox Home Entertainment, 2004.

Thompson, G. R. "Poe and the Paradox of Terror: Structures of Heightened Consciousness in 'The Fall of the House of Usher.'" *Ruined Eden of the Present: Hawthorne, Melville, Poe.* Ed. G. R. Thompson and Virgil L. Lokke. West Lafayette: Purdue University Press, 1981. 379–83.

# *Buffy's* Insight into Wollstonecraft and Mill

### Kevin K. Durand

And then it was over. Seven years, hundreds of puns, vampires and Big Bads dusted and vanquished, the Sunnydale Hellmouth closed, the world saved... A lot. Seven years and the story arc of destruction of patriarchy, empowerment of women, and feminist triumph comes to its conclusion as the Scooby gang looks out over the crater where once their town stood. Slowly, the town sign creaks, gives way, and falls into the crater. It's over. Faith sums it up—"Looks like the Hellmouth is closed for business."

It's a statement of completion. Closed for business. Over. We win. The triumph is complete. Caleb, the paradigm of the patriarchal power and oppression, indeed, the denigration of women, has been conquered; every potential slayer across the globe has been empowered; and the First Evil has been, as Willow puts it, "scrunched." Faith reacts as a triumphant, but exhausted warrior reacts—"I just want sleep, like for a week." And with the image of the Scoobies seeking out all the newly empowered young women, the show closes on Buffy's wry smile and Dawn's question, "Yeah, Buffy. What are we gonna do now?"

Perhaps lost in the imagery and ennui of the beloved show coming to an end is a line from Giles. To Faith's "Looks like the Hellmouth is closed for business," he responds, "There is another one in Cleveland. Not to spoil the moment." He then bends, picks up a rock and tosses it into the crater. Given this line, Dawn's question takes on new depth. There will be no "sleeping for a week." Indeed, Giles's response to the sleep desire had been a wryly put, "We've got lots of work to do."

Winning a battle does not mean that the war is over. Even winning a battle of the epic and apocalyptic sort that closes *Buffy, the Vampire Slayer* does not end the war. There is always more work to be done.

It would seem as if the show "gets it." That is, it "gets" at least two very important features of the struggle, features that are often ignored or forgotten. First, it is impossible to fight the patriarchal structure that systematically oppresses women alone. And second, just because you win once does not mean it is over. Giles paired lines—"There's another one in Cleveland," and "We've got lots of work to do" only serve to drive the point home further. Triumph is fleeting and the gang, as a group, must press forward into a new, yet still dangerous future.

Let us treat these in that order. One of the most commonly commented themes within the Buffyverse is the notion of group dynamics and that it is not a one-person show—everyone, even Jonathan, is important. Buffy can't do it all, Willow cannot, not even all of the Scoobies together ultimately are able to finish off the First. But every one of them is important, critical for the battle. The careful viewer will remember Season Three when Anya first appeared in Sunnydale. In *The Wish*, to spite Xander, Cordelia wishes that Buffy had never come to Sunnydale. In a flash, her wish is granted by the then Vengence Demon, Anyanka. Just that quickly, the world is completely different. Vampires rule Sunnydale and the Master rules them. Xander and Willow have both been vamped, Giles leads a rag-tag band of "white hats" while wondering why the Slayer whom he had come to Watch had never arrived. Eventually, he makes contact with Buffy—in Cleveland—and she arrives, very much the worse for wear. This is a very different Buffy. Indeed, she reminds the viewer much more of Faith than of the Buffy we have come to know. She is scarred and battered, battle hardened and exceptionally practical. Leading the white hats into battle, which mostly amounts to individual skirmishes throughout a large warehouse, most of the good guys are killed— Buffy dies at the Master's hand, Vamp Willow and Vamp Xander both are staked, almost all of the heroes, in whatever incarnation, are destroyed—one at a time; alone.

This "wished" world stands as stark contrast to the one that Whedon envisions as the series is completed. In that vision, the Scoobies win, mostly survive, and women who have been systematically, and often literally, beaten down have been empowered to stand up and throw off that inequity. But, the war isn't over. Giles's comment carries with it a timeless and disturbing experience of the struggle against oppression, at least for the last several hundred years. Just because you win a battle, even an epic one, the fight is not over. This is the second, and perhaps more important of the two to be gleaned.

To reiterate, winning a battle does not mean the war is over. Even if the battle is as apocalyptic and epic as gaining the right to vote, the right to own property, the right to be something more than chattel. Even if the triumph is as powerful as the absolute refutation of those arguments that would deny those rights and deny full personhood to half of humanity. Somehow, again and again, we fail to remember what Giles reluctantly reminds. In heady moments of triumph, it is easy to obscure the difficult work that lies ahead; that inevitably lies ahead given the intransigence of patriarchal power that is, through Wollstonecraft and Mill and others, stripped of its "supporting philosophical basis." Indeed, Giles is a sort of Cassandra here, although much better received than his ancient counterpart. Often there is a sense of discouragement that sets in when the machinery of power refuse to bow to triumphant arguments. And, the victors, those arguing and working and struggling for the recognition of full humanity for all humanity, are like Faith. "We won, why don't we get to rest? We won, but it still goes on? Why can't the revolution just be finished, why does it take so long? Can't we just sleep for a week?" That discouragement leads to complacency in some and to surrender in others.

Season six saw that discouragement, and, indeed despair, very nearly overcome Buffy. Having been ripped from heaven and thrust back into a world where everything was too bright and too harsh, she is in despair. Closing season five, Buffy made the ultimate sacrifice — flinging herself into a vortex to save the world. Again. In the Buffy of season six, we see exemplified, in extreme fashion, the dilemma facing the gang at the close of seven. Buffy wonders why she wasn't allowed to rest. After all, her headstone summed it up — "She saved the world. A lot." Shouldn't such a one enjoy the fruits of that labor and be allowed to stroll the Elysian fields? Yet even Buffy's sacrifice and salvific acts don't provide respite. The world is a desperate place. Her triumph stopped an apocalypse, but it wasn't enough; it didn't end the war. Tired though she was, she had more to do. Not only Buffy was faced with this dilemma. The Scoobies also waged the fight against Glory, and while Buffy was in heaven or in a heaven-like dimension, the war raged on, and they were on the front lines. They, too, were exhausted, and likely wanted to sleep for a week. None got to experience that reality because reality goes on, and winning a battle, even against a cosmic deity, doesn't end the war. There are still important things to do.

Among the important things to do, as Buffy and Giles and Willow and Faith all tell the slayerettes during season seven, is to remind ourselves that battles have been won. While Wollstonecraft and Mill predate the voting rights and property rights victories, they were important wins along the way. Wollstonecraft and Mill are Whedon's ancestors, the fighters who made Whedon's vision of the future possible, rather than the vision that is much more like the nasty, brutish, and short one of *The Wish*. Indeed, it could be argued that without Mill and Wollstonecraft, there couldn't have been a Whedon. Perhaps some look at Whedon's intellectual ancestors is helpful.

John Stuart Mill wins. Within the halls of philosophical investigation, it is a rare thing to truly win. It is perhaps the most stereotypical description of philosophizing that no view is ever truly overthrown. This is not true, of course. Minor and silly views are refuted all the time (although some of them, like Dracula in "Buffy vs. Dracula" managed to hang around as mist for a while and then coalesce again — sillier than they were before). However, even some very thorough views have been overthrown. Leibniz, in his *Theodicy*, drives a stake in the heart of Occasionalism. So much so that a rather popular 17th and 18th century view is all but unheard of today. Alfred North Whitehead buries the Millian underpinning of Utilitarianism (see, Mill doesn't always win). And Mill categorically, unquestionably, and irrefutably devastates the philosophical foundation of the subjection of women.

There are five central arguments within Mill's *Subjection of Women* leveled against those who would argue that women are naturally, socially, physically, emotionally, and rationally inferior to men. His thesis, advanced at the very outset of the book and thus inescapable for anyone who would even begin to peruse it, is quite simple and direct:

> The object of this Essay is to explain as clearly as I am able the grounds of an opinion which I have held from the very earliest period when I had formed any opinions at all on social or political matters, and which, instead of being weakened or modified, has been constantly growing stronger by the progress reflection and the experience of life. That the principle which regulates the existing social relations between the two sexes — the legal subordination of one sex to the other — is wrong itself, and now one of the chief hindrances to human improvement; and that it ought to be replaced by a principle of perfect equality, admitting no power or privilege on the one side, nor disability on the other [Mill 29].

In other words, the subjection of women is morally, politically, socially, naturally, rationally, and experientially wrong, and the consequence of this evil is the weakening, and perhaps ultimate destruction, of the entirety of civilization.

While such a description sounds very much like the opening of a modern character tale — one girl in all the world who alone will fight the forces of evil — it turns out that Mill's arguments are successful. That is, he wins. Before all the credit is given to Mill, however, it is rather important to note that what was true of Sir Isaac Newton is double so of Mill. Newton, in a moment of humility, said that if he had seen farther than others, it was because he had stood on the shoulders of giants. Mill, likewise, owes much to his predecessors, especially Mary Wollstonecraft. Many of his arguments have their beginnings in her work. So, before completing the examination of the Millian devastation of the philosophical underpinnings of patriarchy, we should first look briefly at one of Wollstonecraft's contributions. Then, we shall return to Mill's thesis and the arguments which rest firmly on her shoulders.

Mary Wollstonecraft's voice is one of the first voices of women philosophers generally added to the canon of the Modern Period in Western Philosophy. The absence of women's voices in the canon has come to be understood to be by no means on account of a lack of depth, sophistication, and/or creativity. Rather, contemporary scholars have come more and more to understand the significant loss to philosophical inquiry that resulted from the arbitrary exclusion of the voices of women philosophers. Wollstonecraft's until recent exclusion is a clear case of this arbitrariness and the attendant loss. Her most famous work, *A Vindication of the Rights of Women*, which followed her lesser known work, *A Vindication of the Rights of Men*, by two years, is a powerful criticism of the social, political, economic, and educational oppression of women and a compelling argument for the full inclusion of women in the public arena. It should be noted that *Vindication* precedes Mill's *Subjection of Women* by four decades and the granting of the franchise to women in the United States by 120 years.

Wollstonecraft was a direct victim of the suppression of women's voices. Despite the demonstration of a tremendous intellect from a very early age, she was excluded from "proper" English education and society. Without much formal education, she worked mainly as a writer and an editor, which is itself a testament to the breadth of her self-taught learning. Even with such impressive contributions to the arena of philosophical discourse, she has been, until recently, best known for the work of her daughter, Marry Wollstonecraft Shelley, author of *Frankenstein*.

Wollstonecraft's lack of educational opportunities during her formative years was never far from her mind or her writings. She argues, in *Vindication*, that the subjection of women and the relegation of women to second class status, or worse, tied exclusively to hearth and home, is the direct result of women's having been systematically denied the opportunity of education. As a proto-feminist, Wollstonecraft is sometimes marginalized by the very feminist movement that owes much to her. This is probably due to the fact that she concedes that the women of her era are, in fact, inferior to men in the area of intellect. This marginalization is unfortunate because it reflects a very naïve reading of her work. She is not suggesting that the fact of intellectual inferiority is in any way a natural or essential feature of women. Instead, it is an accidental property of English society, a property caused by male oppression through the denial of education to women. Having been excluded from the opportunity of education, it is small wonder that a person so denied might, as a result, be uneducated. While this denial of educational opportunity will not entail a lack of education, it will tend, in a large population organized under such a system, to produce precisely that result as a common feature of the group thusly denied. Simply put, being a woman did not render one inferior; being systematically denied the opportunity to develop one's intellectual capacity tended to render one less intellectually capable. Since the education actually widely available to women was solely focused on passive aspects of beauty and servility, one should not express surprise that this is the general result. An alteration in the system would result in women having not only educational opportunity, but also in the rightful assumption by women of equal political and social rights. This forms the heart, but not the entirety, of her philosophical view; a view that is picked up by Mill and turned into the kernel of his own philosophical reflections on the nature of humanity and patriarchy.

So, let us return to Mill and examine his triumphant argument. Mill's opponents are familiar ones. They are those who would argue that women ought be subject to men. These opponents, Mill points out, would argue that it is women's *nature* that makes them subject to men. The crux of their view is this: "the passage of legislation that accords with that fact is to be preferred because it is in keeping with *natural law*. Thus, women are to be excluded from the public sector, from owning property, from participation in politics, from education because they are naturally incapable of owning, participating, and learning" (Mill 38).

For these, Mill offers a series of analogies, each making this view more ridiculous than the last. Consider the occupation of blacksmithing. Is it necessary to pass legislation that people who are physically weak, infirm, or intolerant of high heat and pressure should be excluded from this profession? Indeed, isn't the profession itself sufficient to restrict those who cannot perform it, whether men or women, from pursuing it. And, if they pursue it and fail, this is sufficient to demonstrate their inability, quite independent of law. Simply put, if legislation is necessary to restrict action, then the actions are not an outgrowth of human nature; if the inferiority is a feature of nature, then no law is sufficient to enforce it. Thus, Mill puts the opposition in the unenviable, and indeed, untenable position of being caught between incompatible principles. To say that legislation is necessary to restrict women from the public sphere is just to say that nature does not so restrict them. To say that nature restricts them is just to say that legislation is unnecessary. They can have it one way or the other, but not both. Since the only support for such legislation is appeal to nature, that path is cut off. Since the only support for the argument about nature is some appeal to social/legislative/doctrinal assertions, then that path is likewise eliminated. Thus, those who would argue that women are naturally and legislatively inferior to men are thwarted. Further, the arguments to restrict any rights accorded to men to women is refuted. Simple. Elegant. And as a direct as a mystical scythe cleaving a patriarchal demon clergyman in twain.

However, one need not look far to see the evidence of the refuted view still widely present, coalescing like a particularly nasty mist in popular and, unfortunately, scholarly discourse. It is sometimes argued that the disproportionate representation of men in the natural sciences is tied to some innate male intellectual superiority. Women are restricted from the clergy (in most cases) and disproportionately underrepresented in the legislative halls of power based, often, on completely spurious notions of male spiritual or rational superiority. Like the Scoobies, Mill and Wollstonecraft have won — but there is no real respite from the struggle.

Simply put — Wollstonecraft (in the last part of the 18th century) and Mill (in the middle of the 19th) win. Their arguments, first hers and then his, utterly refute those who would marginalize and systematically oppress women. The battles are won. It's over. And yet... And yet, the war continues.

It was nearly a century after Mill's *Subjection* that women gained the right to vote in the United States. In the first part of the 21st century, we are still met with structural and systemic differences that are disadvantageous to women. Despite the success of Mill's arguments in support of his thesis that the subjection of women is wrong, despite the success of Wollstonecraft's arguments that women should enjoy the same education and rights men enjoy, this is still not the order of the day.

Giles's comment — "there's another one in Cleveland. Not to spoil the moment" — is a sobering reminder that winning battles doesn't win the war. Warriors get discouraged. Though, like Cordelia, in *The Wish*, it is important to remember that the world without Wollstonecraft, the world without Mill, the world without Buffy is a much more impoverished, dangerous, and backward sort.

## WORKS CITED

Mill, John Stuart. *Subjection of Women*. London: Longmans, Green, 1911.
Wollstonecraft, Mary. *A Vindication of the Rights of Women*. London: T. Fisher Unwin, 1891.

# PART III. BUFFY, THE SCOOBIES, AND BEYOND

# Buffy's Dream in *Surprise*

## Melanie Wilson

When watching *Buffy the Vampire Slayer*, one notices that Buffy is frequently influenced by her dreams in a prophetic manner. This trend is present from the original movie to the end of the series. It is easy to view these dreams solely as prophecies, but more careful viewing reveals that several of her dreams serve also to illustrate challenges of Buffy's personal life. This is obvious in dreams like the ones in "Restless," but more subtle in dreams like the one at the beginning of "Surprise." Although the dream sequence serves largely as a prophetic tool for Buffy, the dream cannot be interpreted strictly as prophecy. Buffy interprets her dream as a warning that Drusilla is alive and plans to kill Angel, but it is not Drusilla who tries to kill Angel, literally or metaphorically. This begs the dream to be interpreted on a personal level as Buffy's unconscious attempt to work with her own emotional conflicts.

Before beginning an analysis of the dream, it is important to consider the role of Drusilla in the dream and in the larger structure of the show. Drusilla's existence in the dream is one of two things Buffy consciously recalls, making Dru a powerful dream element. Free from the story's implications, as a vampire, Drusilla may represent "dead" issues that have been resurrected. Drusilla's particular situation in this episode emphasizes this interpretation. Not only is she already undead as a vampire, she has also been presumed dead in the fire of "What's My Line?, Part Two."

The idea of a link between Buffy and Drusilla has already been suggested in "Lie to Me," when Angel must choose between Drusilla and Buffy, but in "Surprise," it is strengthened because Drusilla and Buffy are both planning parties. After Buffy wakes from one of her dreams in the library and looks at Angel with fear for what could happen to him, her face fades into Drusilla's, further establishing the link between them. Within the context of the show, Drusilla is Buffy's rival for Angel. Buffy has seen Drusilla as a threat since she first glimpsed Drusilla talking to him in "Lie to Me." While Angel seems to be free from desire for Drusilla, Angelus certainly is not. Angelus can be viewed as an entirely separate character, but, as Angelus himself points out, Angel and Angelus often intermix. When Angel follows his darker instincts, he behaves much as Angelus would. It is probable that Angel harbors and represses his feelings of desire for Drusilla. Buffy senses the danger that Drusilla represents to her relationship with Angel. Drusilla's sexuality is very predatory, following the tradition of Gothic female vampires, as Laura Diehl eloquently explores in her essay, "Why Drusilla Is More Interesting Than Buffy." Buffy knows that Drusilla is not as inhibited as she is. This causes Buffy severe anxiety and self-doubt.

Aside from their mutual interest in Angel, Drusilla and Buffy are both visionaries. *The Monster Book* calls Drusilla's visions "an odd counterpoint to the prescient dreams that Buffy [...] sometimes has" (114). *The Watcher's Guide* also compares the visions to Buffy's dreams (133). In fact, Drusilla had prophetic dreams like Buffy's even before she became a crazy vampire ("Becoming, Part One"). No doubt Buffy recognizes her kinship with Drusilla and unconsciously incorporates her into the dream for a reason. One explanation for Drusilla's appearance in the dream is that Drusilla herself, as a fellow visionary, is invading Buffy's dreams and sending a warning. This explanation is problematic, however; Drusilla seems completely unaware that Buffy knows anything about her being alive. Furthermore, since Drusilla is absorbed in resurrecting the Judge in an attempt to end the world, she probably would not send such an eloquent warning to Buffy. The dream can be interpreted with far more interesting results if Drusilla is viewed as a negative double of the kind Donald Keller describes in "Spirit Guides and Shadow Selves from the Dream Life of Buffy (and Faith)." According to his article, when other characters appear in Buffy's dreams, they serve as spirit guides, aspects of Buffy that she dramatizes by enfleshing them in a person she knows. Specifically, he examines Buffy's dream about Faith in "Graduation Day," Buffy's dream of Angel in "Innocence," and Buffy's dream of Riley in "Hush" with Faith, Angel, and Riley as positive doubles with interesting results. Finally he examines Faith's dreams of Buffy in "This Year's Girl" viewing Buffy as a negative double. Whereas in Buffy's dreams of Faith, Angel, and Riley, her friends provide her with information and warnings, in Faith's dreams of Buffy, Buffy tries to destroy Faith, acting out Faith's feelings of betrayal. In Buffy's dream at the beginning of "Surprise," Drusilla does not provide Buffy with any helpful information, but, like Buffy in Faith's dreams, Drusilla behaves in a destructive way by killing Buffy's love interest.

If Drusilla is viewed as a double for Buffy, as a vampire, she represents urges Buffy represses. Considering Drusilla's role in the narrative, she particularly represents unrestrained sexual urges which Buffy may have thought were dead but are now asserting themselves. She may also represent Buffy's fear that if she gave in to her position as a supernatural being (i.e., the Slayer), she could become the twisted, hysterical being that Drusilla is. On the show, being a Slayer or being supernatural in general is often equated with being empowered, so Buffy may equate her sexual inclinations with being supernatural. Faith certainly does, as she often demonstrates during her tenure on the show. It is not unlikely to presume, then, that Buffy's dreams represent some form of anxiety about her sexual desire for Angel.

The dream begins with Buffy looking on her nightstand and finding her glass almost empty. Water, a traditionally complex symbol, can symbolize the unconscious, emotions, life, and energy. Drinking water is usually symbolic of refreshing the spirit and the heart with the gifts of water, implying a certain need of refreshment. In the original script, the glass Buffy picks up is completely empty. The change from the script may signify that Buffy has resources around her that can help to refresh her, such as her friends, whereas an empty glass would have signified a lack of resources. When she drinks from the glass and is not fully refreshed, it is a clear indication that Buffy is searching for something new in her life to satisfy her thirst. This segment of her dream can be interpreted as her dissatisfaction with an unconsummated relationship with Angel. Being with him is refreshing, but does not completely quench her thirst.

To satisfy her thirst, Buffy leaves her room to refill her glass. In traditional dream theory, the bedroom often symbolizes the private, emotional self. When Buffy leaves her room, she leaves her symbolic sanctuary. Buffy's bedroom is, as Carey Meyer notes in the "Designing Buffy" featurette, the one thing that remains stable throughout her life. The room only becomes confused and disorienting when Buffy herself is excessively confused and disoriented, as in her return visit during "The Freshman." She leaves this sanctuary and enters a hallway, which typically represents transitional periods and beginnings of new spiritual or emotional paths.

Significantly, Drusilla is behind her in the hallway. When Buffy senses Drusilla is behind her and turns quickly, Drusilla vanishes, and Buffy still does not see the danger. Drusilla's disappearance supports the interpretation of Buffy refusing to consciously acknowledge her fears and desires as embodied by Drusilla. Placing Drusilla behind Buffy accentuates the idea that she represents a danger that Buffy does not consciously see, even if she can sense it.

After her encounter with Drusilla, Buffy heads for the bathroom, a private place of cleansing and releasing burdens. Whatever is causing Buffy's thirst is something she does not want to share with the public. Nevertheless, Buffy opens the door to the bathroom to find herself in a rather public place, the Bronze. Clubs and bars often symbolize a desire to escape from stress. Buffy certainly uses the Bronze as this type of escape, as she does in "Dead Things." While escape is often important, it also conveys a desire to resist facing problems or problematic emotions. When Buffy enters the Bronze, she sets the glass on the bar, but she still seems to be searching for something or someone.

The first person she encounters is Willow. In dreams, seeing friends sometimes portends the arrival of good news about them. This could be the case with Buffy's dream, especially since this segment is an obvious reference to Willow and Oz's earlier conversation about animal crackers ("What's My Line, Part Two"). The coffee they are drinking also suggests that they are romantically involved , according both to classic dream symbolism and the earlier coffee text in "Reptile Boy." However, the segment also has a slightly darker tone. Willow may be shorthand for the willow tree, which symbolizes mourning and sadness. Having Oz appear as a monkey being fed by Willow is an interesting choice. Dreaming about feeding a monkey may symbolize betrayal by someone who appears to be loving and genuine, which happens two seasons later in "Wild at Heart." It may seem far-fetched to imply that this segment consciously foreshadows the eventual demise of the Oz and Willow relationship; regardless, the dark undertone to a seemingly happy union underscores the overall mood of the dream. Buffy sees two compatible people in a relationship, but she also sees a possible outcome of the relationship. When she looks at Willow and Oz, she may be viewing a version of herself and Angel, hinting at the source of her anxiety.

After she sees Willow, Buffy finds Joyce, who is drinking coffee from a prominent cup. The segment with Joyce works as her confrontation with her conscience about how to react to her passion for Angel. Joyce can be interpreted as Buffy's conscience, as mothers in dreams frequently are, asking Buffy if she is ready to make the relationship sexual. Joyce asks Buffy, "Do you really think you're ready?" The question here is ambiguous. Even though later, when Buffy is awake, Joyce asks the question about Buffy's driving, the question resonates with the dream's theme of relationships, implying that Joyce is actually asking about Buffy's readiness to have sex. When Buffy hesitates, Joyce drops the saucer, carrying out Buffy's fears of what might happen if she hesitates in making the relationship sexual. When Buffy looks in horror at first the shattered remains of her relationship and then at Joyce, she sees the remains of a relationship that she has let slip through her fingers by listening to her conscience and hesitating.

As Buffy stares at the broken saucer, Joyce calmly turns and walks away, signifying the exit of Buffy's conscience. She turns from Joyce's caution to see Angel and explores a different scenario. The original script describes the dance floor as "alive with sexual energy." Everything oozes with sexuality, even Buffy and Angel's slow movement toward each other. When she sees Angel, everything in the dream appears to resolve, including the music. Buffy no longer seems to be searching for anything. Since he appears in the context of her lover just after an abstract conversation she has had about her sexuality, Angel should be read primarily as a love interest and secondarily as a vampire, but both roles have strong sexual implications. As a vampire, he symbolizes seduction and sensuality, and someone who is charming but possibly harmful. Their movement toward each other broadcasts sexual desire and seduction.

Suddenly, Drusilla stops Angel by staking him. If Drusilla is read as a metaphor for Buffy's darker side in this episode, Buffy's subconscious decision to have Drusilla stake Angel is appropriate. Buffy places her double in a masculine role, reinforcing the interpretation that Buffy fears being aggressive in pursuing a sexual relationship. When a male stakes a female vampire, it is usually interpreted as shorthand for sexual penetration. Having Drusilla, already a sexual being, penetrate Angel only emphasizes her role as a seductress. Not only does she penetrate Angel, however, she also destroys him. If interpreted with Drusilla as a double for Buffy, the dream becomes disturbingly prophetic.

Because of Buffy's sensual desires and initiative, she actually does lose Angel. Buffy takes on the traditionally masculine role, as the series itself eloquently implies in "I Only Have Eyes for You." She feels responsible for destroying Angel in much the same way that heroes in 17th century literature feel responsible for destroying or corrupting virginal women by seducing them. Traditionally, after a sexual encounter, it is the female in the relationship that loses her purity. In this encounter, Angel is the one who loses his purity. He becomes a demonic maniac. Buffy remains innocent, as Joss Whedon states in his commentary to the subsequent episode, "Innocence.

When Buffy wakes up from her dream at the beginning of "Surprise," she only remembers that Drusilla is alive and that Angel may be in danger. She takes these things at face value and rushes over to see Angel. It is immediately obvious that she and Angel are longing to take their relationship to the sexual level. Like the half-empty glass Buffy drains in the first segment of her dream, the time Angel and Buffy spend together is simply inadequate to quench their thirst for each other. The dream leaves Buffy with an unresolved complex of emotion. Either choice she makes regarding sex could be wrong, and either choice could be right, but at least she seems consciously aware of her decision now.

## WORKS CITED

Diehl, Laura. "Why Drusilla's More Interesting Than Buffy." *Slayage: The On-line Journal of Buffy Studies.* 13–14 (October 2004). 1 Sept. 2005. *http://www.slayage. tv/essays/slayage13_14/Diehl.htm.*

Golden, Christopher, and Nancy Holder. *The Watchers Guide.* Vol. 1. New York: Pocket Books, 1998. 3 vols.

Golden, Christopher, Stephen R. Bissette, and Thomas E. Sniegoski. *The Monster Book.* New York: Simon Pulse, 2000.

Keller, Donald. "Spirit Guides and Shadow Selves from the Dream Life of Buffy (and Faith)." *Fighting the Forces.* Ed. Rhonda Wilcox and David Lavery. Lanham, MD: Rowman & Littlefield, 2002.

# Complexes My Mother Left Me
## Spike Meets Robin Wood

BRENT LINSLEY

The full text of Joss Whedon's television series *Buffy the Vampire Slayer* presents a wide range of interpretations for the character of Spike. Spike, a vampire who first appears in the series during its second season, plays many roles throughout the show's course: villain, flunkie, warrior, and even, eventually, savior. As a character blessed with the gift of recurrence, we are allowed to see many different angles of his life, both in human and vampire form. In the seventh season episode "Lies My Parents Told Me," all the different sides of Spike converge, allowing the viewer to see into his mind and soul and establishing him as a different vampire from most, one who is, in his own earlier words from "Tabula Rasa," "a noble vampire"; in contrast, Principal Robin Wood is presented as Spike's near opposite, a human with personal issues that lead him down a path of vengeance and intentional, conscious violence. Both characters are portrayed in a world of opposing grays that lead them to a showdown central to one of the big thematic pushes of the program's final season: that of the power of evil over various parts of humanity.

"Lies My Parents Told Me" opens on a fight scene between Spike and Nikki Wood, a slayer from the 1970s. It then morphs to a similar scene in the present day of the slayer timeline in which Buffy, Spike, and Principal Wood battle a group of vampires in just one of many dark Sunnydale alleyways. Toward the end of the scene Spike dusts a vampire just before it is able to sneak up on Principal Wood and kill him. Thus, Spike symbolically becomes Wood's savior in a personal sense. As the two stand by exchanging banter, we can, in the background, see Buffy continuing to pummel the remaining vampire. As the conversation concludes, Wood clenches the stake he retrieved from his mother, the deceased Nikki Wood, so tightly that his own blood drips from his hand, concluding the teaser scene for the episode.

This scene is especially significant in that it not only sets up the current episode but also reinforces the histories of the characters. Nikki Wood, as regular viewers will remember from the fifth season episode "Fool for Love," is the slayer mother of Robin that Spike kills on a New York City subway. She was the original owner of the jacket Spike wears throughout the series, an integral part of his image system. Her death creates the seed of tension between Robin and Spike, tension which has been mounting. In the previous episodes, the First, in the form of Robin's mother, has been regularly visiting the conflicted principal.

Viewing the opening fight scene in "Lies," from Robin's perspective gives us insight into his mind during the fight. He nearly loses his life, only to have it saved by the very being that destroyed his mother, the very being in the world he most wants destroyed. This irony is almost too much emotional torment for him to bear. He silently rejects Spike as his savior, instead reveling in the pain of long ago wounds, symbolized by the new physical wounds he creates on, by, and with his own hand as a result.

Meanwhile, the First has been employing different tactics with Spike. When Spike returned to Sunnydale with his recently reacquired soul, the First planted a subconscious trigger that would turn him immediately into a vampire, presumably to create an army of vampires to give the slayer problems and likely keep her too busy to worry about the First. The trigger is in the form of a song called "Early One Morning," an old folk song Spike's mother used to sing to him. Spike lies to the Scoobies, telling them she used to sing it to him as a child, when instead it is a song she sings to him as a grown man, before he becomes a vampire. Spike's reference to himself as a child in the days just before his turning is indicative of his self-perceptions and self doubts. He sees his former human state as an embarrassment, as though he were inadequate as a man; by attempting to mask the situation, he further reveals the subconscious inadequacies that continue to torment him.

This difference in the form the First chooses to take with the characters of Principal Wood and Spike is perhaps indicative of the nature of their minds, drawing a contrast between the conscious motivations and subconscious ones in the minds of living and undead. Although the First has come consciously to Spike in many different forms, his rejection of these methods signifies his refusal to believe in the deceptions of evil, mostly significant due to the fact that the vampire, traditionally, is a figure that represents of evil, or at least of the evil in humanity. The only way that the First can get a reaction from Spike is through the subconscious. Through this subconscious trigger, Spike again becomes a human; his soul and his humanity, at that point, become suppressed behind the urges of the demon still inside him, the demon that longs to kill and destroy. It is through no fault of his own that he slides back into the role of killer. The First is using him as a tool of evil in these cases, not a conscious agent.

With Principal Wood, the First's methods of conscious approach are much more effective and much darker in significance. "The show intimates that Wood may be a villain. His early appearances are often accompanied by menacing music, [and] he is shown finding Jonathan's body in the school basement and then burying it in secret" (Jowett). At the end of the seventh season episode "First Date," the First appears to Wood in the final scene of the episode, taking the guise of his mother and revealing to him that Spike is the vampire who killed her. Although Wood consciously knows that the First approaches people to attempt to convince them to do the work of evil, the actions that the First suggest fall in line with the underlying motivations of Wood himself, and he is therefore able to overlook the significance of such a meeting because of his black-and-white mindset over the destruction of vampires. This is particularly true with regard to the specific vampire who killed his mother. This mindset leads him to believe that destroying vampires, even ensouled ones, is always good. He chooses to accept the materialization of the First and later, in "Lies," act accordingly. Hence Wood becomes the conscious agent of evil and the representative of the darker aspects of humanity that deal with personal vengeance and violently aggressive behavior, though he convinces himself on a psychological level that he is acting for the good of humanity.

This difference in reaction is indicative of the strength of mind in both these characters. Whereas Spike, the traditionally evil manifestation of the vampire, dismisses the advances and ploys of the First, Wood consciously accepts them in an attempt to avenge his mother's death. When speaking of Spike and Drusilla in a flashback sequence of the episode, Drew Goddard notes in the episode's commentary, "that's the key to villains in the Joss Whedon universe, [that] they actually have an agenda and care about things, as opposed to just being evil" ("Lies My Parents Told Me" commentary). The situation with Spike, Wood, and the First further illustrates the point that just because something is supposed to be evil it may not actually be so. Evil, just like good, comes in many shades, and sometimes is not found in the areas expected.

The First latches on to both characters by dealing with their mother (not just Oedipal) complexes. With Spike, the trigger attaches itself to the song Spike's mother Anne used to sing to him not because of their relationship during his human existence but instead because their relationship in vampire form. One of Spike's first actions as a vampire is to return home to turn his mother, who is dying from tuberculosis. His actions, however, have consequences he never imagined. Once in vampire form, Anne berates Spike, mocking his poetry. When he mentions something of her callousness, she responds that "I find it so freeing" ("Lies"). Spike, in contrast, has not become callous, but instead remains sensitive and somewhat hurt by her remarks. The reason for this is a much argued controversy in *Buffy* circles, but perhaps has been somewhat clarified by the recent release of the DVD commentary, in which writer Drew Goddard states, "Spike is an anomaly in the vampire world. He has some facet of his soul, even if it was removed when he became a vampire; it's still there. He, still, he has more humanity, as a vampire, than most vampires do ... perhaps something about his character as a man; he's retained that as a vampire."

It is only through the confrontation with Principal Wood that Spike is able to confront the issues he has with his mother and disarm the trigger that the First has planted in his subconscious mind. By allowing the psychology of the past to be addressed, Spike is not only more human than most vampires but also more human than most humans.

It is Spike's soul that most likely gives him the strength to resolve the issues his mother's vampire form caused. Much of Spike's psychology is built upon issues of trust and belonging. As a human, he longed to belong to the world of the aristocracy and impress his peers, though he became known to them merely as William the Bloody, as in William the Bloody Awful Poet. As a vampire, he strives to fit in with the world of Drusilla, the vampire who turned him. Angel and Darla see him as reckless, however, and he is almost always shown in flashback scenes as their subordinate. His mother, in her human form, always supported him and did her best to play the role of a loving mother. In her vampire form, however, Anne's cruelty creates a complex within Spike's mind that fuels the spirit of resentment, itself a part of the First. While reliving the moments with his mother caused by Wood's intentional activation of the trigger, Spike pays attention to the issues at hand, coming to the final realization that it was not his mother speaking to him, but instead that the words of hate and intolerance were from the demon he "let loose" inside her. Upon coming to this point of epiphany, he disarms the trigger and is no longer under even the subconscious control of the First.

Principal Wood's refusal to deal with his mother issues is a relevant point here. As Spike points out in the episode, Nikki chose being a slayer over being a mother, a decision that cost her her life. Robin, still upset over the fact that his mother died (and likely over the fact that she could and would choose the path of the slayer over him), has dedicated his entire life to tracking down the vampire who took her life and meting out vengeance. His mental torment is apparent in the obsessive "sanctuary" he has created for himself, a room where crosses cover nearly every inch of the walls. This structure of obsession has consumed most of Robin's life, and his own life has fallen somewhat to the wayside as a result: he goes out at night in search of the creature who destroyed his mother, leaving little time for an active social life and creating a guarded wall around his personality that makes it impossible for others to enter. His obsession has been distorted psychologically such that he believes himself on a crusade, fighting forces of darkness in a black and white world, where he himself slips into shades of gray.

Through Buffy, herself, these two characters come together as she serves as a substitute mother for both. She first meets Principal Wood while taking Dawn to her first day of high school, where he comments that she must be Dawn's mother: "[a]lthough he soon admits that he has 'heard of' Buffy — and will eventually confess that he knew all along that she was the Slayer — here is the foreshadowing of Wood as the son of Nikki ..." (Rambo). This scene serves not only as foreshadowing of Wood, but as Buffy as well, as she takes on more motherly responsibilities to the entire cast, but particularly for Principal Wood and Spike. The two males are dealing with deep Oedipal issues revolving around the concept of their mothers' rejections of them. Wood finds Buffy's slayer existence to be closely related and thus forms a strong attachment to her, though it never develops into a sexual fruition. "There is a sexual tension between him and Buffy from their first meeting" (Jowett).

For Spike, Buffy is the protector, much as his own mother had been over a hundred years earlier; on many occasions she saves Spike from others who try to bring harm to him, both from outside her group and from within. As the episode resolves, Buffy finds that Spike has beaten Wood badly during the fight in Wood's sanctuary but "gave him a pass, on account of his mother." This statement serves dual purpose, as Spike realizes that, although he would like to exact his revenge on the way Wood has ambushed him, the road of vengeance is the road of darkness, and that killing Wood would likely result in a further rejection by Buffy. Wood, however, chose the road of vengeance, neglecting to seek the approval of Buffy, in fact knowing that she disapproves of such a course of action. It is Buffy, in the end, the symbolic mother to both, who drives the final stake through Wood's past as she tells him, "If you try anything like that again, Spike will kill you. And more importantly, I'll let him." It is this final rejection from the new mother that, ironically, pulls Wood off his path of vengeance.

This final rejection of his path is exactly what Wood needs to be able to once again fight against the First. Although he knows that Spike will kill him, and that Buffy will allow that to happen, should his avenging behavior continue, his mindset is changed, and the mother-figure explaining that vengeance is secondary to the contemporary struggle against the First allows him to put the issues of vengeance aside. Spike, conversely, has dealt proactively with the issues of his mother, coming to a conclusion that leads him to the same path, an unalterable collision course with the First. Through these very different methods, these very different characters arrive at much the same point, revealing that opposites, through opposite means, can be very similar.

# WORKS CITED

Fury, David, and Goddard, Drew. "Lies My Parents Told Me." *Buffy the Vampire Slayer: The Complete Seventh Season on DVD*. Twentieth Century–Fox Home Video: 2002–03, 2004.

Fury, David, et al. Commentary. "Lies My Parents Told Me." *Buffy the Vampire Slayer: The Complete Seventh Season on DVD*. Twentieth Century–Fox Home Video: 2004.

Jowett, Lorna. "New Men: 'Playing the Sensitive Lad.'" *Slayage: the Online Journal of Buffy Studies*. Vol. 13 & 14 (2004). 28 November 2004 <*www.slayage.tv*>.

Rambo, Elizabeth. "'Lessons' for Season Seven of *Buffy the Vampire Slayer*." *Slayage: the Online Journal of Buffy Studies*. Vol. 11 & 12 (2004). 28 November 2004 <*www. slayage.tv*>.

Rand, Rebecca. "Tabula Rasa." *Buffy the Vampire Slayer: The Complete Sixth Season on DVD*. Twentieth Century–Fox Home Video: 2001–02, 2004.

# She Believes in Me
## *Angel, Spike, and Redemption*

### MELANIE WILSON

The popular image of a vampire being repelled by a cross is ingrained in the mind of most devotees of the vampire genre. Usually, the cross-bearer acts as an agent of God, channeling God's goodness to meet the evil personified in the vampire. The vampire fiction that empowers the cross with the ability to repel vampires usually places vampires firmly in the position of irredeemable demons and the cross-bearers in the position of God's agents. The vampires that cower in fear of the cross have undergone a perversion of Christ's resurrection, achieving eternal life through unnatural means. Other vampire fiction eradicates the power of the cross, representing a world void of divine intervention. Vampires in these stories are neither good nor evil. In *Buffy the Vampire Slayer* and *Angel,* collectively known as the Buffyverse, the cross has power over the vampires but does not symbolize moral judgment or divine condemnation. Breaking from most vampire fiction, the moral code of the Buffyverse is dictated by human rather than divine standards. For a vampire to be redeemed, he or she must emulate human behavior. Redemption is possible, but it comes at the painful price of constant self-sacrifice and atonement. The power of the cross over Buffyverse vampires represents the excruciating price of redemption.

To more fully grasp the significance of the role of the cross in the series, it is important to examine the established theological ideology of the show. Despite the common themes it shares with Christianity, the show cannot be categorized as strictly Christian, as many critics have commented. Wendy Love Anderson discusses how often religion and organized worshippers are demonized. In his article about why Jasmine is the scariest villain ever, Steven Harper points out that the most terrifying thing about her was that people like her followers actually exist in the real world. Gregory J. Sakal explores the subtle differences between the Christian concept of terms such as "redemption," "salvation," and "sacrifice," and how these terms are used in the Buffyverse. The show itself certainly provides evidence that the Powers That Be, or PTB, are not the same sorts of beings that Christians expect

God is. They are not necessarily benevolent beings. Angel tells Faith at one point, "To kill without remorse is to feel like a god," suggesting that deities do not care who lives or dies ("Consequences"). On *Angel*, the PTB usually ignore Angel and his sacrifices, refusing to intervene on his behalf except in response to substantial sacrifice. In "I Will Remember You," for example, when Angel offers to sacrifice his happiness with Buffy in favor of becoming a vampire again to more effectively fight evil, the Oracles note his sacrifice with awe and agree to help him. Usually, however, they leave him to make his own choices. Stacey Abbott comments, "[T]he [P]owers are shown to be most fallible by their absence when things turn particularly dark for Angel. [...] It is possible that [...] they themselves advocate choice over a sense of pre-determinacy" ("Walking" 6).

Despite the apparent indifference of the PTB, the show at first seems to insist on the idea that it is possible to be rejected by God. Using this interpretation, the cross, as a symbol of God, naturally acts as a reminder to the vampire that it is irrevocably evil. Some passages of the show seem to uphold this idea. For example, Spike throws a cross at and taunts Angel: "Look at you, thinking you're the big savior, fighting for truth, justice, and soccer moms. But you still can't lay flesh on a cross without smelling like bacon" ("Destiny"). Darla holds a cross up to Angel and says, "No matter how good a boy you are, God doesn't want you. But I still do" ("Dear Boy"). Despite these scenes, the cross does not usually seem to imply divine rejection of vampires as a species. In both of these scenes, it is significant that the link of the cross and God's rejection is provided by vampires, specifically vampires who are trying to discourage Angel. Whereas in traditional vampire fiction, the vampire hunter uses the cross to remind the vampire that it is evil, in the Buffyverse the reminders are provided by beings who share the same limitations as Angel. The reminders may represent Spike and Darla's personal beliefs about redemption. They certainly reflect Angel's beliefs, since he repeatedly comments that there is no way he can be redeemed. They do not necessarily reflect truth; in fact, based on her appearance as a messenger from the PTB for Connor, Darla is apparently redeemed ("Inside Out").

From the beginning of the show, moral absolutes have been overturned. Season one of *Buffy*, which begins by describing vampires as irredeemably evil, almost immediately undercuts this claim with the introduction of Angel. As the series matures, mirroring Buffy's maturing view of the world, vampires become more complex. Perhaps the most obvious example of a complex vampire is Spike, who eventually embarks on a quest for his own redemption.

Furthermore, the shows repeatedly demonstrate that the cross does not react to the spiritual quality of evil; it only reacts to the physical manifestation of the vampire. For example, when an elderly man named Marcus steals Angel's body, the cross burns Angel's body but not Marcus' body ("Carpe Noctem"). If the cross were meant to condemn the spiritual quality of evil, it would still burn Angel, even in another body. Since the connection between the cross and Christianity is never convincingly established, the cross might even appear to be non–Christian. In a discussion about the burn Angel receives in "Angel," Stacey Abbott points out that the cross "simply has a physical effect upon him like an allergy" ("Little" 2). The strength of Abbott's argument lies in her point that the cross does not fill its traditional role as an agent of divine condemnation; however, it still has unique power because it only affects vampires. Other weapons Buffy uses affect almost all of her foes the same way. Joss Whedon's decision to keep the cross as a vampire repellent is certainly problematic given the show's insistently stated rejection of the idea that the PTB will not redeem a vampire.

Despite its problems, the idea of the cross as a vampire repellent resonates with the theology of the series. In his examination of the series, Gregory Erickson takes an alternate view of Angel's burn in "Angel," citing it as the single incident of Christian symbolism: "Here, in Angel, and only here, in the negative image of a symbol burned into the skin of a tormented vampire, does the cross stand for anything remotely Christian. Angel, the eternal soul, has given the gift, and the cross represents his suffering and sacrifice" (114–15). While the example noted is certainly not the only example of Christian symbolism anymore, Erickson's analysis is convincing. The resonance of the cross as a symbol on the show definitely exceeds the limits set on it as a simple allergen.

While the cross does not fill the Christian role it is traditionally assigned in vampire fiction, it still functions as a Christian symbol most of the time. The power of the cross over vampires is particularly interesting because they are classified as demon-human hybrids; that is, they are not pure demons. Humans are naturally unaffected by the cross. Most demons are also unaffected by the cross. In fact, when Angel's pure demon manifests in Pylea, the demon does not seem to be bound by any of the normal restrictions imposed on demon-human hybrid vampires. Angel can run through the sunshine as a demon, and he sees his reflection in a pool of water. Considering these breaks from Buffyverse vampire limitations, it is unlikely the cross would burn him as a pure demon, but there is no conclusive evidence. Possibly, the hypothetical inability of the cross to repel or burn the pure vampire demon is because there is no hope of redemption for such a bestial creature. As Giles explains to Buffy in "Beauty and the Beasts," "In my experience there are two types of monster. The first can be redeemed, or, more importantly, wants to be redeemed. [...] The second is void of humanity, cannot respond to reason or love." Perhaps the cross responds to vampires because they can be redeemed. Angel's pure demon does not want redemption and is not capable of attaining it. Demon-human hybrid vampires, on the other hand, are capable of redemption.

The more a vampire considers redemption, the stronger his or her reaction is to the cross. The Master, for example, states that he fears the cross ("Nightmares"). His reaction to the cross is because he has considered the idea of redemption and renounced it. In fact, the Master is afraid of being "good." Angel's reaction to the cross is often not fear but pain. More than any vampire in the series, Angel touches the cross in spite of its burning. Angel accepts the painful sacrifices he must make to be redeemed. Spike also touches crosses frequently, but takes the precaution of guarding his skin during *Buffy* seasons one through four. Unlike Angel, Spike does not think about redemption during these seasons, so he does not have a strong reaction to the cross.

Both vampires choose Buffy as a savior figure, which is especially interesting considering her Slayer role as the one girl in all the world with the duty to kill them. Significantly, the Slayer must always be female, a life-giver. Though Buffy brings death to many vampires, she brings life to some. In the Buffyverse, death is almost never permanent and is usually followed by rebirth and a change of behavior. Jacqueline Lichtenberg explores the concept in detail as applied to Buffy and Willow in her article, "The Power of Becoming." Angel and Spike choose Buffy because they realize she has the ability to give death and life that they need for redemption. When Buffy kills Angel, it represents a turning point for him. While Buffy does not literally kill Spike, she repeatedly cuts him off from her, metaphorically killing him, which forces him to change his behavior. Examining the paths of Angel and Spike in their quests for redemption demonstrates Buffy's position as savior for both of them.

When Darla turns Liam into a vampire, making him Angelus, she creates a torrent of evil that sometimes surprises even her. After Angelus is cursed with a soul, he tries in vain to return to Darla and regain the kind of life he feels safe with. When Darla finally casts Angel out because he refuses to eat a baby, Angel sails to America. He spends the next 94 years in misery, battling the demon inside him. While the series mythology overtly claims that Angel, his souled identity, and Angelus, his unsouled identity, are independent of each other, it undercuts this claim with Angel's periods of darkness and evil that suggest Angelus' darkness is born of Angel's own darkness and evil. As Darla tells him, "You don't learn that kind of darkness. It's innate. You had it in you before we ever met" ("Dear Boy"). Based on the flashbacks in various episodes, it is easy to see Darla's point. In 1943, Angel goes on a military mission only because he is forced to. He completely abandons the vampire he sires ("Why We Fight"). In 1952, Angel's experience being betrayed by Judy and hanged by a mob leads him to nonchalantly abandon the entire hotel to a paranoia demon ("Are You Now or Have You Ever Been?"). Angelus himself presents an intriguing question about Angel's slowness to rescue the victim of a robbery in the 1980's:

> ANGELUS: Choices, little girl. The ones you make with your heart of hearts.
> FAITH: He was going to save him.
> ANGELUS: Or did he choose to be just a little slow on the draw?
>
> ("Orpheus")

Since Angel's bloodlust has been clearly established earlier in the episode by his pained gaze at a customer's neck, Angelus' question is all too unsettling. Clearly, the return of Angel's soul does not redeem him from his darkness. As Stacey Abbott points out, "These flashbacks demonstrate that it was not the curse and the return of his soul that set Angel onto the path of goodness, but rather, it was Buffy" ("Walking" 5). For Angel, Buffy is salvation. He emphasizes this point by giving her a large silver cross necklace. His choice of a cross is interesting given that he professes that he fell in love with her the first time he saw her ("Helpless"). Why would he then present Buffy with an object that should keep him away from her? The answer is that he knows Buffy symbolizes his redemption. By working with Buffy, he can become a force for good, even though the sacrifices he must make will be painful. The cross is the perfect symbol for him to give her, and this is perhaps why the final scene in the episode "Angel" is so potent. When Buffy walks away from Angel leaving a deep burn from the cross in his chest, it is clear that by engaging in a relationship of any kind with Buffy, Angel will be fundamentally altered. Parts of his personality must be burned away, leaving him a stronger person.

During the time he is close to Buffy, Angel rarely does anything ambiguous. His dark side is so notably absent that Stacey Abbott argues: [A]ngel's representation seems too neatly split across polar oppositions: the good Angel versus the evil Angelus. [...] It is only when Angel is moved from peripheral love interest to the central protagonist of a new series that his representation breaks from strategically polarizing his good and evil sides. ("Walking" 1)

Countless other critics have agreed with her, arguing that *Buffy*'s Angel is too polarized to be interesting. Nevertheless, carefully observing Angel's behavior during the first season of *Buffy* demonstrates that Angel still retains some of his innate darkness. Though present through much of early season one, Angel's darkness becomes evident in "Angel." As Laura Resnick points out, it is Angel who tells Buffy, "I wanted to kill you tonight," not Angelus (54). Again, it is Angel who almost drinks Joyce's blood in the same episode, even after he saves Joyce from Darla. As Resnick concludes, "Angel may have stopped feeding on humans years ago, but it's not as if he doesn't still *want* to; and it's not as if we can ever be sure he'll never do it again" (55). At the end of "Angel," Angel is forced to choose between Darla and Buffy. Considering Darla's symbolic position as his sire and his earlier struggle to gain her acceptance, Angel's staking her is significant. He appreciably breaks with his past and prepares himself for change by destroying a symbol of his past. This episode marks the beginning of real change in Angel and the end of his dark period. A few episodes later in "Prophecy Girl," Angel risks his life to help Buffy, though he cannot save her. A scene cut from the episode includes Collin threatening Angel with a fate worse than death if he intervenes in the events. It is Angel's love for Buffy that convinces him to intervene. Xander tells him, "I don't like you. At the end of the day, I pretty much think you're a vampire. But Buffy's got this big yen for you. She thinks you're a real person. And right now I need you to prove her right." Significantly, when Xander enters Angel's apartment, he is able to repel Angel with the cross. The above speech is delivered to a sullen Angel avoiding redemption because of its price. After Angel overcomes his fear of the Master, another figure inextricably linked with his past, he touches his future, symbolized by Buffy. Having Buffy nearby to reinforce his good behavior makes it easier for Angel to avoid falling into true darkness, and that is why his moral ambiguity is practically nonexistent in the first two seasons of *Buffy*.

During *Buffy* season two, Angel helps and supports Buffy in her battles, growing stronger through her acceptance and love. Unfortunately, by losing himself in Buffy, he loses sight of the redemption he must achieve. The emergence of Angelus at the moment of Angel's complete happiness emphasizes that Angel can never let himself rest in his quest for redemption or he will revert to Angelus, his shadow self. Angelus is mortally afraid of being redeemed and can be repelled by the cross again. In "Innocence," Xander holds a cross, and Angelus backs away snarling. Angelus also devotes almost all his energy to destroying Buffy, the initiator of Angel's salvation.

When Angel returns from the hell-dimension Buffy eventually has to send him to, he realizes that, though Buffy initiates his salvation and serves as a guide for him, Angel cannot let her do the work for him. He must transition from being a sidekick to taking initiative. He is fighting the good fight for the wrong reasons. His love for Buffy inspires him to do great things, but cannot redeem him. The glimpses of Angel's dark side that appear *Buffy* in season three are caused by Angel's fear of seeking redemption alone. He knows seeking redemption will be difficult. Sliding back into old habits of darkness seems easier to him. In "Amends," the First Evil torments Angel with visions of his past victims. Angel's interaction with Buffy in this episode is dominated by dark moments. When he goes to Buffy for help, he cannot tear his eyes from her neck. He clearly longs to take the advice of the First Evil and bury all his frustration and guilt by drinking her blood and taking the easy way out. The First Evil tries to distract him from his mission of redemption by tempting him to give in to his desires and embrace his demon nature. Angel does not ultimately succumb to the temptation, but chooses instead to kill himself by waiting for the sun to rise instead of taking the difficult way of true self-sacrifice. He believes he is irredeemably evil, and longs for the cleansing purification of the sun's fire. The First Evil responds to Angel's intended suicide by stating, "You're not supposed to die. This isn't the plan," and then, when Angel is out of earshot, "but it will do." These comments imply that the First Evil is on a mission to destroy Angel, not Buffy. When Buffy finds the First Evil, she proclaims, "You won't get Angel," again acting as a redeemer for Angel. Buffy reaches him just before sunrise and tries to convince him not to give up. After a heated argument, Angel shows signs of acquiescing to Buffy's pleas, but the decision is taken from him by a miraculous snowfall, possibly sent by the PTB. The end of the episode is uncomfortably ambiguous, leaving Angel's acceptance of his responsibility open for interpretation.

In the final episode of season three, Buffy evokes Angel's dark side to make him feed on her so that her blood can cure him of a poison Faith exposed him to. When he recovers and realizes what he has done to Buffy, Angel knows he must leave Sunnydale. Buffy's blood acts as a strengthening agent, echoing the cleansing and saving power traditionally associated with the blood of Christ, again suggesting Buffy's role as Angel's savior. Through this experience, Buffy gives Angel the strength to seek salvation through his own merit.

When he moves to Los Angeles at the end of *Buffy*'s third season, Angel begins a life as a vigilante. Cut loose from Buffy's stabilizing influence, Angel is forced to face his dark side alone, which accounts for his sudden change in personality. Though Angel has friends and co-workers who care about him, none of them fills the role Buffy previously held. The change can easily be seen on the crossover episodes of *Buffy* season four. Laura Resnick comments: When Angel revisits Sunnydale in "The Yoko Factor" (4–20), Riley Finn finds his manner so dark, menacing, and "king of pain" that he mistakenly assumes Angel has gone evil again, and he's stunned when Buffy explains that no, this is how Angel behaves *with* a soul (55).

The change is also evident in "Pangs," so much so that everyone automatically assumes he is evil again. Finally, in exasperation, Angel interjects, "I'm not evil again! Why does everyone think that?"

In Los Angeles, Angel's dark nature makes occasional appearances. In "Eternity," Angel tries to protect a fading movie star from a stalker. When the starlet learns that Angel is a vampire, she tries to turn him to Angelus so that he will make her a vampire. When he realizes what she is doing to him, Angel violently drags her into the kitchen and forces her to drink some of the blood he has in the refrigerator. Suddenly realizing that he is not behaving characteristically, he asks her what she did to him. His treatment of Rebecca is not at all characteristic of Angelus. He approaches Rebecca with anger, an emotion Angelus never displays. Angel later tells Cordelia, "That thing that Billy brought out in others, hatred and anger, that's something I lost a long time ago. [...] I never hated my victims. I never killed out of anger. It was always about the pain and the pleasure" ("Billy"). When Angelus surfaces a moment later in "Eternity," all of Angel's anger is gone, leaving an apparently playful creature set on causing pain for his own pleasure. Before he reverts to Angelus, Angel has reached an intense state of darkness on his own.

Most of *Angel* Season One, however, demonstrates Angel's growing faith in his purpose. He consistently chooses to find redemption the hard way instead of the easy way, as he demonstrates by destroying the Gem of Amarra in "In the Dark" and by sacrificing his happiness with Buffy so he can do more good as a vampire in "I Will Remember You." The second season of *Angel* brings a crisis of faith to Angel via Wolfram & Hart's resurrection of Darla in human form. After an intensely dark period and an accompanying epiphany, Angel becomes more masterful at living a balanced life. The third and fourth seasons of *Angel* rarely find him in extended periods of darkness, which is remarkable given the sheer volume of horrible things that happen. During *Angel* season five, Angel again descends to his darker nature. Besides the obvious problems he faces with the increasingly ambivalent problem of running Wolfram & Hart, he becomes alienated from his friends. With Cordelia in a coma, no one forces Angel to open up about his feelings. His jealousy of Spike is particularly large in his mind, as revealed in "Soul Purpose." He believes Spike is doing a better job than he is of helping the helpless. In his fevered dream, he sees Spike having sex with Buffy, symbolizing his fear that Spike is much closer to salvation than he is.

Many people argue that Spike is, in fact, more advanced than Angel is. An argument between Spike and Angel in "Destiny" summarizes the positions of both sides. Angel says, with a bit of disdain, "Like you're any different?" The "from me" is understood, not only by the viewer, but by Spike. Spike responds, "Well, that's just it. I am. And you know it. You had a soul forced on you — as a curse. Make you suffer for all the horrible things you'd done. But me... I fought for my soul. Went through the demon trials. Almost did me in a dozen times over, but I kept fighting. 'Cause I knew it was the right thing to do. It's my destiny." Angel is so disarmed by Spike's insight into the differences between them, that he is left only with the feeble comeback, "Really? Heard it was just to get into a girl's pants."

Angel supporters believe Angel is superior because his quest for redemption is not motivated by love, conveniently forgetting that Angel's quest for redemption is initially inspired by Buffy. The vampires are more similar than most viewers realize.

Unlike Angel, who views his siring as a form of damnation, Spike views his siring as salvation. In his episode commentary, Douglas Petrie, the writer of the episode, mentions William's behavior: "Usually when someone [is turned] into a vampire, [the] victim is terrified or frightened or confused, but William is still into it." Unlike Liam, who is sired with his eyes closed, William looks into the vampire face of Drusilla and accepts her bite ("Fool for Love"). "Becoming a vampire is a profound and powerful experience. I could feel this new strength coursing through me. Getting killed made me feel alive for the very first time," he tells Buffy ("Fool for Love"), again emphasizing the role of death as an agent of change. Drusilla represents this profound change to Spike. He reiterates the point later, describing Drusilla's importance to his life: "This is the face of my salvation. She delivered me from mediocrity" ("Crush").

When Spike first appears in Sunnydale, it is evident that he is evil, but he is more unique than the vampires previously established on the series because he is in love with Drusilla. Countless critics have pointed to the moment when Spike turns to give Drusilla his jacket as the moment when shades of gray were introduced to the series. Nevertheless, the mayhem Spike creates in Sunnydale establishes him as a force of evil, clearly not in the game as a force of good. In *Buffy* season four, when the government implants a chip in Spike's head that renders him incapable of harming any living thing, Spike begins his reluctant journey to redemption. For most of season four, Spike continues to act for selfish reasons. Spike does display the beginning of redemption in this season. When Buffy and Riley are trapped in a house by a cluster of poltergeists that feed on sexual energy, Spike initially volunteers to help rescue them: "I know I'm not first choice for heroics, and Buffy's tried to kill me more than once, and I don't fancy a single one of you all, but... Actually, that all sounds pretty convincing," at which point he wanders off in search of other entertainment ("Where the Wild Things Are"). The Spike of the first three seasons of *Buffy* would never even have considered helping someone if he got nothing from the deal. Like Angel's denial of his soul during his dark period between 1898 and 1996, Spike's denial of the chip does not remove its power over him. Although Spike resents the presence of the chip, it begins to influence his actions for good. As unsettling as the implication is, Dawn may be correct when she answers Buffy's insistent claim that Angel was different because he has a soul with the simple statement: "Spike has a chip. Same diff" ("Crush"). The chip, acting as the scientific equivalent of a soul, is beginning to change Spike.

Like Angel, Spike finds the beginning of true redemption through his love for Buffy. Buffy treats Spike more harshly than she treats Angel, but the difference ultimately benefits Spike. After Spike realizes he is in love with Buffy, he begins trying to do the right thing to please Buffy. In the subsequent episode, Spike shyly greets Buffy when she discovers him lurking in the bushes outside her house. Buffy abruptly responds, "Don't take this the wrong way, but," and follows it with a punch to the face ("There's No Place Like Home"). With such a lack of positive feedback for his efforts, it is amazing he seeks a soul at all, but Spike seems more determined than ever to win Buffy's approval.

He continues to push himself to change despite painfully disappointing results. Though souled behavior seems uncomfortable to him, he works to emulate it. In "Into the Woods," Spike catches Riley paying vampires to feed on him. When Spike takes Buffy to see Riley's infidelity, Buffy's reaction frightens Spike. Although Buffy is genuinely unconcerned about Spike's role in the scenario, Spike believes he has angered her ("Into the Woods"). The next episode finds him offering apologies and a box of chocolates to a mannequin dressed like Buffy, playing with the idea of behaving like a good man. He begins rehearsing an apology. As he rehearses, he imagines Buffy's response, and replies, "Oh, I'll insult him if I want to! I'm the one on your side! Me! Doing you a favor! And you being dead petty about it. Me getting nothing but your hatred and venom." At this point, he loses control and begins beating the mannequin over the head with the box of chocolates in his hand, screaming, "Ungrateful bitch!" The most interesting part of this scene is that he calms himself down, straightens the rumpled mannequin and crushed box of chocolates, and starts over in an attempt to correct his error. His role-playing stretches him morally, but does not guarantee him Buffy's approval.

In "Triangle," Anya and Willow accidentally conjure Olaf, a troll-god, to Sunnydale. When Olaf takes his rampage to the Bronze, Xander suggests that Spike fight Olaf. Spike replies, "Yeah, I could do that, but I'm paralyzed by not caring very much." His attitude changes drastically when Buffy arrives, however. Spike fights Olaf to impress and protect Buffy. After Olaf leaves the Bronze in shambles, Spike tries to help a victim, self-righteously telling Buffy, "I'm not sampling, I'll have you know. I mean, look at all those lovely blood-covered people. I could, but not a taste for Spike, not a lick. I know you wouldn't like it." Buffy stares at Spike in disbelief before asking incredulously, "You want credit for not feeding off bleeding disaster victims?" Spike's frustrated, "What's it take?" is understandable. Not feeding off disaster victims is a step forward for him.

In "Fool for Love," after Buffy humiliates Spike by shoving him to the ground and tossing the money she has promised at him before leaving him broken in the streets, Spike characteristically returns to his crypt to get a gun, prepared to kill Buffy before he lets her humiliate him again. Spike reaches a turning point at the end of the episode. When he stalks into Buffy's backyard, he finds Buffy sobbing on her porch. He struggles for a moment with his desire to kill her before he lowers the gun and asks, "What's wrong?" He then joins her on the porch and awkwardly pats her back in comfort, demonstrating tremendous growth from his former behavior. Buffy does not acknowledge or praise this growth, but she does not reject it, either.

Later, Spike ties both Drusilla and Buffy up and tries to make Buffy choose his future for him ("Crush"). Spike is trying to find a reason to establish Buffy as his new "sire," just as Angel did when Angel killed Darla ("Angel"). Buffy refuses to be bullied, insisting that she could never love someone without a soul. This actually benefits Spike because, unlike Angel, Spike never has the luxury of letting Buffy fight the good fight for him. Buffy's coldness ultimately allows Spike to grow on his own.

The simple act of being in love with Buffy is what sets Spike on the path to redemption. At first, Laura Resnick comments, "Spike does have a moral code, and he states it plainly to Buffy: 'I don't hurt *you*' [("Entropy").]" (62). Spike tries to explain this to Buffy: "I've changed, Buffy. [...] Something's happening to me. I can't stop thinking about you. And if that means turning my back on evil... [...] This is real here. I love y-," at which point Buffy cuts him off ("Crush"). She is incapable of accepting him as a soulless demon. It is when Buffy completely shuts him out of her life that Spike learns to do good without hope of a reward, as he demonstrates with his anonymous bouquet in "Forever" and his refusal to betray Dawn in "Intervention." Though he has made great moral strides, Spike is not worthy to save the world (Wilcox 3). In the final moments of "The Gift," Spike tries to save Dawn but fails. When Doc asks him, "I don't smell a soul anywhere on you. Why do you even care?," Spike's response is, "I made a promise to a lady," illustrating that Spike still has no internal concept of good and evil. His moral center is still Buffy. Like Angel before him, Spike lets Buffy make his decisions for him.

Spike is finally driven to seek a soul when he completely loses sight of his moral code and attempts to rape Buffy. Spike, exhibiting his typical behavior pattern on the heels of lost power, tries to force Buffy into admitting her feelings by raping her. When she stops him, he is so disgusted with himself that he seeks a legendary demon who can restore his soul ("Seeing Red"). Considering that he is soulless, Spike's realization that he has committed an evil act is praiseworthy, as Buffy later points out to Dawn ("Him").

Buffy continues to act as Spike's savior when he returns with a soul. After he tells Buffy his motivation for seeking a soul, Spike embraces a large cross. Like Angel, Spike realizes that he will have to make painful sacrifices, symbolized by the cross scorching his skin, to be redeemed. A few episodes later, when Spike realizes that he has been killing again, he calls Buffy and confesses. Buffy meets him where he has buried the bodies, and the First Evil brainwashes him again, ordering him to kill Buffy. Spike licks some of the blood from a wound in Buffy's arm, which pulls him out of the trance. He consciously sees every victim he has killed through the First Evil, and quickly becomes a quivering mass of remorse. Like Angel, Spike is cleansed and saved by Buffy's blood. After Buffy has killed the other vampires, Spike begs her to kill him, too. She refuses to let him take the easy way out.

In the following episode, "Never Leave Me," the First continues to manipulate Spike, using him to nearly kill Andrew. When Spike realizes what he has done, he again begs Buffy to kill him. He then proceeds to dismiss his changed behavior as "window-dressing," punctuating most of Buffy's response: "Be easier, wouldn't it, it if were an act, but it's not. You faced the monster inside of you and you fought back. You risked everything to be a better man. And you can be. You are. You may not see it, but I do. I do. I believe in you, Spike." When the First kidnaps him soon after and tortures him in "Bring On the Night," the next episode, Spike is able to maintain his integrity. The First, who has significantly taken the form of Drusilla, the symbol of his former life, taunts him, "What makes you think you will ever be any good at all in this world?" Spike firmly replies, "She does. Because she believes in me." Buffy's faith and forgiveness enable Spike to forgive and accept himself, making him worthy to save the world.

Nineteen days after he sacrifices his life to save the world, Spike is accidentally resurrected in Angel's office. When Spike returns from the dead in "Conviction," he must learn to be worthy without Buffy. Like Angel, Spike finds himself in Los Angeles fighting for redemption. Though his first inclination is to call for Buffy, he soon realizes he must remain moral without her. By "Shells," the sixteenth episode of *Angel* season five, Spike is willing to stay and work with Angel, fighting evil for the intrinsic reward of being good. As Nancy Holder eloquently states, "At the end [of *Angel*], he stands on Angel's right side, ready to fight an unwinnable fight. Not for Buffy, not for Angel, but because Spike has become a champion in a champions' world" (165).

Despite their inability to see good in each other, Angel and Spike are clearly connected, not only through their similar lives but also because they are the only two vampires with souls in the Buffyverse. Both vampires demonstrate that redemption in the Buffyverse is fraught with painful sacrifice, death, and resurrection. The cross traditionally represents all three elements, so its symbolic presence on the series speaks to the vampires as a reminder of their condition. Willing to pay the price, Angel and Spike actively seek redemption for its intrinsic rewards. By wrestling with their animal natures, they are able to allow their human souls to dictate good actions. Unlike vampires from most other fiction, the vampires of the Buffyverse can find redemption through sacrificing their demon desires in favor of human behavior.

# WORKS CITED

Abbott, Stacey. "A Little Less Ritual and a Little More Fun: The Modern Vampire in *Buffy the Vampire Slayer.*" *Slayage: The On-line Journal of Buffy Studies.* 3 (June 2001). 17 February 2004. *http://www.slayage.tv/ essays/slayage3/sabbott.htm*

_____. "Walking the Fine Line Between Angel and Angelus." *Slayage: The On-Line Journal of Buffy Studies.* 9 (August 2003). 17 February 2004. *http://www.slayage. tv/essays/slayage9/Abbott.htm.*

Anderson, Wendy Love. "Prophecy Girl and the Powers That Be: The Philosophy of Religion in the Buffyverse." South 212–26.

Erickson, Gregory. "'Sometimes You Need a Story': American Christianity, Vampires, and *Buffy.*" *Fighting the Forces: What's at Stake in* Buffy the Vampire Slayer. Eds. Rhonda V. Wilcox and David Lavery. Lanham, MD: Rowman & Littlefield, 2002. 108–119.

Harper, Steven. "Jasmine: Scariest Villain Ever." Yeffeth, *Five* 49–56.

Holder, Nancy. "Death Becomes Him: Blondie Bear 5.0." Yeffeth, *Five* 153–166.

Lichtenberg, Jacqueline. "Power of Becoming." Yeffeth, *Seven* 121–136.

Petrie, Douglas. Commentary. "Fool for Love." *Buffy the Vampire Slayer* 5 ep. 7. Perf. Sarah Michelle Gellar, Nicholas Brendon, Alyson Hannigan, Marc Blucas, Emma Caulfield, Michelle Trachtenberg, James Marsters, Anthony Stewart Head. WB. 2000–2001. DVD. Fox, 2003.

Resnick, Laura. "The Good, the Bad, and the Ambivalent." Yeffeth, *Seven* 54–64.

Sakal, Gregory J. "No Big Win: Themes of Sacrifice, Salvation, and Redemption." South 239–253.

South, James B., ed. Buffy the Vampire Slayer *and Philosophy: Fear and Trembling in Sunnydale.* Popular Culture and Philosophy 4. Chicago: Open Court, 2003.

Wilcox, Rhonda V. "'Every Night I Save You': Buffy, Spike, Sex and Redemption." *Slayage: The On-Line Journal of Buffy Studies.* 5 (May 2002). 17 February 2004. *http://www.slayage.tv/essays/slayage5/ Wilcox.htm.*

Yeffeth, Glenn, ed. *Five Seasons of* Angel. Dallas, TX: Benbella, 2004.

_____. *Seven Seasons of* Buffy. Dallas, TX: Benbella, 2003.

# Cordelia Chase as Failed Feminist Gesture

## AMIJO COMEFORD

"Then Laforgue's prayer will be answered: 'Ah young women, when will you be our brothers, our brothers in intimacy without ulterior thought of exploitation? When shall we clasp hands truly?'" So quoted Simone de Beauvoir at the conclusion of her chapter "Myth and Reality" from *The Second Sex* (297). On the surface, the thought contains affirmative possibility, an achievement of de Beauvoir's notion of reciprocity, the ability of men and women to relate to each other as real people, mystery and myth having been vanquished by lived experience. When we probe deeper, however, an alarming undertone manifests itself, one which speaks to a traditional dogmatic approach: gender equality necessitates women's forced abandonment of "womanhood" and an active movement toward becoming "brothers." Womanhood, then, is relegated to the realm of *immanence*, a term de Beauvoir defines as a state of non-progression and static paralysis, while masculinity remains as the opposite: *transcendence*. Though de Beauvoir's text is nearly sixty years old and the women's movement has had significant success in reclaiming womanhood from areas of male appropriation, a disquieting residue of de Beauvoir's concluding statement stubbornly remains in effect. This is true even among writers of *Buffy the Vampire Slayer* and its spinoff series *Angel*, writers who have gained a reputation for creating characters with an unequivocally contemporary female power. In short, within twenty-first-century popular culture, writers still struggle with distancing themselves from the damaging need for Feminine renunciation as a means for women to gain and maintain power.

Cordelia Chase is an especially promising case study for investigating this complexity. More than any other female character, Cordelia most clearly illustrates the potentially paralyzing Feminine myth, as de Beauvoir characterizes it, throughout *Buffy*, but she then destabilizes that same paralysis rather dramatically when she enters the predominantly masculine world of *Angel*. Throughout *Angel*, unlike the early seasons of *Buffy*, Cordelia learns to convert her overt femininity into sheer power; in fact, she participates and succeeds in the violent masculine world precisely because she is highly feminized. This transformative process from immanent Feminine Myth to transcendent Real Woman, culminating in the Third Season episode "Billy," is one of the most interesting storylines in *Angel*.

Early on in *Angel*, Cordelia begins her evolution from catty, self-centered "Sunnydale Cheerleader" to strong, new, Third Wave Feminist "Vision Girl," a solid representative of a movement whose impetus for social change is rooted in popular culture, with its "twists and transformations," rather than in more traditional political and legislative avenues (Rowe-Finkbeiner 88). In effect, Cordelia potentially embodies the new feminist who embraces the Feminine myth and subjects it to her own interests rather than being enveloped by it, thereby radically "turning traditionally confining pop-culture images of women around to empower." Tragically and dangerously, from a socially progressive perspective, with the end of Cordelia's character, the writers undermined Cordelia's strength by forcing upon her the consequences of age-old, damaging stereotypes, especially in season four. Cordelia, though a brilliant example of a Third Wave feminist in her most ideal form, is tossed rather callously aside in season four — disappointingly for her and for her fans, turning out to be a failed feminist gesture.

When audiences first meet Cordelia Chase in *Buffy*, she is a wealthy, upper-class, snobby cheerleader with a penchant for an acerbic wit. In fact, Cordelia's function in the early seasons of *Buffy* is arguably as a hyper-feminine character whose interest in clothes, shoes, fashion, and fraternity boys is almost mythical, as we are reminded in the conversation between Doyle and Angel in *Angel* season one's episode "Rm w/a Vu" when Angel describes Cordelia and her group as the "Cordettes," or rich girls who ran the school: "it was like the Soviet Secret police if they cared a lot about shoes." Cordelia is carefully juxtaposed with Buffy as that hyper-feminine character through the first three seasons, most prominently in the second season episode "Halloween."

At the episode's beginning, viewers find themselves amusedly watching Cordelia entertain Angel at the Bronze while he waits for Buffy to arrive for their first official date. When Buffy finally appears, she is, as she confides to Willow the next day, "looking trashed," having experienced "unscheduled slayage." While Angel unconcernedly reassures Buffy that she "looks fine," Cordelia appears in the frame directly behind Angel and smugly comments, "Buffy, love the hair. It just screams street urchin." Buffy's response is to accept Cordelia's assertion of her feminine inadequacies and admit to Angel that unlike Cordelia who thinks about "nail polish" and "facials" (both interests that are socially accepted feminine markers), she thinks about "ambush tactics, beheading, not exactly the stuff dreams are made of." In essence, Buffy accepts the dichotomous premise of rejecting these feminine markers in order to participate more effectively in the violent world of killing demons and embracing her role as a hero.

Her sacrifice is made hyperbolic throughout the episode, as Buffy, loathe to shed her feminine side in real life chooses to hyper-feminize herself for Halloween. Her decision's poignancy is clear in her comment to Willow that Halloween is "come as you aren't night." By choosing to be "the kind of fancy girl [Angel] liked when [he was her] age," desiring to "be a real girl for once" with the princess dress, coifed hair, and damsel-in-distress attitude, Buffy is, according to her own logic admitting that she is not and cannot adopt that feminine nonpareil version of herself in everyday life; in fact when Buffy "becomes" this very hyper-feminized figure (remember that here the term feminine is being used in regards to attributes historically accepted as feminine markers), her life and the lives of others are put at risk. Only when she returns to her non-feminized self, "Just little old twentieth-century me" (in a basic black tank top and oversized gray sweatpants no less), is she able to quell the danger and shield those around her.

Ironically, before the Ethan Rayne–induced Halloween horror breaks loose, Cordelia comments to Buffy, after having just applied a fresh coat of lip gloss, that when it comes to "demonology or whatever," Buffy might be the slayer, but when it comes to dating, says Cordelia, "I'm the slayer." Here Cordelia embodies and even thrives on her feminine traits, while Buffy is weakened by accepting them, which is the basis for the season three episode "Homecoming." When Buffy decides to run against Cordelia, among others, for Homecoming Queen — the clearest marker of traditional femininity in adolescence — she appears surprisingly vulnerable. Not only does she lose the contest, but she loses her entire support base. Each member joins Cordelia's campaign. Buffy is "Scooby-less" for the entire episode. As the episode proceeds, it does so in abnormal fashion. Something is not right: Buffy is uncharacteristically vulnerable — that is until the end when she defeats the monsters who have targeted her and Cordelia (mistakenly believing Cordelia to be Faith).

When we turn to Cordelia, however, especially as her character is developed throughout *Angel*, she becomes a powerful fighting force with Angel Investigations without renouncing her tie to the same feminine markers that seemed to weaken Buffy in those early seasons. In defiance of "Laforgue's prayer," Cordelia refuses to choose between her tie to social ideas of the Feminine and her ability to fight evil effectively in a very masculine world, eventually becoming an invaluable and crucial center for Angel's team.

By season two's conclusion, Cordelia is very much part of Angel Investigations and is as serious about her role fighting evil as Buffy is in Sunnydale, "resembl[ing] the Slayer, and shar[ing] her role as mystical protector" (Battis 5.2, para 1) even giving up fame and royalty for a life of demon fighting and possible death. Yet, this devotion to her calling and her effectiveness within the group is still offset with her character's ties to fashion and shopping, the Feminine. After Angel realizes in the episode "Epiphany" that "if what you do doesn't matter, then all that matters is what you do," and he attempts to rejoin the group he previously abandoned, Wesley counsels him that Cordelia is not the same girl anymore. She is serious about her work with the helpless in L.A. She is *not* the shallow fashion-plate from the early seasons of *Buffy*. In the episode that follows, "Disharmony," Cordelia informs Angel, rather abruptly, that "we're not friends." Angel, visibly hurt by this assessment, tries valiantly throughout the episode to champion Cordelia's side against the others (even when he believes she is wrong) and make amends with her, but to no avail ... that is until he appeals to the Cordelia that only he seems to really discern, the Cordelia whose interest in the Feminine is as strong as anything else about her, that she can be both fighter and feminine. He gives her new clothes.

Almost concurrent to this moment in the episode, Wesley attempts to counsel Angel about Cordelia's need for time to build trust again, in effect drawing on what he knows about the "serious" Cordelia, the one whom he assumes has shed her more "shallow" feminine interests. Wesley's understanding of Cordelia at this point illustrates the traditional notion that feminine interests and helping the helpless, in this case, are mutually exclusive. However, Angel has already discovered that Cordelia can indeed embrace both endeavors. In recognizing this duality, Angel alone finds the way to win Cordelia's forgiveness. Cordelia and Angel's relationship is mended effectively. While plenty of similar examples of Cordelia's tie to both the Feminine and fighting abound throughout Seasons 1–3 of *Angel*, the culminating point occurs in Season Three's "Billy," and the opening scene in particular: Angel training Cordelia, at her request, to fight with a broadsword.

When the scene opens, Cordelia's dress utterly overpowers the audience with her female body. While one might suggest that she is working with a sword and requires, therefore, tight clothing, the argument is not sustainable since Angel is obviously not dressed in any sort of male equivalent. He is wearing his usual attire. Cordelia is not. The shirt is short and low-cut, emphasizing cleavage and an open midriff, and her body-hugging clothes emphasize the hour-glass figure that has come to represent the perfect female physique. But more importantly, this scene emphasizes one of my central arguments: that Cordelia takes on the potentially paralyzing and immanent Feminine myth, represented here by the hyper-feminized stereotype of the varsity cheerleader, and makes it into a fighting, transcendent force — not just a fighting to "stave" off danger, but a slaying force. We are reminded of Cordelia's power in this regard when she points her cross-bow at the demonic and violently misogynist Billy at the episode's end and reminds him that "actually, I'm feeling superior because I have an arrow pointed at your jugular. And the irony of using a phallic shaped weapon? Not lost on me."

In this episode's opening scene, Cordelia literally smashes through the box, though an admittedly large and nicely furnished box, that she has inhabited throughout much of the series, in which Angel is the heroic, saving male, a point Angel elucidates when he admits to Cordelia that his purpose is to teach her to "stave" off danger until he arrives to save her. Cordelia replies in her characteristic charming, insouciant, though deceptively simple, manner, "Men folk not always around to protect the women folk, you know?" Still, the scene is fraught with intricacy. While Angel defines his transcendence in relation to Cordelia's immanence — the mythical female image that "exist[s] only in relation to the protagonist (who is male)" (Russ 202)⁻and essentially admits that his status as male hero depends on her status as helpless damsel, Cordelia utterly explodes that paradigm by converting her feminine cheer-leading experiences of wielding a drill team flag into the physical power of fighting with a broadsword. This conversion challenges the dichotomous paradigm that governed much of the series to that point. As a result, Angel is forced to acknowledge her newly acquired dominance. Angel's acknowledgement does not occur through masculine markers but through feminine ones, in this case Cordelia's cheerleading experiences. With a sword at his throat, Angel can make no other reply than weak concession to Cordelia's power and his own new position as the effeminate recipient of that power. Cordelia literally expels her "feminine" weakness— by conversely internalizing and harnessing its potential power — as something not part of her essential being, compelling the source of that socially expected weakness, the dominant male, to reply simply, "Go team."

The episode is also notable for the scene between Cordelia and Lilah, wherein they spar on the issue of fashion for several rounds before Cordelia abruptly ends the match and addresses the issue at hand — Billy's brutality against Lilah through Gavin. Again, we return to Cordelia as a Third Wave feminist, as one who "reclaim[s] stereotypical femininity and [makes] it [her] own — with lipstick and push-up bras [...] short dresses and attitudes[...]" (Rowe-Finkbeiner 90). Significantly, Cordelia ends the conversation, showing she, not Lilah, controls the encounter. Once Cordelia establishes her power in terms of her fashion knowledge, she trenchantly moves on to the purpose of her visit and the exchange — the need for women, exemplified here by Lilah, to exert their own power over the masculine which oppresses them, which Lilah does in the end when she shoots and kills Billy. This type of confidence in the ownership of the Feminine is remarkable in a show that is so defined by its masculinity.

Even before "Billy," in the opening episode for season three, "Heartthrob," Cordelia powerfully reclaims her feminine power through not just her fashion knowledge but her physical sexuality as well. The opening scene finds Angel returning from a meditative retreat to deal with Buffy's death (in *Buffy's* season five finale "The Gift"). He presents each team member with a unique souvenir from his travels. Cordelia's gift is, not surprisingly, a beautiful pendant necklace — a nod to her "feminine" interest in fashion. Cordelia immediately puts it on. The next frame is noteworthy in that we find the entire male cast standing together opposite Cordelia, a visual reminder that in this male world, Cordelia stands alone in opposition to them. Significantly, however, none of them are actually gazing at her directly until, that is, Cordelia draws their attention by proclaiming with unabashed sang-froid and aplomb, "And look how it brings out my breasts!" Angel, Gunn, and Wesley all turn toward her, somewhat surprised and even uncomfortable, to which Cordelia replies, "I know you were all thinkin' it." Again, the men appear ill at ease with Cordelia's open direction of their gazes toward her sexuality. What they are uncomfortable admitting about her, she entirely claims. In this moment, she reconfigures herself not as object but as subject — a necessary controlling partner in the visual consumption of herself as Feminine/Woman. She not only participates in but actually creates (since they were not even looking at her prior to her comments) and directs toward herself that usually objectifying and degrading male gaze that sees the externally created object rather than the self-created subject. In this moment, however, the men are gazing on her terms, making her the active controlling subject rather than the passively controlled object.

By mid-season of season three, then, Cordelia Chase has emerged as a new feminist who reclaims feminine "stereotypes" and defeats the historically destructive and paralyzing consequences of the Feminine. Sadly, this power could not last, as Cordelia in the end is destroyed in a manner utterly plagued and defined by centuries-old, misogynist stereotypes. What viewers witnessed in the closing episodes for season four seems to me to contain a disturbing undercurrent of a very old text — the *Malleus Maleficarum*, or the *Hammer of Witches*.

This text was one of, if not the, most influential and comprehensive texts on the physical relationship between material demons and witches during the Early Modern Period, as well as being a detailed handbook on how to deal with or "hammer" those witches, as Gianfrancesco Pico della Mirandola wrote in 1523 in *Strix*: "...And you can have this hammer, if you want to use it against those who are hardheaded, and don't want to believe the truth; so you can either bend them to believe what they are supposed to, or else smash them into a hundred thousand pieces" (Stephens 32).

The *Maleficarum* was written and compiled by two Dominican Friars, Heinrich Kramer and Jacob Sprenger, in 1486. As evidence of the text's prominence, between 1486 and 1520, the *Malleus* had undergone fourteen editions, and later between 1574 and 1669, the *Malleus* was printed in sixteen more editions (Summers viii). And should we attribute these editions to small and cornered niches throughout Europe, we would be sadly mistaken since Pope Innocent VIII in 1484 had issued a papal bull against witchcraft that became the preface for the *Malleus* just two years later. In fact, Kramer and Sprenger were commissioned by Pope Innocent VIII to be inquisitors into the practice of witchcraft in Northern Germany, placing them at the center of religious clerical authority (viii). Montague Summers, in his preface to the 1948 edition of the *Malleus*, for which he also served as translator, notes: "The *Malleus* lay on the bench of every magistrate. It was the ultimate, irrefutable, unarguable authority. It was implicitly accepted not only by Catholic but by Protestant legislature" (viii).

In a recent thoughtful and convincing study entitled *Demon Lovers: Witchcraft, Sex, and the Crisis of Belief*, Walter Stephens has pointed out that the *Malleus* is much more complex than its most famous misogynist section would suggest, though "the *Malleus* has been justly condemned for its remorseless misogyny," (Stephens 33) and that larger issues for the clergy about the material reality of demons is what underscores and drives the *Malleus* and other similar texts: what "[clergy] wanted to see was not hidden behind bedroom walls or memories of their mothers" but rather "closed off by the barriers that separated life from the afterlife, humanity from the demonic and the divine" (Stephens 32) Though Stephens' argument is a compelling one, these larger metaphysical questions about the evidence of the demonic world were still, at least in the *Malleus*, played out on the landscape of a woman's body and depended on misogynist stereotypes, particularly in this case her physical sexuality and the assumption that she was much more susceptible to demonic influence than was a male:

> But because in these times this perfidy is more often found in women than in men, as we learn by actual experience, if anyone is curious as to the reason, we may add to what has already been said the following: that since they are feebler both in mind and body, it is not surprising that they should come more under the spell of witchcraft [*Malleus*, I.vi].

During the Early Modern Period, the idea of women's inherent weakness being taken as an indisputable fact, and even more than indisputable, as mythically obvious, is clear. Take for example the following excerpt from the

*Homily on Matrimony* published under Bishop Jewel's direction in 1563, the text of which was a translation from a much earlier sermon by Veit Dietrich of Nurnberg (1507–1549): "For the woman is a weak Creature, not indued with like strength and constancy of mind, therefore they be the sooner disquieted, and they be the more prone to all weak affections and dispositions of mind, more than men be, and lighter they be, and more vain in their fantasies and opinions" (St. Clair 350). Moreover, one need look no further than the generally historically held view in Christian theology that fault for Adam and Eve's fall is solely on Eve's shoulders—a weakness in woman that is not present in man, in this case Eve's susceptibility to the devil's temptation but Adam's apparent inherent resistance.

This weakness is directly linked to sexual proclivity in the *Malleus*, wherein the male clergy, by focusing on issues of demonic copulation with women during the interrogation process, were engaging in their own metaphorical sexual power over these women on the grounds that women were indeed physiologically, psychologically, and spiritually weaker (and the same could be said about the specific sexual nature of interrogations aimed at men, though men were not the focus of the *Malleus* and women were, indicating an obvious discrepancy between the two groups as far as clerical theory on witchcraft is concerned). The very term used by Kramer and Sprenger to signify "witch" is a feminine one, malefica — the heresy of witches (maleficarum) instead of the heresy of wizards (maleficorum) (Stephens 33).

The basic assumption in the *Malleus* is the deep-seated notion that a woman, being sexually "insatiable," would be more vulnerable to being sexually involved with a demon than a man would: Again from the *Malleus* directly, "All witchcraft comes from carnal lust, which is in women insatiable ... wherefore for the sake of fulfilling their lusts they consort even with devils" (I. vi). I must add here, though, that this is not to say there are no documented cases of accused males who, under torture, also admitted to having sexual relationships with demons; such cases do exist (Stephens 4). Even so, we still we have to deal with texts like the *Malleus* that single out women for sexual advances from devils based on what clerics thought about a woman's carnal nature when compared to men.

One can likely see at this point how the *Malleus* is crucial to the storyline for Cordelia: she gives birth to a demon after having her body co-opted and controlled by that same demon, in order to have sexual intercourse that will provide a physical body to the demonic Jasmine. Notably, this occurs after Cordelia accepts Skip's offer to move on to the next plane of existence as a higher being. In doing so, she opens herself– albeit unknowingly—to be used by Jasmine, which places her alongside the Early Modern women who unknowingly agreed to demonic consort since the victims often were ignorant that their paramours were devils until after the intercourse had occurred, after which the devils would take on their demonic form again (Stephens 2–6).

What is even more disturbing in Cordelia's case is that her death in season four is the culmination of the undercutting of her strong Third Wave feminist character by a pattern of her physical subjection to the demonic. No other character in *Angel* is so often either physically or mentally "raped" by demonic forces. Some might object to my use of the word "rape," but I do not use it lightly. Rape is the unwanted and unsought penetrative and (even non-penetrative) force exerted over one's body by another who seeks absolute and uncontested physical and emotional control, which is what happens to Cordelia *five* different times within the first four seasons of *Angel*.

She is impregnated by demon spawn in the season one episode "Expecting;" her mind is literally penetrated and taken over by the demonic at the end of season one in the episode "To Shanshu In L.A.;" she is again impregnated in season two's "Epiphany;" her mind and body is taken over by the demonic in the season three episode "That Vision Thing," which leads to Angel releasing Billy from Hell; and finally and most assuredly she is taken over completely by the demonic in season four. What we might also consider is the layering in season four of the "hijacking" of Cordelia's body. Her body is first taken over and controlled by the power that wants Jasmine born, but most disturbing of all is that same power also forces Cordelia's body to be used for intercourse to give Jasmine a human form, as I think we can all agree that Cordelia would never have engaged in a sexual relationship with Connor on her own. In effect, for the Jasmine story arc, Cordelia is raped twice.

The pattern of Cordelia's consistent subjugation to demons ends with her actually giving birth to Jasmine, a demon goddess—the ultimate demon born of woman—a strange perversion of the Christian immaculate conception, and a reminder of old myths about the woman as susceptible to demonic sexual intercourse and the instigator and bringer of evil—the downfall of humanity, a situation that again the *Malleus* makes clear is perfectly possible: "It is with this intention, that through the vice of luxury [devils] may work a twofold harm against men, that is, in body and in soul, that so men may be more given to all vices. And there is no doubt that they know under which stars the semen is most vigorous, and that men so conceived will be always perverted by witchcraft" (*Malleus* I.iii). The offspring of demonic sexual encounters born to a woman will be perverted and evil, which is exactly what Jasmine is.

No other character is so often compromised in the *Angel/Buffy* universe as is Cordelia. Is it because she is a woman? Because she is the ultimate example of successful female strength that takes back feminine stereotypes and makes them part of her power? Certainly not consciously. Neither Joss Whedon nor any other writer in the Whedonverse harbors the misogyny that drove and characterized texts like the *Hammer of Witches*. Perhaps writers do not yet know how to handle this type of strong Third Wave feminist figure, even if they are her creators: once the myth is destroyed, so is the woman. All that is left for her is yet another myth — a beautiful, dead young woman, kept in perfect feminine form by Wolfram and Hart, as Lilah acknowledges in season four's final episode, "Home": "Cordelia's safe and sound. Probably getting a manicure and a blow-dry as we speak... Still in a coma. But hey, it doesn't mean she can't look her best" ("Home"). And Cordelia does look her best from the moment she "awakens" from the coma in season five's "You're Welcome" (though of course, it is her spirit in the form of the still comatose Cordelia who actually seems to be functioning in the episode).

Regardless of authorial intent, what is undeniable is that in the end, Cordelia is a failed feminist gesture who is returned to centuries-old misogynist situations that lead to her degradation and an ignominious death — not one of dramatic self-sacrifice of her choosing, as with Buffy, Doyle, or Wesley, but one that is forced on her, she being what Elizabeth Rambo, in a thoughtful analysis of Cordelia's death, referred to as a "victim of overwhelming forces" (Rambo 6.3, para 14). Cordelia's death is forced on her because she is a woman, susceptible to sexual breach not of her choosing that led to a demonic offspring. What is most alarming of all is that the Cordelia character arc was undoubtedly *not* consciously done with an eye toward undoing her feminine power. "You're Welcome" from season five seemed to be an attempt by the writers to do justice to the Cordelia character and satisfy fans, but the damage had already been done and was essentially irrevocable at that point. Or as Rambo observed, "Although the angelic Cordelia who makes her final appearance in "You're Welcome" *is* stronger and more effective in almost every way than before, she is also only present and active for one day." (para 15).

As we think about the Buffy/Angelverse and the importance of examining the Cordelia Chase character, we must recall again the relationship between feminism and popular culture, a connection that Sherryl Vint shares with Kristin Rowe–Finkbeiner, author of *The F Word, Feminism in Jeopardy*: feminism does indeed have "a particularly close relationship with the stuff of popular culture" (Vint *Slayage* 2.1, para 1). The failed feminist gesture of Cordelia — combined with Fred's death, as her death mirrors that of Cordelia's, effectively ridding *Angel* of any real feminine presence at all — in a fictional universe explicitly declared as one that empowers women, teaches us that even today at the dawn of the twenty-first century our stories and our narratives are still shaped by our past. As enlightened and as progressive as we might consider ourselves, we are still subject to and perhaps controlled by the attitudes and myths of those predecessors who bequeathed to us their powerful concepts of human experience, concepts that we must never be foolish enough to believe we have eradicated, even with all of our linguistic flexibility, progressive mindsets, and conscious efforts at magnanimity and social equity.

## WORKS CITED

Battis, Jes. "Demonic Maternities, Complex Motherhoods: Cordelia, Fred, and the Puzzle of Illyria," in *Slayage* 5.2, Par. 1.

de Beauvoir, Simone. "Myth and Reality," in *The Second Sex*, trans. H.M. Parshley (New York: Vintage, 1952).

Kramer, Heinrich and James Sprenger. *The Malleus Malificarum*, trans. Montague Summers (New York: Dover, 1948),

Rambo, Elizabeth L. "'Queen C' in Boys' Town: Killing the Angel in Angel's House," in *Slayage* 6.3, Par. 14.

Rowe-Finkbeiner, Kristin. "Signs of the Times: Defining the Third Wave," in *The F Word, Feminism in Jeopardy* (Emeryville, CA: Seal, 2004), 88.

Russ, Joanna. "What Can a Heroine Do? or "Why Women Can't Write," in *Feminist Literary Theory and Criticism: A Norton Reader*, eds. Sandra M. Gilbert and Susan Gubar (New York: Norton, 2007), 202. Originally published in Susan Koppelman's *Images of Women in Fiction: Feminist Perspectives*, 1972.

St. Clair, William, and Irmgard Maasen. *Conduct Literature for Women, 1500–1640*, Vol. 2, eds. (London: Pickering & Chatto, 2000), 330.

Stephens, Walter. *Demon Lovers: Witchcraft, Sex, and the Crisis of Belief* (Chicago: University of Chicago Press, 2002).

Summers, Montague. "Introduction to the 1948 Edition," in *The Malleus Maleficarum* (New York: Dover, 1948), viii.

Vint, Sherryl. "'Killing us Softly'? A Feminist Search for the 'Real Buffy,'" in *Slayage* 2.1, Par. 1.

# Why the Cheese Man Is an Integral Part of *Restless*

## MELANIE WILSON

"Restless," the final episode of *Buffy the Vampire Slayer*'s fourth season, is a fascinating and enlightening journey through the subconscious of each of the main characters that encapsulates the essential struggles that each character faces. Since the episode is a series of dreams, there are many irrational elements, but the most prevalent is the infamous "Cheese Man" who appears in each dream. In Joss Whedon's often-quoted Bronze posting, he declares that the Cheese Man has no real meaning: "The cheese man means nothing. He is the only thing in the show that means nothing. I needed something like that, something that couldn't be explained, because dreams always have that one element that is just *ridiculous*. Thus, man of cheese. Plus funny. (to me)." Despite Whedon's protestations, the Cheese Man's recurring presence in each dream and later in "Storyteller" begs further interpretation.

Before exploring the role of the Cheese Man, one must first examine the possible meanings of the cheese. The cheese serves different roles in each dream: in Willow's dream, it is an object to be arranged; in Xander's dream, it is a failed form of protection; in Giles's dream, it is an article of clothing; and in Buffy's dream, it is a warning sign. The differences between these roles suggest that the cheese is malleable, able to shift to the varying needs of each character — symbolic of the essence of life itself. Whedon would not be the first writer to use cheese as a symbol for the unknowable, mysterious essence of life. In "The Open Boat," Stephen Crane's shipwrecked correspondent repeatedly laments, "Was I brought here merely to have my nose dragged away as I was about to nibble the sacred cheese of life?" (894). This comparison is useful since the protagonists of both "The Open Boat" and "Restless" confront their deepest fears of annihilation. As the First Slayer guides and manipulates their dreams to mine their worst fears, the Scoobies discover that they have not defeated the *real* Big Bad of season four: their own fears and shortcomings. Confronting these fears leads the characters to question the meaning of life. The cheese serves to symbolize the mysterious, supernatural forces hidden behind the ordinary façade of life. The Cheese Man, offering cryptic or farcical responses to the First Slayer's attempts to reveal the weaknesses beneath the characters' strengths, becomes a caricaturized version of the coping mechanisms each character employs when confronted with "the sacred cheese of life."

The Cheese Man's first appearance is in Willow's dream. Although she was the "spirit" element of the enjoining spell in "Primeval," this dream reveals that Willow defines herself not in terms of her internal spirit but in terms of her external appearance and accomplishments. Nowhere is this deficiency more obvious than in "Doomed." Willow laments that she has not been a nerd for a long time, immediately adding: "Hello! Dating a guitarist! Or at least, I *was*." She defines her social success in terms of her boyfriend, and her belated remembrance that the relationship is over leaves her self-image ambiguous and unstable. She fears that the changes she has undergone in the last year are merely part of her persona and not her Self. The First Slayer is able to prey on these doubts. This interpretation of her dream is fairly straightforward. Willow responds fearfully to Tara's statement that everyone else will find out about her and reject her. Her acting class turns into a play in which Buffy believes Willow is already in costume, again demonstrating Willow's feeling of being disingenuous. Of course, the clincher is when Buffy forcibly removes Willow's "costume" to reveal Willow's spiritless, nerdy, season one self.

The Cheese Man appears during the chaotic play. As Willow edges away from the stage in search of reassurance, the Cheese Man tells her, "I've made a little space for the cheese slices." His method of approaching the cheese is to control both it and the space around it. The script describes his statement as "conspiratorial," indicating an affinity between the two characters heightened by the common root shared by "conspiratorial" and "spirit." The Cheese Man, dutifully organizing his cheese in the midst of a chaotic, nonsensical play, represents Willow's approach to life's chaotic, nonsensical moments. Her respect for systems and order has always been important to her character; it is one of the reasons she practices magic in the first place. As a Wiccan, she manipulates the sacred cheese of life more than most characters, which gives her a great deal of power. Because of this connection, she can do things like empower an entire generation of Potentials.

This power can be destructive, however, when Willow perceives a breakdown of order. Willow's reliance on order and systems removes her from the true wisdom of relying on her own spirit. She clings to outward forms, like a guitarist boyfriend, that serve as concrete proofs of her identity. Her need for control and order becomes dangerous in "Something Blue," where she tries to work magic on herself to control her emotions and ends up inadvertently causing mayhem for her friends. Again, the dark side of her need for control leads her to erase Tara's and then all of her friends' memories in "As You Were" and "Tabula Rasa," respectively, to fix their emotional problems instead of dealing with them. Finally, her thwarted desire for control and order leads her to kill Warren and cut a swath of destruction through Sunnydale, damaging even herself by using dark magic. She is angry about Tara's senseless death, and when she realizes that there will neither be divine intervention for Tara nor divine retribution for Warren, she takes matters into her own hands. In every case, she imposes order so that she can restore things to the appearance of normalcy, so that the outward form will reflect her idea of order. The Cheese Man mimics her behavior.

As with Willow's spirit, the First Slayer reveals the weakness within Xander's strength of heart. Throughout season four, Xander has been saddled with a general lack of direction. Xander's dream is, as Giles states, "all about the journey." He has always felt out of place among his powerful friends, but "Restless" reveals that he feels out of place everywhere. The world of prophecies and mystical power is not his world, which he seems to realize in the playground segment of his dream. In this segment, Xander begins by situating himself among Buffy, Giles, and Spike, all of whom are inextricably entwined with the supernatural. Eventually, the focus shifts to an alternate Xander in an ice cream truck who is watching himself interact with the group. The more mundane life is the one that resonates with Xander. If he belongs in the mundane world, however, he faces another problem, the possibility of recreating the patterns his family has enacted during his whole life.

His dream repeatedly tries to force Xander to face his fear by bringing him back to the basement. The basement, while obviously referring to his current residence and the shame that comes with living there, also represents the unknown unconscious. For Xander, this unknown basement is not only a symbol of his directionless life; it also contains the seeds that explain his aimlessness. Throughout the dream, every time Xander finds himself in the basement, he ends up gazing in horror at a rattling door. He responds by telling himself, "That's not the way out." Behind the door are his family and their dysfunctional life. Xander wants to be an adult, but not an adult like his parents. Ultimately, his aimlessness is rooted in his fear that he will not be able to break away from the behavioral patterns they have established for him.

Not surprisingly, the Cheese Man appears in Xander's basement. The Cheese Man holds the cheese on a plate and warns Xander, "These will not protect you." Like the Cheese Man, Xander approaches life with skepticism toward anything that appears impractical. He is immune to the siren's call of the esoteric. Xander realizes that intense connections to the source of life will not protect him from what he fears: becoming his parents. As the only Scooby without any mystical abilities, Xander believes that he is ultimately power-less in the face of true evil, the evil he carries within himself. This mistrust is not merely instinctual. It is based on his experience. His few attempts to connect with the mystical source of life have proved disastrous, as in his experiment with a love spell in "Bewitched, Bothered, and Bewildered." His power is always strongest when he approaches a situation without supernat-ural aid, as when he single-handedly stops a group of zombies from blowing up the school in "The Zeppo." Season Six amplifies the strengths and fragility of his heart. He hides his fears about marriage from Anya and even himself until his wedding day, and when those fears erupt as a result of demonic intervention, he leaves Anya at the altar. Most viewers immediately list this as one of his most deplorable actions. His consistent reliance on practical solutions to complex mystical problems also gives him the power to save both Willow and the world in "Grave." The Cheese Man enacts Xander's practi-cal nature, both the strength and fragility of his heart.

Giles's dream focuses on his reluctance to abandon his role as Watcher. Of course, he has wrestled with this problem throughout Season Four, most notably in "A New Man" as he experiences a literal version of a midlife cri-sis when he wakes up to find that he is a Fyarl demon. Other episodes also dramatize his attempts to pursue his own interests. In "The Freshman," he initially refuses to help Buffy solve her problem so that she will have to think for herself. "Where the Wild Things Are" finds him playing his guitar in the local coffee shop. Ultimately, though, his attempts to break away are ineffec-tive, partly because he knows he will not be able to leave his Watcher role as long as he is near Buffy, and partly because pursuing his own interests is not very fulfilling. There is something deeper at work, though, and this dream reveals it: he is afraid that if he abandons his duties as Watcher, disaster will ensue. Willow asks him, "Do you know this is your fault?" Giles offers half-hearted excuses about pursuing his own life, but he obviously does not believe them himself. Perhaps he is right not to; his departure in season six *does* indi-rectly result in disaster on an epic scale.

His death scene further illuminates his fear. "I know who you are," he tells the First Slayer. "And I can defeat you. With my intellect. Cripple you with my thoughts. Of course you underestimate me. You couldn't know... You never had a watcher..." He is wrong, however; he is ultimately powerless against the physical violence of the First Slayer. He is obviously afraid that primal forces will overpower his intellect. His dying words also represent something subtler: a supposition that the primal power of the Slayer requires the intellectual power of the Watcher to balance it. This is a particularly patri-archal paradigm which resonates with Giles's opening statement to Buffy that she has to "stop thinking. [...] This is the way women and men have behaved since the beginning, before time." Giles, as a representative of the supremely patriarchal Watchers Council, has been trained to impose these codes onto his Slayer. Although Giles has largely abandoned his training, it is so deeply ingrained that he cannot entirely escape his fear of an uncontrolled Slayer. On some level, he is afraid that if he leaves, Buffy will revert to primitive, uncontrolled power. This explains his reaction to the mud-caked face of Buffy earlier in his dream. The script describes her as "wild and primeval, breathing hard through her nose." Giles's response is a "shocked" whisper, and no wonder. In this scene, Buffy personifies one of his deepest fears—not that she will die, but that she will degenerate.

Giles meets the Cheese Man in Spike's crypt. The Cheese Man, wearing two slices of cheese on his head, tells Giles, "I wear the cheese. It does not wear me." Giles believes that he has a certain amount of control over the supernatural. The location of the cheese—the Cheese Man's head—mirrors Giles's reliance on his intellect, a reliance which is further symbolized by Giles's role of "Mind" in the enjoining spell. In the original script, the Cheese Man was supposed to wear a mask of cheese complete with eyeholes. To a certain degree, Giles is a wise sage, one who has dealt with the supernatural for so long that it is like a second face. However, he knows he is not the infallible pillar of wisdom that the Scoobies believe him to be; he feels like a fraud. Underscoring this fear, Spike poses for the cameras, presenting an idealized version of himself as vampire. Everyone seems to love him in this archetypal role, just as everyone seems to love Giles in his own archetypal role. Ultimately, though, they are both acts, acts that rapidly become stifling. Since the Cheese Man's quotation is also an allusion to *The Man in the Iron Mask*, the cheese mask also serves to imprison him by concealing his true identity. He does not know how to escape from the muzzle and express his true identity in any meaningful way.

Giles is the first character to verbally respond to the Cheese Man. He laments, "Honestly, you meet the most appalling people." Giles rejects this image of himself, and it foreshadows his eventual recognition of the fact that he must leave Sunnydale and pursue his own interests, both for his own sake and for Buffy's, regardless of the consequences. He cannot help being a Watcher, but he must stop viewing it as a role and recognize that to be a good Watcher, he must be himself. The end of his dream supports this interpretation. He manages to sort through the tangled wires, which Joss Whedon describes as a literal depiction of Giles's life, to find a watch. With its complex coils, it also represents his brain. The watch buried at the center of his life and mind is both a visual pun on the word "Watcher" and also a warning that time is of the essence. This dual meaning represents the truth that being a Watcher is not just a role to Giles; it is part of his identity. Paradoxically, he must abandon the role so that he can embrace the reality, even if his absence results in disaster.

Buffy's dream dramatizes her conflict between the proscribed behavior of a traditional Slayer and her desire to have a life of her own. Throughout the series, Buffy wrestles with this conflict, frequently voicing her fear that being a Slayer means that she has to be alone. Buffy's encounter with Riley in her dream is particularly helpful in understanding Buffy's fears. "We're not demons," she says in response to Adam's insinuation that he shares a common source of aggressive power with Buffy. The "we" in this case does not seem to refer to Adam, since Buffy has consistently viewed him as a monster. Rather, the "we" refers to both Buffy and the First Slayer, who appears in the frame with her as Buffy speaks the line. Despite her protestations, Buffy seems far from secure about her humanity. As she reaches into her bag of weapons to help Riley fight the escaped monsters, she finds only mud. Instead of recoiling in disgust, she slathers it all over her face. The script describes her "face now looking just a little like it was when Giles saw it. Animal." She shares with Giles a common fear that the primal power of the Slayer is dangerous and primitive at heart. Although her power is in her hands, according to the enjoining spell, this power is a fearful one with the potential to dehumanize her. The "scolding look" on Riley's face confirms her fears that, if she truly embraces her Slayer identity, the primality of her power will drive all of her friends and family away. As with the other characters, Buffy's fears come to fruition in season six. Emotionally isolated from her friends and family as a result of her death and resurrection, she withdraws almost completely from them. Spike becomes the mud that she clings to as she uses him to punish herself for, as she believes, coming back as a demon, but she remains emotionally isolated even from him. She is even more disgusted with herself when she realizes that she is not a demon and that the explanation for her changed behavior is not external but internal.

The other important element of Buffy's dream, the one that saves her from being defeated by the First Slayer, is her refusal to accept proclamations from any authority. The First Slayer states, "I have no speech. No name. I live in the action of death. The blood-cry, the penetrating wound. I am destruction. Absolute." Slayers, according to her, are essentially weapons who must sacrifice everything that makes them truly human — not only their friends but also their identities, including their names and their speech, qualities which have always made Buffy unique. When Buffy retaliates with a poetic response about her individuality, the First Slayer angrily responds, "No friends. Just the kill. We are alone." The intervention of the Cheese Man at this point is significant. He leans over the shoulder of the First Slayer to "dangle the cheese slices invitingly," according to the script. His proximity to the

Slayer associates him with her. The cheese slices in this particular segment are symbolic not only of the First Slayer's assertion but also of all prophetic and supernatural mandates. His role changes slightly from the other dreams. He is a caricature of the First Slayer instead of Buffy. This represents the power shift from the First Slayer to Buffy during this dream. In the end, it is the First Slayer's nightmare instead of Buffy's. Of this scene, Whedon says in his commentary, "When [The First Slayer] makes the poignant part about being alone, here comes the Cheese Man to say, 'Okay, it's a dream.'" Of course, in every dream, the Cheese Man signals to the dreamer and the viewer that the sequence is only a dream. Buffy is the only one to respond to his signal, however. The Cheese Man serves as a catalyst for Buffy's rebellion because she immediately sees the absurdity of letting the First Slayer take her power from her. It is, after all, a dream, and she can wake up. By reclaiming her power, she is able to defeat the First Slayer and the fears she represents. As Buffy tells her, "You're not the source of me."

The Cheese unexpectedly reappears two seasons later in "Storyteller." During Andrew's flashback of a dream he and Jonathan share, the Cheese Man appears sandwiched between flashes of the Turok'Han and the seal of Danzelthar. This dream is similar to the ones Buffy has in "Lessons" and "Beneath You." All three dreams foretell dire events, and two of them end with the sentence, "From beneath you, it devours." Andrew and Jonathan's dream clearly foretells doom and apocalypse with a disturbing finality. The Cheese Man footage is taken from Willow's dream in "Restless," which associates Jonathan and Andrew with Willow. All three characters approach life with a similar reliance on order. They have each "made a little space for the cheese slices." Andrew and Jonathan demonstrate their desire for control throughout their tenure on the series. Jonathan's most dramatic attempt at gaining control is when he casts a spell in "Superstar" to make himself the most popular, accomplished person in Sunnydale. Andrew's obsession with order manifests itself in his tendency to view every event as part of a larger story, one that he constructs himself. This habit culminates in "Storyteller," where Buffy forces him to see that he is deluding himself. What this mindset means for both Andrew and Jonathan is that they do not resist fate. Like Willow, they let self-doubt cloud their power. The Cheese Man's appearance in this episode also serves to undercut the finality of these prophetic dreams. Buffy can fight against it and win as she did in "Restless." The Cheese Man is a signal that a paradigm shift is eminent in the Buffyverse, and one ensues in the series finale, "Chosen."

When the Cheese Man is present, the characters can be heroes and change their circumstances. Jacqueline Lichtenberg eloquently discusses the concept of the hero versus the victim in her article, "Victim Triumphant." According to Lichtenberg, Buffy and Angel represent different types of protagonists. While Angel survives by adapting to circumstances and learning to cope with the consequences, Buffy repeatedly manages to change the circumstances. In other words, "the goal [Angel] pursues in each episode [...] is not his own" (134). Buffy, on the other hand operates differently: "Her heroism lies in her ability to take the cards she's dealt and refuse to play the hand. When faced with an acceptable choice, she doesn't choose the lesser of two evils—she finds another way. Buffy is a hero because she makes her own rules" (135). Angel's strategies work for him in Los Angeles, but they would not work for Buffy as she confronts the First Evil. It is her willingness to change the circumstances that allows her to realize that nothing is truly inevitable and that mystical messages are the equivalent of a "skittish, balding, bespectacled little fellow" pathetically dangling cheese in the desert ("Restless").

## WORKS CITED

Crane, Stephen. "The Open Boat." *Stephen Crane: Prose and Poetry.* New York: Library of America, 1984.

Lichtenberg, Jacqueline. *Five Seasons of* Angel. Ed. Glenn Yeffeth. Dallas, TX: Benbella, 2004. 133–38.

"Restless." By Joss Whedon. Dir. Joss Whedon. *Buffy the Vampire Slayer* 4 ep. 22. 1999–2000. DVD. Fox, 2003. Transcript.

Whedon, Joss. Commentary. "Restless."

# Wesley as Tragic Hero

## Rebecca Bobbitt

*I'm not interested in the people destined to be heroes, but the ones who want to run away... If someone's pulling a sword from a stone, I want to know what happened to the third guy on the left, who couldn't get the sword out of the stone but the responsibility falls to him anyway... Those are the people I speak for because that's who I am.*

— Joss Whedon

Why is it that the main character of a TV show is rarely anyone's favorite? In Whedon's shows about the outcasts and little guys of the world, the supporting characters become the "third guys on the left" who are even more inspirational than the heroes because they come to the fight without the superpowers and responsibility, but they fight all the same. And sometimes these supporting characters have issues with their leaders, such as the Scoobies' attack on Buffy in season seven's "Empty Places." In one of her many speeches that season, Buffy tells her army that they need someone to lead them. Anya answers, "And it's automatically you. You really do think you're better than we are. But we don't know. We don't know if you're actually better." Anya says that the slayer legacy gifts Buffy with "certain advantages," but that doesn't make her better, only "luckier."

Wesley is a better person than his leader. In fact, Wes is almost too much of a good person to be a Whedon character. He has no past cruelties to atone for, and he has never tried to end the world. He once tried to kill Fred while under a spell that made brought out his scary male misogynistic tendencies in "Billy," but unlike Xander, possessed by a hyena spirit, he did not even eat the school mascot ("The Pack"). Wes does seek redemption, but his initial crime was just being a ponce and an overly sycophantic acolyte of the Watcher's Council. When Wes joined the *Buffy* cast in season three, he was a nerdy, bossy jerk who refused to adjust his role to Buffy's world. In "'Nobody Scream ... Or Touch My Arms: The Comic Stylings of Wesley Wyndam-Price," Stacey Abbott describes Wes as a "comic foil" for Buffy. He fulfills the role of the blind and incompetent authority figure who must be mocked and disobeyed to emphasize the superiority of Buffy's method of world-saving. But as we have seen on *Angel*, Wes is well-suited to rebellion against traditional authorities (he must be to desire to become a rogue demon hunter). Had he not betrayed the Scooby Gang by aiding the Watcher's Council in capturing Faith, Wes might have eventually gained a trusted position in Sunnydale.

This leads to Wes's tragic flaw. He wants to fight the good fight, but he has had to let go of his rigid view of good and evil. He has had to turn his back on the Watcher's Academy to follow first a teenager and then a vampire. And it is Wes who usually ends up being the member of the group who argues that Angel is different because of his soul (to his father, to Gunn's former gang, to Holtz, etc.). In season four's "Spin the Bottle," we realize how much Wes has changed when we see his return to the Watcher's Academy's Head Boy — obnoxious and over-confident.

"Spin the Bottle" is an important episode for understanding Wes's character. In season six of *Buffy*, during the episode "Tabula Rasa," the Scooby Gang (and Spike) lose their memories after Willow's memory spell goes awry. Despite being unaware of her superior strength and long history as the leader, Buffy asserts herself from the beginning, encouraging the others to organize and find a solution. She instinctively protects the group, comforting Dawn and staking the vampire threatening Spike. While her Slayer powers might have influenced the last bit, this episode argues that Buffy (not just the slayer) is a natural leader. Angel is not. That is part of the beauty of *Angel*, that Angel has overcome his nature and obstacles and become a champion. Angel has not just Angelus to overcome, but also Liam the drunken idiot. However, the interesting part is that Wes steps up to lead the Fang Gang in "Spin the Bottle." He is not very good at leading; everyone, especially Gunn, resents his officiousness. His leadership style here harkens back to his attempts to lead in Sunnydale. However, Wes is best-suited to lead the amnesiac team because he uses his knowledge of the supernatural to solve the problem presented. And he is right when he says that there is a vampire lurking in the hotel. Unfortunately, Wes nearly gets Angel killed by convincing the group that Angel has been placed there to kill them all in a scenario created by the Watcher's Council.

"Spin the Bottle" highlights Wes's good qualities. He is intelligent, educated (not as well as he thinks), and brave. He attempts to protect Cordelia and Fred from Angel, even though he lacks any discernible skill at fighting (his ka-ra-te is merely laughable). Indeed, the wrist gadget that so plagued Wes at first once again becomes a cool and competently-wielded weapon as Wes takes a defensive stance against the vampire threat. What is shown in this episode is that Wesley, like Buffy/Joan in "Tabula Rasa," has the heart of a hero, but he lacks the superpowers that make "Joan" the Boss. Stacey Abbott argues that the slapstick humor surrounding Wes during his early days on *Angel* was meant to redeem the character for his transgressions on *Buffy* by "generat[ing] sympathy or identification" within the audience. She states that the return to slapstick in season four had a different purpose — to create nostalgia for that fun guy who had not yet become a "brooding and isolated 'Byronic Hero.'"

The focus of this essay is Wes's transformation into a tragic hero, a transformation that mirrors Angel's own development — but with less brooding, isolation, and rats. We can see the beginnings of this in the episode "Guise Will Be Guise" in which Wes pretends to be Angel and shows how much of the hero is in the reputation and the long black coat. Wes has always played the Giles role of exposition guy, there to translate the Sumerian or demon language and explain what the monster intends to accomplish with its dark, sacrificial ritual. His transformation into a fighter was not complete until he endured isolation as a result of betraying Angel. Like Angel, he spent time (though not nearly as much) fighting alone because he felt unworthy of human contact. So Wes runs his own crew for awhile, and in "Spin the Bottle," he starts sporting the wrist gadget, a versatile weapon that erupts from his sleeve. It mirrors Angel's retractable wrist stakes from the pilot, "City of...," but is even cooler because it can be a stake, a throwing stake, or a sword. In season four, Wes, though always reticent, becomes a tortured and isolated hero who chooses to continue fighting the good fight even after, as he says, "I had my throat cut and all my friends abandoned me" ("Spin the Bottle").

In "A Sense of the Ending: Schrodinger's *Angel*" Roz Kaveney states that Wes is "the character who has most consistently acted as Angel's shadow and surrogate." In "Deep Down," the fourth season opener, Wes becomes the hero as he rescues a helpless Angel from the bottom of the ocean. But for Wes, being the hero has a price, and he succumbs to behavior that mirrors Angel's during his disillusionment in season two. When the love of Angel's unlife, Darla, is resurrected by Wolfram & Hart to seduce and/or torture Angel into regressing to his evil alter ego, Angelus, Angel loses the mission and starts on a downward spiral into darkness. After learning that real hell is on earth in the episode "Reprise" (2015) and failing to save a human Darla, Angel surrenders and seeks to lose his soul by having sex with a re-vamped Darla. This is after he allows Darla and Drusilla to kill several of Wolfram & Hart's lawyers by locking them all together in Holland Manners' wine cellar in "Reunion." Angel is ultimately forgiven for these transgressions. In fact, sex with Darla results in Angel's beloved son, Connor, and in an epiphany that allows Angel to return to heroism (the Powers let him save Kate).

When Wes loses his illusions and slips into darkness, he also starts a relationship with the wrong woman, Lilah, the evil lawyer. This self-inflicted misery is directly linked to his abduction of Connor because he and Lilah discussed the dangerous possibilities of the child of two vampires, a discussion that influenced Wes's decision to take Connor. Like Angel's night with Darla (and Buffy and Spike's sexual marathons), Wes's sexual relationship with Lilah is degrading and monstrous for them both. However, Wes and Lilah do have affection for each other (she buys him nice presents), and the relationship does much to humanize Lilah.

Still, they also use each other to a great extent, as she cons him into giving information to Angel that results in Lorne's brain being raided for details on the season's apocalypse. Wes is using Lilah to punish himself and as a substitute for his real love, Fred. When in a fit of jealousy, Lilah dresses as Fred to seduce Wes, he sours her joke by exposing how he feels about Fred — he commands her to leave her costume glasses on while they have sex ("Supersymmetry"). Unlike Angel and Darla who are rewarded for their act (Darla says Connor is the "only good thing" she has ever done), Wes and Lilah are punished. First, Fred finds out about Lilah, though she does eventually forgive Wes. Then possessed Cordelia kills Lilah, and Wes has to decapitate her dead body to prevent her possible return as a vampire.

To rescue Angel from the ocean, Wes must first find him, so he kidnaps Justine and keeps her locked in a closet to help him in the search. That last part really has no connection to his search for Angel because Justine had already admitted what she and Connor had done to Angel. She was of no more use in finding him, though Wes does use her to scuba dive. Therefore, Wes was holding her captive in retribution for her involvement in the botched abduction of Connor (and for slitting his throat). Like Angel letting the Darla and Dru kill the lawyers, Wes steps over the line, letting revenge guide him. Justine's description of the new Wesley is telling — "The great Wesley Wyndham-Price, the shining beacon of all that's good and pure. But, oh, wait, no. That's before he started banging the enemy and keeping the slave girl in his closet" ("Deep Down").

However, Wes is merciful after he finds Angel, throwing Justine the key to her handcuffs and advising her to leave the revenge business. And he is rewarded for finding Angel when Angel forgives him for kidnapping Connor. Yet the damage to Wes is not so easily undone, and he does not make a full return to Angel Investigations until the apocalypse makes it unavoidable.

When Angel does eventually kill his son in "Home" and accepts leadership of Wolfram & Hart, everyone's memories of Connor are erased, including Wes's kidnapping attempt. For awhile, Wes regains his trusted position in the family, but Angel, who retains his memories, has moments of doubt about Wes. In season five's "Lineage" (5.7), Angel berates Wes for taking Fred to a meeting with his former arms dealer where she is injured. Although Wes does not understand that Angel's anger is based on his abduction of Connor (because he does not remember it), he feels guilty for endangering her and failing to protect her. Angel's argument denies Fred an active role in the group by placing her as a damsel in distress. Of course, Angel usually does not make that call regarding Fred. In "Habeas Corpus," Angel expects Fred to join the fight against the Beast, a creature that has proven to be nigh impervious and has nearly killed Angel. Angel says to Cordelia, "Cordelia, I don't want you there. It's dangerous. Way too dangerous. I can't risk it. Fred, get a move on."

And yet, Angel is right in not trusting Wes's judgment, or rather, that Wes should attend to Angel's judgment. This is highlighted in "Origin." Wes discovers that Angel commissioned Wolfram & Hart to perform the mind-altering spell, and he enlists Illyria's help in discovering what Angel had changed. Despite Angel's insistence that Wes should trust his choices, Wes drops the ball, literally, and releases the erased memories of kidnapping Connor. This works to Angel's advantage because Connor is able to receive these memories and forgive Angel, leading to a reconciliation between father and son that helps defeat Hamilton, the bad ass liaison to the Senior Partners. Wes, however, receives another blow to his confidence.

Because Wes is a good person, a hero in his own right, these failures and bad judgment calls are even more significant. Kaveney describes him as "a character whose essence is to lose and yet lose so honourably as to be admirable." Wes, even more so than Angel, shows us what it means to be a hero because he is so rarely rewarded for his sacrifices. The one thing he ever really seemed to want, Fred, was only his for a brief time. He even (sort of) killed his father to save Fred (robot dad in "Lineage"). After pining for her for three seasons, Wes finally receives her love only to see her die and be invaded by Illyria. Throughout the rest of the season, Wes has the daily suffering of seeing a creature who looks like his dead girlfriend. This destroys Wes to the extent that his death in "Not Fade Away" seems like a mercy.

The sympathy for Wes's loss persists even as Fred's death propels him to kill a human, Knox, who intentionally exposed Fred to Illyria's sarcophagus to infect her with the demon. In the aftermath of Fred's death, Wes mirrors Angel's actions after Connor's abduction. Angel nearly suffocated Wes as he lay in the hospital, and Wes stabs Gunn for allowing the sarcophagus into Wolfram & Hart and then lying about his involvement. Wes is depicted as righteous in this action, because Gunn then mirrors Wes's isolation in season three, suffering remorse and alienation in a hospital bed. Even Harmony shows disgust toward Gunn. Knox's death is even played for comedy. Angel is explaining to Illyria why he would protect Knox even after being betrayed by him: "You're about as low as it gets, Knox, but you're a part of humanity. That isn't always pretty, but it's a hell of a lot better than what came before. And if it comes down to a choice between you and him, then yes, I would fight for his life, just like any other human's. Because that's what people do. That's what makes us—." He is interrupted as Wes shoots Knox, killing him.

Angel then turns to Wes and says, exasperated, "Were you even listening?" ("Shells").

Despite the fact that the main rule of both *Buffy* and *Angel* is never to kill a human, Wes kills Knox, barely raising an eyebrow. Wes finally gets by with something, though he could hardly have cared. Wes also shoots a Wolfram & Hart employee who argues that Fred isn't their biggest issue, but that also seems kind of comedic, forgivable (and forgettable!).

Although Wes does nearly lose his mind after Fred's death, he continues to help humanity by staying with Angel and helping Illyria. And he finally defies Angel with good results by refusing to kill Illyria in "Time Bomb." Despite Angel's order to kill her before she explodes and destroys most of California in the process, Wes engineers a machine that will weaken her and prevent the explosion. Wes's defiance saves Illyria, who ultimately helps Angel in his plan to defeat the Circle of the Black Thorn. His defiance also allows for Illyria's redemption in "Not Fade Away." Kaveney describes Illyria's offer to be Fred for Wes as he dies as "an outward sign of genuine inward change." This change is certainly due to Wes's humanizing presence in her life. Wes has done something Angel could not do, socialize the god-king and make her a member of the team. What the result of that change would have been is unfortunately unknowable because of the show's cancellation.

Wes's influence on Illyria mirrors Angel's pivotal role in Faith's redemption. Wes failed with Faith, as she liked to remind him, and he failed with Lilah. An undead Lilah tells him, "For all your supposed darkness, your "edge of the razor" mystique, there was always a small part of you that thought you could pull me back from the brink of my evil, evil ways. Help me find redemption ... Angel's influence I suppose. The whole 'not giving up on someone no matter how far he or she has fallen'" ("Salvage").

Although he was a good person, Wes had to suffer isolation and the destruction of his idea of himself to become a hero — to discover what it means to fight for the world. He needed to understand darkness, to realize that he did not always know what was right.

Wes has long been fighting the good fight, but Angel's influence transformed Wes into a hero. Unfortunately, the path to becoming a hero damaged Wes even more so than it did Angel. Wes's death in the show's final episode, according to Kaveney, "demonstrat[es] that the mission is about self-sacrifice," but it also prevents Wes from being The Hero and from fighting the last battle with his friends. Yet he does not die alone, and he dies looking at his final good deed — the transformed Illyria. Because Wes did not have the safety of being the title character of the show, his actions were less productive, less heroic. And he was ultimately expendable and tragic. Yet because he was not the hero, his journey has a resonance with the audience that

Angel's, chosen champion of the Powers that Be and supernaturally strong vampire with a soul, cannot. Like us, Wes must fight the good fight without real muscle to fall back on.

## WORKS CITED

Abbott, Stacey. "'Nobody Scream ... Or Touch My Arms': The Comic Stylings of Wesley Wyndam-Price." *Reading* Angel: *The TV Spin-off with a Soul*. Ed. Stacey Abbott. London, New York: I. B. Tauris, 2005.

Kaveney, Roz. "A Sense of the Ending: Schrodinger's *Angel*." *Reading* Angel: *The TV Spin-off with a Soul*. Ed. Stacey Abbott. London, New York: I. B. Tauris, 2005.

Miller, Nick. "Laying Demons to Rest." *The West Australian* 24 September 2005, Metro: 15. Lexis Nexis Middle Tennessee State University.

# The Battle Against the Patriarchal Forces of Darkness

### KEVIN K. DURAND

"Are you ready to finish this?" Not the most subtle of lines, to be sure. However, Caleb is not a subtle character. Caleb is obvious. Indeed, Caleb is almost too obvious. Fans of *Buffy* have come to expect a little more complexity, a bit more nuance in our Big Bads. Even the underlings or instruments of the Big Bads have more inflection to them. Caleb, on the other hand, is almost a caricature of the woman-hating, deeply patriarchal cleric. Indeed, upon his arrival in Sunnydale, viewers are given only the briefest moment to think of him in any way other than a loathsome, powermad, blasphemous creature; as the Turuk-Hon are to vampires, Caleb is to humanity. His message to the Slayer is similarly lacking in subtlety — a knife to the belly and a girl left to die.

It might well strike the careful viewer of the Buffyverse as quite odd that in the final season of the show, in the culmination of a story arc that has rarely lacked for subtlety and twists and turns that we should get so obvious a character. However, I will argue here that Caleb, obvious though he may be in most ways, is actually a lens through which perhaps the most significant twist in the Buffyverse is made clear. Caleb, the Watchers Council, and the Shadow Men are not warriors in a cosmic and metaphysical battle of Good versus Evil. Rather, they are all essentially instantiations of the archetypal First and only through a radical reimagination of the nature of power is the conflict between Good and Evil to be truly understood.

As season seven unfolds, we are given to believe that the battle lines are drawn. This seems obvious, too. Travers has uttered the obligatory Winston Churchill line, "We are still masters of our fate, we are still captain of our souls" (*Never Leave Me*). The good guys (The Council, the Scoobies, the potentials) are under siege; the bad guys (The First, the Bringers, and very soon, Caleb) are on the offensive. The apocalyptic battle is before us.

Yet, the impotence of the invocation of Churchill is striking, as the Council is exploded within moments of the expression of the "stiff upper lip." This is more than just irony. This moment encapsulates the Council; its role, its place, its very being. The Council is not, nor has it ever been, what it appears to be, nor even what it perceives itself to be. Season Seven, particularly through the lens of Caleb, makes it impossible to see the Watchers Council as anything more than a self-deluded tool of the First. With this revelation, the obvious battlelines are not nearly so obvious anymore and that this is more than a story of two medieval fantasy armies arrayed against each other.

To make this point, let us first look at the obvious archetype of Evil — the First and its tool, Caleb. "Archetype" may be too strong a word. Indeed, it may be too respectful. In many ways, Caleb is a caricature; or would be if that which he caricatures were not so given to some of his own rhetorical and symbolic excesses. In a way, he seems overdrawn. Yet, tragically, not. Simply put, the viewer is to be put in the mind of the Church and its clearly patri-archal hierarchical nature. This is not the forum nor does this paper have the scope to address the many ways in which denominational hierarchies struc-ture themselves, from Episcopal through Congregationalist systems. However, in whatever ways denominations order themselves, the pervading model, whether Roman Catholic or evangelical protestant, is hierarchical and patri-archal. This is not controversial. It is also clear that Caleb represents that structure.

In his Roman collar, the Catholic symbolism cannot be lost on the viewer. His Eucharistic language reinforces this connection. At the same time, his deeply southern drawl and riffs on evangelical themes aligns him symboli-cally with that wing of the church. In *Empty Places*, for example, Caleb employs a standard political mantra of the evangelical right. Pressing an encounter with Buffy at school, he says, "This here's a, uh ... public school, ain't it? Kinda deserted. Only just, I suppose. Folks work so hard at keepin' the Lord out, and look what happens in return.... He abandons you." Here the caricature is not so remote from that represented. As Pat Robertson told the Dover School District, "I'd like to say to the good citizens of Dover: If there is a disaster in your area, don't turn to God. You just rejected him from your city." Indeed, Caleb elevates himself to the level of deity, opining in *Dirty Girls* that, "I work in mysterious ways."

Connected to both structural wings of the church, Caleb is also repre-sentative of the institutionalized misogyny that has been a marker of the established church for much of its existence. A great deal has been made in recent popular fiction and reflective scholarship of the systemic repression of women's voices within the patriarchal hierarchy of the church. From Pope Gregory I's character of assassination of Mary Magdalene to the systematic restriction of women from the majority of leadership roles within local churches and larger church structures, the stain-glassed ceiling is a clear and present reality. While not nearly so explicitly oppressive and denigrating of women, one need look no further than some of the ancient Doctors of the Church — St. Thomas of Aquinas, St. Augustine, Tertullian — to name a few, to find Caleb's sentiments expressed in perhaps more subtle ways. The patriarchal oppression and, further, dehumanization of women is clearly borne by Caleb; obviously so. Even the most novice literary critic cannot miss the phallic and deeply Freudian use of the Caleb's knife into the potential's belly. In short, Caleb is obvious.

As such an obvious character, with the symbolism so blatant, one might be given to wonder why Whedon would take such an obvious tack; it lacks subtlety, it lacks finesse, and it lacks the punch of Whedonesque creations. If Caleb is merely taken as an obvious token of some metaphysical evil Type, that is. However, if we suppose that Caleb is a lens, a lens through which our understandings of the entire power structure of the Buffyverse can be seen and re-imagined, then Caleb is a subtle and nuanced epistemological catalyst.

Intriguingly enough, the first of the twin scenes that unites between Caleb and the Watchers as functional tools of the same power of darkness happens prior to Caleb's debut. While out of order, let us examine first the scene in which Caleb's power is restored by the First. Caleb and the First have suffered a series of small setbacks, culminating in Buffy's reclamation of the scythe. In rage, Caleb flings a barrel of fine, full-bodied merlot against the wall. In the guise of Buffy, The First says, "Face it. Your strength is waning. It has been quite some time since we've ... (looks at him seductively) merged." Lured from anger toward violence of a different sort, Caleb responds (and sniffs), "Maybe you're right. OK, let's do it." The obvious sexual innuendo is lost neither on The First or Caleb, and Caleb's stereotypically male response to the proffered "merger" is not lost on the viewer. On the off chance that it was, The First's response leaves nothing to chance. It says, "Boy, you sure know how to romance a girl. No flowers, no dinner, no tour of the rectory. Just, "OK, I'm ready. Let's do it." Help me. My knees are weak (rolls her eyes)." Caleb is taken a bit aback by the sarcasm and asserts both his perceived status and his masculinity, admonishing the one who clearly has the power in the relationship by say, "Watch what you say now. You're starting to sound like her. This is a sacred experience for me." The First is unimpressed by the show of machismo and replies with sighing exasperation, "And for me as well."

The First then briefly transforms from its Buffy guise into the demon and enters Caleb in what is clearly a sexual experience for him. He is infused with power and his eyes glow black. So willingly has he embraced the darkness that he utters reverently, with good King James inflections, "I am thy humble servant and I am ready to serve thee." While the infusion of power is clearly sexual, it is also clearly a power transfer. Caleb is much stronger, physically, following the "merger." He is much more connected to that patriarchal power structure and at the same time, subservient to it.

Caleb is the anti–Buffy, and she is the anti–Caleb; at least that is how the powers want it to be. Good and Evil are in eternal conflict; Buffy and Caleb are the instruments by which they fight. The encounter with the Shadow Men rearranges our understanding, however. Good and Evil may be in an eternal conflict, but who belongs to the side of Evil is understood differently. While Caleb is an instrument of the First and the Watchers Council is the descendent of the Shadow Men, they are fighting an internecine war amongst themselves; or simply put, they are like two rival mob families locked in combat to be the most powerful representative of the block called Evil. Caleb and the Council, the Shadow Men and the First — they are all functionally equivalent. To make this more clear, we should turn from Caleb and his infusion by the first to the scene from earlier in Season Seven that is its twin.

When Principal Wood encounters the Slayers in Training, the full gravity of the situation compels him to pass along to Buffy the bag of mystical heirlooms he has preserved from his mother. Within those heirlooms is a box that only the Slayer can open, a box that transports Buffy to the original Shadow Men and to the beginning of the Slayer line. Buffy's ensuing encounter with the Shadow Men, an encounter prefigured by the encounter of the First Slayer with these same Men, throws into stark relief the stakes involved in the coming battle with the First and its minion, Caleb. More interestingly, though, it readjusts the moral and ethical terrain of the entire Buffyverse, reconfiguring the perceptions of the true meaning of the timeless battle that Buffy has always thought she was fighting. Buffy responding to the cryptic responses of the Shadow Men, says, "Look — I got a First to fight. You three have clearly had some time on your hands. Tell me what I need to know. I came to learn." One of the Shadow Men responds in a way that seeks to reject Buffy's reconfiguration, "We cannot give you knowledge. Only power."

They knock her out and drag her to a cave. Meanwhile, back in Sunnydale, Willow is enraged; eyes go dark, Dawn and Kennedy blown across the room like they touched a live electrical outlet, Willow roars.

When Buffy awakes, chained to the wall, she gets the story of the violent beginning of her line. The Shadow Men, in time immemorial, psychically and spiritually raped the first slayer. They are dismissive of Buffy — when she says that she doesn't need power, but knowledge, they respond that "The first Slayer ... did not talk so much." Buffy's "Bastards!" only begins to cover the character of those who sought to protect themselves from the powers of darkness by utterly and phallically subjugating another. Buffy fights back.

Even after the mist enter her, she fights. The Shadow Men say of the first slayer, "She begged for us to stop. We did not then. We will not now." And, then prefiguring words of the Watchers Council who descend from them, they say, "We only want to help you."

Willow, with one of the most long awaited lines in all of spellcasting says, "Screw it. Mighty forces, I suck at Latin, okay?" and while the lines that followed might be obscured by a chuckle or two, they are crucial. She goes on, "I am in charge here and I am telling you, open this portal *now!*"

Not only does Buffy fight off the Shadow Men and their attempt at physical and metaphysical rape, Willow demonstrates that Buffy's later claim is right. When the final plan is given to the gang, Buffy recalls a line from the encounter with the Shadow Men, "You are just men." They are just men and this woman, Willow, is stronger than all of them combined. While the Shadow Men try to reinstitute the hierarchical system of patriarchy that is now revealed as no better than the "evil" is seeks to fight, Buffy has gained not brute power but knowledge. So, what does she know?

She knows that the First Evil and its representative tool, Caleb, are just like the Shadow Men, their descendents, the Council, and its representative tool, the Slayer (at least through Buffy). The Shadow Men are right, just not in the way they think. Buffy is the last of her line; and the first of a radically new line, a line that breaks with all of the incarnations of evil — Caleb and the Council.

The destruction of the Watchers Council is prefigured in Buffy's rejection of the Shadow Men and their doom is sealed by their own inability to imagine a world in which the hierarchical worldview that supports their claim to elevated status is overthrown. Rather than join the Slayer in a united front against the First, the hold on to their own self-importance and secretive machinations. After Buffy calls and asks them for help in finding Giles, Travers says, "The girl knows nothing." Not only does he continue to denigrate the young girl who he still views as an instrument of the Council and creation of the Shadow Men, he assumes that she knows nothing of value. Indeed, Buffy does not even recognize yet what she knows, and does not even really know until taunted by the First in *Chosen*. However, what Buffy knows and Travers cannot fathom is that the tables have actually turned, that she has power they know not of, and, more importantly, she has knowledge. Only after the Shadow Men showed her the vastness of the army arrayed against her, could Buffy have the epiphanic moment that reveals that the entire power structure is flawed; that the Shadow Men and the First are essentially of a piece, and that only through radical shared power (and knowledge), can a system that is built on the patriarchal oppression of women be overthrown. No, Travers is right in one sense — "The *girl* knows nothing." Buffy does not know where to locate Giles nor the secret and self-important machinations of the Council. Where he is wrong is that she knows far more than he does, and indeed, far more than he could. Trapped as he is in the internecine battle for power, not between good and evil, but *for* power, Travers cannot see the power of shared power. This lack of foresight and ignorance of his own impotence has immediate repercussions for him and for the line of the Shadow Men as the Watchers Council building explodes before his grandiose speech about taking the fight to the First can even reach its first phase. For Travers, for the First, for the Shadow Men, for the Council, for Caleb, power is something that is accumulated and wielded like a hammer. For Buffy, power, she is coming to see, is something that is shared and thereby multiplied.

To complete this series of connections we must show that the Watchers Council is functionally equivalent to their ancestors and essentially instantiations of the archetype of Evil that is the First must be made. It is no small thing to lump the "good guys" with the evil ones. Yet, from Season Three, grave suspicions about the Council arise. That the Council would not help Buffy save Angel's life might be dismissed as the act of a hidebound and shortsighted bureaucracy, convinced in its conceptions of the world — Vampires bad, tree pretty. However, pairing that with the Council's intentional poisoning and testing of Buffy in *Helpless*, one cannot help but be left with the view that the Watchers Council, like the Shadow Men, view the Slayer as not only something of their own creation, but as a tool to be used in their own power struggles. Travers' claim of "fighting a war," is met with Giles's retort of "You are *waging* a war. She's fighting it." The incredibly important distinction is immaterial to Travers who, prefiguring the Shadow Men's interaction with Buffy, says essentially, "this is the way it has always been done." More precisely, he says, by way of justification of the physical invasion of Buffy's body without her consent, "It's been done with way for a dozen centuries. It's a time-honored rite of passage."

The sexual connotations are clear. The Shadow Men psychically and metaphysically raped the Primitive to create the first Slayer. In an effort to continue the dominance of Council to Slayer, the Council infuses each Slayer privileged enough to reach 18 years of age. The phallic needle takes back from the current Slayer that which the primordial rape imbued her; yet her plight is the same — still she must face a vampire, still she must fight. The Primitive was chained to the ground; Buffy was drugged by a crystal. The patriarchal and explicitly phallic hierarchical domination of the "chosen" girl makes explicit the moral equivalence of the Shadow Men and their Watcher descendents.

Travers should have seen the Watchers Council full descent into impotence and final destruction coming long before it happened. In season five,

Buffy finally puts the Council in its place, at least verbally. Just two years previously, he came face to face with the reconstructed power structure in the Shadow line. Faced with a runaway god in Glory, the Council is faced with an inversion of almost everything they have assumed. However, their blind spot is ultimately their own devastation. Glory is a female, to be sure, but she is a female patriarch. She deals in a form of power with which the Council is familiar — top down, wielded with no concern for underlings. Glory would have understood Quentin's chastisement of Giles in *Helpless*, "You have a father's love for the child and that is useless to the cause." No one can charge Glory with love of anything or sympathies for underlings. This is a power that is familiar, that is obvious. In the line of the Big Bads, Glory fits perfectly. The structure and implementation of power is exactly the same, only the names have changed — The Master, the Mayor, Adam, Glory — every one of them a patriarch in a highly ordered power structure. And all of them with exactly the same blind spot. Each is overcome, not with a David and Goliath battle to the finish; each is overcome through a sharing, through a joint empowering of others beyond the one with "obvious" power.

Quentin and the Council minions blow into town to "test" Buffy and through threats, coercions, and superciliousness. Just to make sure she understands "her place," he asserts what he thinks is still his hierarchical authority over her (odd, since the Slayer has not been under the "direction" of the Council in a couple of years). Quentin, sensing the opportunity to right what he thinks is wrong, namely the understanding of place and who is actually in charge, tells her, "The Council fights evil. The Slayer is the instrument with which we fight. The Council remains. The Slayers ... change. It's been that way from the beginning." This is the system and you must know your place and we are in charge.

In one of the most popular scenes in the Buffyverse, Quentin is shown the blind spot he and all of the patriarchal instantiations of the archetype of evil have. They are fundamentally impotent. Their power is illusory. He does not truly see the impotence because at this point it is still in the language that he understands — power, with a bit of violence. But knowledge is dawning on Buffy. It is nascent at this point, an epistemological kernel that still needs time to fully germinate, but the Council (with an assist from the Knights of Byzantius and Glory) give Buffy the beginnings of true knowledge of power (a knowledge that the Shadow Men, with an assist from the First provide her again at the Finish).

Buffy sums her conclusions and puts the Council in their place, "There isn't going to be a review. No review. No interrogation, no questions you know I can't answer, no hoops, no jumps ... and no interruptions. See I've had a lot of people talking at me, last few days. People just lining up to tell me how unimportant I am. And I finally figured out why. Power. I have it. They don't. This bothers them." She tells them that Glory, the other dimensional god, had come to her house; not to thrash her or to kill her, but to talk. In the talk, Glory told Buffy that she was inconsequential, unimportant. In this way, the Council and Glory were similar — both whistling through the cemetery because they lacked power and hoped that their "slayer" and their adversary, respectively, didn't recognize her own. Buffy sums it up for the Council, "You didn't come all the way from England to determine whether I'm good enough to be "let back in." You came to beg me to let *you* back in. To give your jobs, your lives, some semblance of meaning again." Nigel, of course, is indignant and interrupts, Oh, this is beyond insolence...." In response, Buffy throws a sword and embeds it inches from his head. As it quivers in the pillar, Buffy reminds them all, "I'm fairly certain I said no interruptions." Then, putting them in the place they know is theirs, she refines for them their world. "You're Watchers. And without a Slayer you're pretty much just watching Masterpiece Theatre.... So here's how it's going to work. You're gonna tell me everything you know. Then you're gonna go away. You'll contact me if and when you have more information."

The Watchers attempt to reassert control, to reassert the power of their ancestors over the Slayer is thwarted and their impotence clear to all. Hidden in this interchange is the kernel of shared power that ultimately overturns the patriarchal archetype. After thwarting the Council, she meets their questions about the qualifications of the Scoobies to meet the Glory challenge by running down the strengths of the *team*. Individual strengths, to be sure, but strengths that are magnified into something far beyond the sum of their parts when in concert. Buffy still views power as power *over*, at least in her assertions to the Council. However, for nearly five seasons, the views of the show have seen the debate over the following sorts of power — power *over* and power *with*. Again, in the fight against Glory, it is power *with* that triumphs. It is this power that the Watchers, the Shadow Men, the First, and Caleb cannot see.

So, let's finish this.

Sides have been drawn in the timeless conflict between Good and Evil and while there have been some defections from one side to the other that have altered our perceptions at the margins of the conflict (Angel, a vampire with a soul; Spike, a vampire with a chip; Faith, a rogue Slayer), the core has remained unchanged. Following the encounter with the Shadow Men, it becomes clear that obvious enemies (Caleb, for example) and the Watcher's Council are all of a piece — instances of a patriarchal archetype, particular incarnations of The First, the power of darkness that seeks to oppress and destroy. It takes a while for Buffy to realize that the battle is fundamentally different than she thought. Buffy, at first, assumes the same role — the General, the Commander, the Master, the "Chosen." Consumed with her own power, she tells the potentials and the Scoobies, "I'm the Slayer. The one with power. And The First has me using that power to dig our graves. I've been carrying you. All of you, too far, too long. Ride's over." When Xander says that they've been waiting on her only because she told them to, that "You're our leader, Buffy. As in 'follow the...'" she responds, "Well from now on, I'm your leader as in 'do what I say.'" However, in this role, Buffy would lose. Only by participating in a sharing of power that radically turns the hierarchical patriarchal power on its head, does Buffy, the Scoobies, and the newly minted Slayers thwart the First.

Caleb is obvious. He is also a subtle and decisive lens. On the one hand, he is an obvious and overt patriarchal actor. From the beginning, he is symbolical representative of a patriarchy, the phallic perversion of which is manifested almost immediately in the "message" he sends to the Slayer, a young girl with a knife in her stomach. He is initially presented as an apparent perversion of sacred symbols and the forces of good, clearly one of the "bad guys." On the other hand, and lest the viewer become comfortable in simply assigning Caleb to the "evil" camp, Whedon uses the very obvious Caleb to unmask that which is less obvious on first viewing but nigh inescapable as Caleb takes the stage and the frightening similarities between "evil" and "good" in this cosmic battle. It is not that Caleb is one of the "bad guys;" rather it is that through Caleb we see that the "good guys" — the Watchers Council, the Shadow Men — are also the "bad guys," perhaps deluded by their own self-importance, but all of a piece nonetheless. They are all part of a patriarchal power that is fundamentally corrupt at its core. While Caleb is a willing, nay joyful servant of the First, the Watchers are perhaps unwitting servants. In Caleb, and the connections between him and the Shadow Men and their descendents, the Watchers, Whedon presents a masterful critique of "the forces of good," even more damning than the critique of the forces of Evil. The kernel of this critique is that patriarchal, hierarchical structure and exercise of power, whoever wields it and to whatever purpose to which they lay claim, is itself merely an expression of the power of darkness, the First Evil.

# PART IV. *BUFFY* AND THE CLASSROOM

# Concepts of Identity When
## *Nancy Drew* Meets *Buffy*

LAUREN SCHULTZ

*I'm cookie dough.*

— *Buffy Summers*

*How is it that I can both "be" one, and yet endeavor to be one at the same time? ... How and where I play at being [a specific identity] is the way in which that 'being' gets established, instituted, circulated, and confirmed. This is not a performance from which I can take radical distance.*

— *Judith Butler*

They may be blondes, but Nancy Drew and Buffy Summers are both stronger and smarter than many of their predecessors in literature, film and television. These girls are able to solve mysteries and outwit their (often male) opponents— if not best them in an out-and-out fight. They come from very different eras— Nancy solves her first cases during the Great Depression of the 1930s, while Buffy is "called" as the Vampire Slayer in the late 1990s— and so they have very different attitudes and methods. While Nancy will ingeniously find and use threads torn from the coat of an assailant to match his clothing, Buffy will observe and critique the "carbon dated" outfit of the suspect while he is trolling for a date. However, despite their differences, the two young women similarly rely on mental prowess and physical strength which are significantly more developed than the talents and abilities of most female characters. They each have a strong sense of their own identity which gives them an unusual and desirable confidence, and for this reason, Nancy and Buffy have been claimed as feminist heroines, role models that illustrate independence and persistence for adolescent girls.

This commonality between Nancy and Buffy, however, can be much more thoroughly interrogated in terms of how each series models the formation of identity, in general, and gender roles, in particular. The discussion can be framed within the fields of feminism and psychology, which have investigated such concepts as rigidity and foreclosure, performativity and fluidity. In the mid–Twentieth century, psychologist Erik Erikson expanded upon the Freudian stages of development, creating separate categories for puberty and young adulthood, and suggesting that the adolescent's central task is to become comfortable with and achieve identity foreclosure (Crain 281–283). This is essentially the notion that although identity formation is a life-long process, young adulthood begins the usual and appropriate time to accept compartmentalized social roles (283). According to the social learning theories developed by Albert Bandura, children and young adults learn a great deal and develop their identities at least in part by imitating the behavior of others (194–6, 208–9), and while young children certainly imitate and learn from their parents at first, as they grow older, "children are spontaneously interested in models whose behavior is slightly more complex than their own" (205). Thus, children and adolescents tend to seek out teenage role models with the expectation that they will demonstrate appropriate behaviors. Bandura's research specifically notes that symbolic models, such as those found in books or on television, are as influential as live models (195) such as parents, teachers and friends; this puts significant pressure on Nancy, Buffy, and other fictional characters to model the behaviors that society has deemed healthy, appropriate, and desirable.

Feminist theory, however, has critiques these accepted psychological concepts, questioning — the ideas that only a certain set of behaviors is appropriate for women and that there is some sort of necessity that women take on rigid, compartmentalized, or permanent social roles. Nancy and Buffy have often been praised for subverting traditional, genteel female roles with their take-charge attitudes and their success in male-dominated spheres, but an examination of the two heroines and series reveals very different underlying conceptions of female identity. Nancy and her friends do not exhibit any role confusion and seem to have already come to the point of what Erikson calls identity foreclosure, since they are each comfortable with their limited, compartmentalized social roles. The characters of *Buffy*, however, are consistently depicted in the midst of being and becoming an individual, an on-going process which can be helpfully examined through the lens of Judith Butler's writings on performative identity. A Butlerian analysis of both the Nancy Drew series and *Buffy* reveals that over the course of the Twentieth Century, fictional role models for female adolescents have become much less rigidly constructed, not only in terms of the roles they can adopt, but the ways in which female characters can renegotiate those roles, due to a new conception of identity as an on-going and fluid performance.

*New Republic* magazine proclaimed in the fall of 1926 that the Twentieth Century was the "Century of the Child" (Rehak 95), and in the early decades, children and teenagers followed characters from the pages of *The Youth's Companion* and *St. Nicholas* magazines (Miller 62) and dime novels like those written by Horatio Alger which featured rags to riches stories (*Drew and Company* 4). As Sherrie A. Inness notes, however, these predecessors to series books were largely intended for boys, and did not provide young girls a very wide range of female characters from which to choose. She writes that, "when a girl or woman did dare to step into an Oliver Optic or Horatio Alger tale, she was likely to be someone's sister or mother, and never had a chance to do much, except, perhaps, to marry the hero" (4). Though it had been proclaimed the "Century of the *Child*," publishers geared dime novels, comics and series paperbacks toward young boys until they realized that girls craved adventure stories as well.

Thus, Nancy Drew was born out of the tradition of the dime novel, conceived by publisher Edward Stratemeyer. In the early part of the century, the Stratemeyer Syndicate was a factory of ideas for children's literature with a network of ghost writers turning out book after book in dozens of series (5), and Stratemeyer sought to capture not only the male but the female reader. By placing female characters into the center of the already successful adventure genre, Stratemeyer helped not only to increase the *number* of girls and women portrayed in children's fiction, but the *type* and *range* of females portrayed as well (Rehak 91). Instead of melodramatic characters, Syndicate fiction featured young women such as the Motor Girls, who loved cars are were ready for adventure, and career-oriented "modern" girls Dorothy Dale and Ruth Fielding (93, 103). With these and other characters, fictional girls escaped domestic settings and began to illustrate for their readers ways in which to be independent, confident, and successful.

The most beloved and long-lasting of Stratemeyer's heroines, however, was and continues to be Nancy Drew, and her character was shaped as per the original plans of the Syndicate's creator. Though he did not live to see the product of his imagination go to print, the character of Nancy more than fulfilled his description for a heroine and a girls' series that was "less about niceties and more about being brave and adventurous" (Rehak 114) than other popular girls' fiction at the time. As early as the 1930s, Nancy was pushing the boundaries of what was considered acceptable or appropriate behavior, leading the way for feminism to begin questioning gender roles nearly a half a century later.

Nancy is a determined and active role model who effortlessly steps into the male-dominated world and gets things accomplished. Critics Kismaric and Heiferman note that

> Convention [and conventional children's literature] has it that girls are passive, respectful, and emotional, but with the energy of a girl shot out of a cannon, Nancy bends convention and acts out every girl's fantasies of power. She performs faultlessly as a bareback rider at the circus. Her beautiful larkspurs win first prize at the annual Blenheim

Charity Flower Show. She sends secret messages by tap-dancing in Morse code. She reads Chaucer in Old English [sic] and drives her blue roadster with astounding skill [8].

Essentially, Nancy is able to overcome convention and do all of these things because she is both physically and mentally adept. She plays tennis and golf well enough to win many a match, and even a championship in *The Haunted Bridge* despite an injured wrist. She rides a horse like an expert; she skis, swims, sails, and scuba dives. Conveniently, all the physical fitness and skills that these leisure activities require mean that Nancy is able to escape whenever she is trapped — in cellars, closets, boats, mines, caves and other uncomfortable places. Nancy's physical capability in these situations demonstrates to readers that young women are able to take care of themselves and can be as independent as males, despite traditional expectations and roles that often dictate otherwise.

Nancy's familiarity with both the sciences and the arts likewise explodes traditional gender expectations— not only can she draw, paint, sing, act, dance, read and speak several languages, but she also has an impressive knowledge of science, history, anthropology and archeology. Since Nancy is presented with a wide variety of clues to decipher and must sometimes go undercover, she finds her many academic interests and artistic skills are as equally helpful to career in detection as her physical abilities. Thus the character has many opportunities to present an extremely wide range of roles for young women, modeling feminist sensibilities and identities for each new generation that reads the *Nancy Drew* series.

Having mastered all of these skills without regard to their traditional gender affiliations, it seems that Nancy is able to do anything and be anything, and so she effectively transcends and reconciles contradictory images of femininity. Many fans and critics alike have credited Nancy's ability to reconcile contradictions as a significant part of what endears Nancy to her faithful readers (Sunstein 98); Deborah L. Siegel explores this in-depth, writing:

> The appeal of Nancy Drew ... lay in the character's ability to transcend paradox. During a time when competing codes of feminine conduct raised questions about standards of behavior for women-in-training, an adolescent heroine — half woman, half girl — cruised gracefully onto the scene and offered an ideal of girlhood that resolved all contradiction.... Suspended at the threshold of childhood and adulthood, marrying the Victorian and the modern, Nancy's character bridged many worlds ... [and] "solved" the contradiction of competing discourses about American womanhood by entertaining them all [171].

Nancy certainly began her detective career at a historical crossroads when many women were questioning traditional roles; in the texts, not only does she assume both traditional male and female roles, but she embodies every desirable — and contradictory — social characteristic. She manages to have both a modern sensibility and nearly flawless etiquette that simultaneously aligns her with more traditional values. She hangs out with the teens and yet easily handles herself amongst adults, even instructing the police on their next course of action at times. "Her persona — equal parts girl, boy, teenager, and adult — allows her to blossom in a man's world without giving up the perks of being a girl and frees her and her readers from a prison of gender expectations" (Kismaric and Heiferman, 8). Her ability to transcend these various social boundaries is key to her successful career, both as an accomplished detective and an inspiring fictional heroine, and remains a cornerstone of her identity. But while thousands of readers credit Nancy as their inspiration to pursue more difficult goals, both personally and professionally (Sunstein 104, 111), others have pointed out that Nancy's well-rounded perfection is rather problematic.

Nancy's long list of achievements is quite unrealistic, and many readers have been alienated by her almost inhuman ability to master any and every skill. One woman, speaking at the 1993 Nancy Drew Conference at the University of Iowa, declared that "Nancy Drew was everything I *couldn't* be, *not* everything I *could* be" (101). In other words, one of the problems with such an accomplished heroine is that she is inimitable. Even if a young girl of eighteen had managed to study all of the skills and subjects that Nancy is portrayed has having mastered, it is unlikely that she would be so naturally talented at all of them — yet Nancy is depicted as having a natural aptitude for history, science, art, and most of all, detection. Many readers report that they admired Nancy, for this kind of flair is certainly admirable to a certain degree, but others report that they found Nancy's superior talents and intellect to be ultimately deflating (Sunstein 101, de Jesús 230).

Even more problematic than Nancy's unrealistically wide range of skills, however, is the static nature of her character. The texts are able to present her as possessing these skills *only* because she *already possesses* them; Nancy has already achieved all the knowledge and skills necessary to solve her mysteries, and so the text does not need to devote any time to her acquisition of those skills. Nor does she seem to need time to think through her decisions. She never wrestles with moral questions or dilemmas over the ethical use of her power; Things come too easily to her — the police follow her lead almost entirely without question, her father and friends give her what she wants with little complaint, and even criminals who have resisted police interrogation cave in and confess once Nancy asks them nicely. Consequently, Nancy's example is not helpful in preparing readers for the challenge of developing an identity and constructing a moral schema. Nancy can *inspire* readers with her practically super-human accomplishments, but she can also alienate them, and because of the static nature of her character, she cannot be a truly functional role model.

Unfortunately, the series does not include any more realistic role models either; although Nancy is almost always accompanied on her adventures by her best girlfriends Bess and George, critics have observed that these two function primarily to elevate and emphasize Nancy's character. Kismaric and Heiferman note that Nancy is always "looked up to by her small circle of well-bred, privileged girlfriends" (84) and others have suggested that Bess and George specifically operate as reflections of Nancy's own contradictory nature (Heilbrun 16). Bess echoes Nancy's more feminine traits, while George reflects her more masculine characteristics and modern feminist sensibilities. Thus, the two cousins are not truly three-dimensional characters in their own right. When they are first introduced in *The Secret of Shadow Ranch*, Bess is characterized as a "pretty, slightly plump blonde" (1) and her cousin George as "an attractive tomboyish girl with short dark hair" (1). The first page of the novel quickly establishes them as visual opposites, and the next few paragraphs continue to show that they symbolically contrast each other in many other ways. Bess is easily upset and fearful, while George is blunt, calm, and practical. Once this characterization of the two is established, Bess and George remain locked into their roles, even more static than Nancy herself because they are not able to transcend the gender boundaries established to delineate their personalities. Their continuing imprisonment within symbolic roles is obvious in the introduction to another of the series' early novels:

> "The price [of that perfume] would have discouraged me," spoke up Bess's cousin, dark-haired George Fayne. Her boyish name fitter her slim build and straight-forward, breezy manner. "Twenty dollars an ounce!"
> Blonde, pretty Bess, who had a love for feminine luxuries, laughed. "I *was* extravagant, but I just couldn't resist such yummy perfume. After all, Dad gave me money to buy something frivolous, so I did!" [*Red Gate Farm*, 1].

In this passage, the dark/light and male/female dichotomies that characterize the cousins are quickly reiterated, and their dialogue emphasizes their different temperaments. This novel is only the second in which the characters appear, but forty books later, Bess and George's first appearance in *The Spider Sapphire Mystery* emphasizes the same dichotomies:

> Nancy stopped her convertible in front of Bess Marvin's home. At once the front door opened and the pretty, blond-haired girl came out to the car, carrying a rather large suitcase.

"Hello, Nancy. Please forgive the big bag. No telling how long this mystery might last" [...]

There was little conversation for the next few blocks as they rode to George Fayne's house. The slender-dark haired girl ran down the steps, swinging a small overnight bag which she tossed into the back of the convertible, then hopped in [21].

Here, the size of each girl's suitcase serves as shorthand to convey the cousins' opposite sensibilities, and they are, as always, depicted in visual contrasts as well. In this passage, it is not only their appearance, but the way that they move that helps to establish their differences. Bess is weighed down by her suitcase, while George moves quickly and lightly. Any changes to the series formula and characterizations are always related to the *way* in which the cousins' differences are conveyed, but their identities never waver. The cousins are as static as Nancy, and much more limited.

The fixed nature of these characters' identities can create a sense of comfort for readers who wish to retreat to a safe and stable fictional world, but this sense of stability and fixity is diametrically opposed to Judith Butler's position regarding identity. She writes in the essay "Imitation and Gender Insubordination," that "the prospect of *being* anything ... has always produced in me a certain anxiety" (13), since "identity categories tend to be instruments of regulatory regimes, whether as the normalizing categories of oppressive structures or as the rallying points for a liberatory contestation of that very oppression" (13–14). By this definition and understanding of social roles, Nancy and her friends represent the two ways in which women can become trapped. After all, Bess and George often function to normalize the roles deemed acceptable by traditionally oppressive society, roles which Butler explains must be performed again and again in order to maintain their status as normative ("Imitation" 22–23). As already discussed, Nancy herself is a feminist rallying point and occupies a greater number of roles than her friends are allowed, but has also been ultimately limited by her static identity.

In contrast to the identities of Nancy and her friends, which are constructed from fixed and compartmentalized social roles, Butler conceives of identities as flexible constructions that are created and maintained through an on-going performance; she writes that "the 'I' is the site of repetition ... the 'I' only achieves the semblance of identity through a certain repetition of itself" (18). An individual's performance can therefore either reinforce or renegotiate the sense of identity that he or she has previously established, and that is why "this is not a performance from which I can take radical distance" (18). An identity is built and then maintained through repetition; "being" is a constant process and struggle in which every choice can have profound consequences for an individual. A functional role model, then, would demonstrate a series of choices, some of which would maintain the character's current and established personality traits, and other choices which would alter their identity over time.

In contrast to Nancy, Bess, and George, the female characters of *Buffy the Vampire Slayer* are consistently depicted as struggling between competing values and feminine roles in their attempt to construct and maintain a coherent identity. Buffy, her sister, closest friends and larger peer group are all functional role models, so the text is able to illustrate multiple ways of performing identity. Although Butler speaks of identity categories as stumbling blocks (14), the various roles performed by *Buffy* characters could be seen as building blocks instead. Each character is engaged throughout the series in constructing an identity out of the various roles that they play. The idea that an individual must put together these building blocks (roles) to form a coherent identity is not out of line with Butler's desire to resist fixed constructions; after all, she acknowledges that "any consolidation of identity requires some set of differentiations and exclusions" (19). It is simply the ability to *reconfigure* that identity construction which Butler values so highly, and this is an ability that the text of *Buffy* demonstrates through multiple characters.

*Buffy* foregrounds the process of identity building at different ages, and during the later seasons, when most of the cast has reached young adulthood, the show uses Buffy's younger sister Dawn to refocus on the confusion of early adolescence. Her first line on the show, in "Real Me," is, "Nobody knows who I am. Not the real me," and she continues her speech with a somewhat unsuccessful attempt to define who she is—against the competing example of her older sister. Dawn is both determined that she is not at *all* like Buffy, and paradoxically, that she could be a *better* Buffy. She says, "*I* could so save the world if somebody handed me superpowers ... but I'd think of a cool name and wear a mask to protect my loved ones, which Buffy doesn't even." Dawn's search for her identity is dramatized through the revelation that she is not just a regular teenage girl, but The Key—a mystical ball of energy that unlocks the gateways between dimensions. This upsetting discovering shows Dawn that her previous conceptions of her own identity have been false, and she is left with feelings of confusion, emptiness and futility. She lies in bed, refusing to go to school. She burns her diaries and destroys her possessions, markers of her previous specific identity. She must ultimately reconstruct her identity through deliberate decisions and performances, but first she must discover all that she can about her origins. As a last resort, she makes cuts in each of her arms, watching the blood flow and demanding, "This is blood, isn't it? It can't be me. I'm not a key. I'm not a thing.... What am I? Am I real?

Am I anything?" ("Blood Ties"). In burning her treasured diaries and cutting herself, she makes radical breaks with her former self; the diaries had been a tool that she had used to construct herself on a linguistic level, and her body was the physical form which she associated with her past identity, a lie that she wanted to strip away. After this radical break, she is left with few illusions and must then begin the process of reconstructing a new identity for herself.

In the sixth season, Dawn flounders a great deal in this identity building process; feeling abandoned after her mother's death, she begins to shoplift and develops a resentful attitude toward her equally floundering older sister. By the last season, however, Dawn has constructed a more mature and stable identity — in part due to Buffy's increased attention and guidance. The finale of the sixth season has Buffy and Dawn fighting and clawing their way out of the ground together, and the seventh season episode opening likewise shows the sisters training and fighting together, implying that between the seasons Buffy has made good on her promise to stop trying to protect her little sister, and instead show her the world ("Grave"). Overall, Dawn is portrayed as a much stronger, more capable person by this time, something that Xander notices and praises in the episode "Potential." He acknowledges that she handles power and responsibility well, and that she is a hard worker despite her lack of superpowers. When viewed in the light of her earlier irresponsible and flippant behaviors, it is clear that this is an identity she has slowly constructed over time, through repeated performances. Though some viewers find Dawn aggravating, a careful comparison between the ways in which she and Buffy behave, each at the age of fifteen, reveals remarkable similarities. Especially in the first two seasons, Buffy herself is often whiny and selfish; on one occasion, Giles sees fit to remark on her immaturity, and she replies with a great deal of snark, "You know why? I *am* immature. I'm a teen. I have yet to mature" ("What's My Line? Part One," (2009). When scenes of Dawn from the fifth and sixth season are juxtaposed with these sorts of earlier exchanges, which show Buffy at resentful odds with authority figures, it becomes clear that Dawn's whiny and selfish nature is an important parallel to Buffy herself. Because her presence allows the show to return somewhat to its former focus on early adolescence, her character brings the viewer new insight into Buffy, and in similar ways, they are both excellent role models specifically because they begin their trajectories on the show as a whiny spoiled girls who slowly build their more responsible, mature identities.

Viewers can also follow the trajectory of Willow, who is fairly naive and disempowered when she first meets Buffy, but ultimately becomes a powerful heroine with a complicated narrative of identity construction. Her progression as a character over seven seasons is so complex that for the purposes of the current discussion, it will be helpful to examine her development through a narrower lens: her interactions with her romantic partners. When Willow first meets Buffy in "Welcome to the Hellmouth," she is too shy to make more than "a few vowel sounds" around a boy but is soon inspired by Buffy's advice to "Seize the moment, 'cause tomorrow you might be dead." Over the first two seasons, Willow slowly grows more confident by following Buffy's advice and example, and she eventually ends up in a fairly successful romantic relationship with Oz. I judge Willow and Oz's relationship as "fairly successful" since the ultimate demise of that relationship was due to Oz's werewolf nature and subsequent departure. It is debatable whether or not Willow would have eventually broken up with Oz to be with Tara had he not initially departed and given the opportunity to grow closer, and so I judge the success of the Willow/Oz relationship without regard to Tara's presence. In this relationship, it is not infrequent that Willow takes the lead—initiating their first kiss in "Phases" and even suggesting that the two have sex in "Amends." These self-assured actions would have seemed unbelievable to the Willow that appeared in the first episodes of the show; when comparing the two as though they were different people, the change between them seems remarkable—and yet, Willow has so slowly and subtly altered the performance of her identity from day to day that the changes she makes seem natural and believable. Eventually, after Oz has left Sunnydale, Willow has enough confidence in herself and her own identity to choose a lesbian relationship, and fully takes the lead in that relationship with Tara. She is often depicted as the more powerful and dominant of the two, both with magicks and in their other interactions.

It becomes more obvious by the sixth season, however, that Willow's self-confidence is not as stable as Buffy's, something that is foreshadowed in a set of parallel scenes from "Nightmares" and "Restless" that are particularly relevant to the discussion of performative identities. In both sequences, Willow's nightmares about stage performance are literally enacted, and while each situation has different supernatural causes, Willow's nightmares are strikingly similar. In the first season episode, Willow suddenly finds herself backstage at a concert hall, dressed in a silk kimono and receiving instructions from the stage manager. "There's an ugly crowd out there tonight," he tells her. "All the reviewers showed up." In the background, the announcer's voice announces her as "the world's finest soprano." "But I—I didn't learn the words," Willow stutters, stepping back from the curtain with a terrified look on her face. She is, in essence, saying that she lacks the verbal skills to perform the identity of the soprano, and this can be read as a reflection of her larger fear—that she will fail in the performance of her own identity. The similar sequence from "Restless" begins in the same way; Willow finds herself backstage before a performance. This time, however, she is not wearing a costume, only the clothes that she had on in the previous scene. In contrast, everyone around her is wearing elaborate costumes—she passes people in a soldier's uniform and a princess's gown before Harmony and Buffy hurry up to her, dressed as a Swiss maid and a 1920s flapper. This emphasizes the idea that Willow feels herself incapable of performing an interesting and valuable part amongst her friends and peers. This continues to become more apparent throughout the dream sequence; Riley steps up next, wearing full cowboy get-up, and tells her, "Well, you showed up late, or you'd have a better part!" Because of his big grin, it is easy to see that he is comfortable performing his role, but Willow's face reflects her confusion. She does not seem to have a part at all, since she is dressed in her normal clothing. Yet, this is apparently not true, because a moment later, Buffy whispers to her, "Your costume is perfect. Nobody's going to know the truth—you know, about you." Her friend's comment concisely reveals Willow's biggest fear—that her performance of identity will fail, and that she will be revealed as weak and uninteresting.

Willow imagines there is an inherent difference between herself and her friends—that they are comfortable assuming different roles, while she obviously feels off-balance in this environment. "I was given to understand that a drama class would have, you know, *drama class*. We haven't even rehearsed! ... I just think it's really early to be putting on a play, I don't even know what—"and in the unfinished line, she may have been about to say, "I don't even know what *part I have*." Willow, after all, makes the most dramatic switches of any of the main characters on *Buffy*, and while some of her character develops through a slow progression, the show sometimes emphasizes the idea that Willow has changed too quickly. This particular judgment is often connected to Willow's move into use of more complicated and dangerous magicks. While her ability to move between roles could make her a more flexible person and therefore a more functional and helpful role model, she does not seem to have given herself enough time to become comfortable with any one identity performance. She has moved so rapidly between roles that she is now unsure of her part in the play.

The backstage scene from "Restless" also reenacts the instructions that Willow received from the stage manager in "Nightmares." Buffy first echoes some of the same lines, telling Willow that, "the place is packed! Everybody's here! Your whole family's in the front row, and they look really angry." Then Giles appears, taking on the role of the stage manager, and telling the cast, "Everyone that Willow's ever met is out in that audience—including all of us—that means we have to be perfect. Stay in character, remember your lines, and energy! Energy! Energy!" This emphasizes yet again not only does Willow feel incapable of maintaining a consistent performance of her own identity, but that there is a pressure on her to be perfect, with little room to make a mistake. She feels that she must always remember to "stay in character" and never falter, but the show is careful to counter her fear and demonstrate that because identity is performative, each moment gives an individual a new chance to recreate him or herself.

Through Willow's own struggle with powerful magic, which temporarily leads her into a morally ambiguous position, she becomes one of several characters who illustrate the process of reconstructing an identity once negative choices have influenced a person's character. By season six, Willow has become too dependent on both her magical skills and her relationship with Tara to believe in her own self-worth outside of those roles. After Tara is killed, she breaks down and admits that she believes "the only things I had going for me ... were the moments—just moments—when Tara would look at me and I was wonderful" ("Two to Go"). After her cataclysmic breakdown at the end of the sixth season, Willow is shown reconstructing her identity based on roles other than her magical skill, illustrating how performances of identity can be altered. Her rehabilitation in the seventh season is depicted as emotionally challenging, and therefore illustrates something that the Nancy Drew series overlooks almost entirely — that an identity is not simply the activities in which a person engages and how well they perform, but a moral outlook and an overall attitude toward life which must be built with a complex set of beliefs and preferences. Willow's particular choices which *Buffy* depicts as negative are an extremely helpful aspect of the text because they show adolescent viewers that while all choices have consequences, they do not limit a person to a certain identity. Willow's struggle to construct and reconstruct her identity is therefore an extremely helpful model for young women; her character illustrates that while power is a challenging and sometimes dangerous thing to wield, a carefully constructed moral outlook helps an individual to make responsible decisions and create a desirable identity.

Finally from amongst the various role models on *Buffy*, there is Buffy herself, whose personal growth and change over seven seasons demonstrates a concept of performance that is much more fluid than Nancy Drew's static identity. Buffy's role as the Slayer could be conceived as the very kind of fixed identity that distresses Judith Butler; at times, her superhero status certainly seems to be one of those "identity categories [that] tend to be instruments of regulatory regimes" ("Imitation"). As the Slayer, she is required to face many dangerous obligations, and the time commitments of her calling limit her other activities and choices. Yet Buffy consistently resists being trapped into a fixed identity; she may not be able to escape being the Slayer, but when she realizes that she cannot break away from her responsibilities, she seeks to redefine the meaning and office of the Slayer itself. She insists again and again to numerous authorities, pseudo-authorities, and opponents that she will not be defined by the role of Slayer, but that she will instead define the role for herself. This positions Buffy as beyond the control of a fixed identity, strong enough to redefine and move between roles—and indeed, shatter those roles altogether, as she does in the finale of season seven. So radically does she alter the role of Slayer by sharing her power that the end of the series is really a beginning—of Buffy's newfound freedom to create an entirely new identity for herself. In the final shot of the show, Buffy is standing and looking into the rising sun, as though the horizon reminds her that she no longer has to perform the role that has constricted her for seven seasons ("Chosen").

Before this freedom, however, Buffy resists becoming a fixed character and unrealistic model in a variety of ways. It is especially helpful and important to compare Buffy with Nancy on some of these points, since as the main characters, their identities are central to and help to shape the structure of the overall texts. While Nancy is another Mary Poppins, "practically perfect in every way," Buffy lacks talent in many areas, and fails consistently. While fighting, she is verbally and physically suave, but in social situations, she often lacks the same verbal grace and is unable to stay convincingly under cover, even for a few minutes. She does not seem able to satisfy her mother, teachers, principal, or The Watchers Council very often. She is not a very good substitute parent, and cannot even "hold onto" a boyfriend. Additionally, as already noted, her one special "talent" or position—that of the Slayer—is, in fact, what isolates Buffy and sabotages the other interests and pursuits in her life, such as cheerleading ("The Witch"). Nancy's many skills earn her praise and admiration, while Buffy's skills as the slayer go overlooked in mainstream society, or are seen as deviant behavior. Further, this deviance from the norm cannot be a passing thing, but rather is a pattern that is likely to continue into the future. As Dawn observes, "Buffy's never gonna be a lawyer, or a doctor. Anything big..." and when Xander insists that being the Slayer is "way bigger," Dawn is astute enough to know that in many ways, Buffy may be condemned to mediocrity ("Doublemeat Palace"). In spite of her failures and certain mediocrities, however, Buffy still manages to save the world many times, and the fact that succeeds is all to her credit; Nancy's success comes without a personal price tag (and in fact, often gets charged to Daddy's credit card), but in order for Buffy to save the world and raise her sister, she must give up the things she loves one by one throughout the years. The show's insistence that heroine be consistently thwarted in her real-world success is the complete opposite from Nancy's customary successes, and demonstrates the difficulties in constructing and performing an identity.

Buffy also helpfully models another aspect of constructing an identity; viewers are able to watch her construct an ethical philosophy as she seeks to define right and wrong for herself. Over the course of the series, she comes to an understanding of the world as a complex, terrible, wonderful place, and all facets of her perspective prove to be crucial to Buffy's navigation through life's events, especially her existential crisis in season six. Her depression and moral ambiguity is perhaps an even more crucial model than Willow's struggle to reconstruct her identity, given that Buffy has what is arguably the strongest self-confidence and most stable identity of any of the show's characters. Buffy certainly changes in some ways over the seven seasons, but her most important preoccupations, character traits, and guiding convictions remain the same throughout the show. Even at Buffy's darkest moments in the sixth season, when she believes she is no longer acting like herself, the fact that she can compare her current actions—such as having sex with Spike—to a set of behaviors that she believes to be inherently "Buffy" suggests that the character indeed has a stable identity. Prior to this crisis, she has performed this identity enough to be convinced of its permanence, and so she is able to insist that there must be something wrong with her once she has returned from the dead—otherwise she would not be engaged in a relationship that disturbs her so much. As she begins to break down, she says to Tara, "This just can't be me, it isn't me. Why do I feel like this? Why do I let Spike do those things to me?" ("Dead Things") Here, Buffy is convinced that there is a baseline "me," from which her current behaviors deviate. But Buffy's depression and sexual relationship simply reflect that no person has a totally coherent identity—no one can perform a role exactly the same way at every moment. Buffy is simply human, and her various struggles throughout the seven seasons show that even a strong woman will encounter hardships and failures, but that the most important part of constructing an identity is perseverance. As K. Dale Koontz observes, in Joss Whedon's world, "redemption ... must involve sincere repentance coupled with *ongoing action* ... it is the *continued attempt* to do right towards [sic] others that is truly important" (144, emphasis mine) despite whatever an individual may have done. Although Buffy may seem to give up on herself during a part of the sixth season, she ultimately chooses to continue fighting.

Because that choice restores her to her former identity, it can be said that over the course of the show, Buffy undergoes a process of maturation more than alteration. This is a process that she herself sums up with the explanation that "I'm cookie dough. I'm not done baking. I'm not finished becoming whoever the hell it is I'm gonna turn out to be. I make it through this, and the next thing, and the next thing, and maybe one day I turn around and realize I'm ready. I'm cookies" ("Chosen"). This explanation strengthens the idea that Buffy has held onto the core of her identity throughout the show, despite some minor changes in her performance of identity; cookie dough, after all, does not change while baking — it simply becomes more firm, until it is ready to eat. The chocolate chips are still there, though a little melty — but the main difference is that the batter isn't gooey any more. So, Buffy's metaphor for her identity and personal growth is quite accurate: the changes she undergoes throughout seven seasons do not really alter the core of who she is — they solidify her character. She is given a chance to re-evaluate the ways in which she performs her identity, and ultimately reaffirms most of her original choices. Her commitment to family, friends, and the safety of the world remains intact, despite the constant enticements for her to abandon these difficult responsibilities.

Buffy, along with the other characters on the show, illustrate Butler's assertion that "how and where I play at being [a specific identity] is the way in which that 'being' gets established, instituted, circulated, and confirmed" (18). Each of the show's characters demonstrate the kinds of investments and consequences that are involved in the act of identity-building. Examining *Buffy* through Butler's theories of performativity reveals some of the changes in mass media over the course of the Twentieth century, specifically the ways in which literature, film and television model adolescent identity. Butler insists that "is not a performance from which I can take radical distance" (18), and while the Nancy Drew Series and other young adult mass media have left teens without functional models of identity performance in the past, *Buffy* recognizes that identity-building carries great personal consequences. The show does not depict people within the confines of static constructions, but gives each viewer the opportunity to think of identity-building as on-going — a process in which most people are "not done baking."

## Works Cited

Brown, B. Bradford, Reed W. Larson and T.S. Saraswathi, eds. *The World's Youth: Adolescence in Eight Regions of the Globe.* New York: Cambridge University Press, 2002.

Butler, Judith. *Gender Trouble.* New York: Routledge, 1999.

_____. "Imitation and Gender Insubordination." *Inside/Out: Lesbian Theories, Gay Theories.* Ed. Diana Fuss. New York: Routledge, 1991. 13–31.

Crain, William. *Theories of Development: Concepts and Applications.* Englewood Cliffs, NJ: Prentice Hall, 2000.

de Jesús, Melinda. "Fictions of Assimilation: Nancy Drew, Cultural Imperialism, and the Filipina/American Experience." Ed. Sherrie A. Inness. *Delinquents and Debutantes: Twentieth-Century American Girls' Cultures.* New York: New York University Press, 1998.

Heilbrun, Carolyn G. "Nancy Drew: A Moment in Feminist History." *Rediscovering Nancy Drew*. Ed. Carolyn Stewart Dyer and Nancy Tillman Romalov. Ames: University of Iowa Press, 1995. 11–21.

Inness, Sherrie A. "Introduction." *Nancy Drew and Company: Culture, Gender, and Girls' Series*. Ed. Sherrie A. Inness. Bowling Green, OH: Bowling Green State University Popular Press, 1997. 1–13.

Keene, Carolyn. *The Secret of Red Gate Farm*. New York: Grosset & Dunlap, 1989.

_____. *The Secret of Shadow Ranch*. New York: Grosset & Dunlap, 1993.

Kismaric, Carole, and Marvin Heiferman. *The Mysterious Case of Nancy Drew and The Hardy Boys*. New York: Simon & Schuster, 1998.

Koontz, K. Dale. *Faith and Choice in the Works of Joss Whedon*. Jefferson, NC: McFarland, 2008.

Levine, Elana. "*Buffy* and the 'New Girl Order': Defining Feminism and Femininity." Ed. Elana Levine and Lisa Parks. *Undead TV: Essays on Buffy the Vampire Slayer*. Durham, NC: Duke University Press, 2007.

Miller, Leslie R. "The Power of Black and White: African Americans in Late-Nineteenth Century Children's Periodicals." *Defining Print Culture for Youth: The Cultural Work of Children's Literature*. Ed. Anne Lundin and Wayne A. Wiegand. Westport, CT: Libraries Unlimited, 2003.

Lotz, Amanda D. *Redesigning Women: Television after the Network Era*. Urbana: University of Illinois Press, 2006.

Rehak, Melanie. *Girl Sleuth: Nancy Drew and the Women Who Created Her*. New York: Harcourt, 2005.

Siegel, Deborah L. "Nancy Drew As New Girl Wonder: Solving It All for the 1930s." Ed. Sherrie A. Inness. *Nancy Drew and Company: Culture, Gender, and Girls' Series*. Bowling Green, OH: Bowling Green State University Popular Press: Popular Press, 1997.

Stevenson, Gregory. *Televised Morality: The Case of Buffy the Vampire Slayer*. Dallas, TX: Hamilton, 2003.

Sunstein, Bonnie S. "'Reading' the Stories of Reading: Nancy Drew Testimonials." *Rediscovering Nancy Drew*. Ed. Carolyn Stewart Dyer and Nancy Tillman Romalov. Ames: University of Iowa Press, 1995. 95–112.

Walker, Renee. *The Dark Side of River Heights: Observations of the Untold and the Unflattering*. Lulu, 2004.

# The High School Education of Buffy Summers

## KEITH FUDGE

Joss Whedon has never made a secret of his motive for the character of Buffy Summers. In so many words, Whedon said, "I wanted a scene where the petite blond went into the dark alley with the big bad — and then she kicked its ass." But even in creating "the chosen one who would save the world," Whedon gave us so much more: a feminist role model, a fashion-conscious teen, a purveyor of new language, and whether he realized it or not, a figure who represented how America's youth struggles with the public school experience both academically and socially. And, what is even more interesting concerning the last of these characteristics is the fact that Whedon never attended a public school but has captured the experience with remarkable insight.

In a June 2003 interview, Joss Whedon spoke of his own secondary education noting the differences he witnessed in private education in America and in England. During the interview he also noted that today American education stresses testing that does not include what he called, "your grown-up understanding of what you're doing," and he went on to add that "Testing — multiple-choice, memorization, standardization — is the death of American education." Interestingly enough, in this same interview, Whedon also acknowledged that he was intrigued by lectures on the arguments that co-education is bad for girls in the present state of the country. Also, he noted a feeling of loneliness in his all-male private-school life, but added, "I was lonely, but I was just as lonely when I was around girls as when I wasn't." Another interesting comment regarding his time in school dealt with a feeling of being "the other," a feeling subsequently experienced by many of the characters in *Buffy the Vampire Slayer*. Furthermore, when asked if he ever felt as if he were different from anyone else, he responded, "I've always felt that I was the outsider in every group I've ever been in, except my staff."

In Whedon's fictional public education settings of Sunnydale High, and later of UC–Sunnydale, the concept of "the outsider" and his or her struggles is also consistently present in episodes of *Buffy*, but it is even more pronounced and prevalent in the high-school experience of Buffy and the Scooby Gang. Ultimately, in Buffy Summers, Joss Whedon gave viewers a character who must embrace (or suffer) education vocationally, academically, and socially, and soon after her arrival at Sunnydale High, viewers begin to recognize the conflict that Buffy must endure in becoming a good slayer and learning from her watcher (Giles), and trying to excel academically and socially.

Now while this scenario may seem like enough pressure for any teen, Whedon takes the character of Buffy Summers one step further because upon closer examination it becomes apparent that soon into her first year at Sunnydale High School that Buffy takes on an even more daunting task: Not only is she a slayer, a student, and (when occasion allows) a typical teenage girl, but she also soon becomes the teacher, the facilitator, and the "decider" in terms of high-stakes situations. And, all of these roles converge upon Buffy after little more than a few hours in her new school. Consequently, when viewers go back into the first season of the show they will begin to see where all the roles that Buffy plays define themselves and subsequently redefine themselves in terms of her situations.

For instance, in the first episode of season one of *Buffy*, we find Joyce Summers dropping off her high school sophomore daughter for the first day of school in Sunnydale and offering her this cheerful piece of advice, "Honey, try not to get kicked out" ("Welcome to the Hellmouth"). While this might be an appropriate suggestion to some children, how could this plea possibly relate to a 15/16-year-old girl who seems fit for anything rather than for expulsion? Later, viewers realize that Joyce's message has intense meaning because of Buffy's history, so to speak, and that her move to Sunnydale is the result of the divorce of her parents, her mother's new job, and primarily the fact that she has been expelled from her last school for burning down the gym.

Upon her arrival, she meets with Principal Flutie who promises her a fresh start, even going to the point of tearing up her permanent record (that is until he reads it), and yet still tells her that she will have every opportunity to excel at Sunnydale High while he clumsily tapes her permanent record back together. Thus begins the story of Buffy Summers at Sunnydale High School, arrived at the Mouth of Hell to save the world; however, as previously noted, it is not just a journey for Buffy as a slayer, but also as a high-school student who must also conform to all the pressures of academia, socialization, and most importantly in the eyes of her peers, as the totally cool "new kid" in school.

It does not take Buffy long to adapt to her surroundings, and in fact, she becomes academic rather quickly in terms of jargon and vocabulary. At one point she refers to her new watcher, Giles, saying, "You're a textbook with arms and legs," and when speaking of vampires she adds, "It's not like I'm going to get extra-curricular with them." Yet, as we endure random vamps and an introduction to the "big bad" of season one, The Master, it is at the end of the episode when Giles tells her that it (the bad guys) will get worse and at that point Buffy replies, "Well, I gotta look on the bright side; maybe I could still get kicked out of school." While Buffy says this comment half-heartedly, even teasingly while walking away with Xander and Willow, we see that school is a priority for Buffy, either good or bad, and that she sees success or failure in it as a monumental event.

There has been notice of "Buffy-demics" from others as well, and in her article, "The Buffy Factor: What Educators Could Learn From the Vampire Slayer," Laura Thomas shows that Buffy is not only a role model for teenage girls but further asserts that Buffy is in fact *the* ideal role model for teachers and administrators, particularly since the profession is dominated by the number of women in teaching positions. Thomas writes:

> Education, a field dominated by women (at least at the front lines), carries with it an expectation of passivity, respect for the hierarchy, and obedience. (All traditional values of womanhood.) We are to do as we're told. Those who push back are labeled troublemakers, ignored, ridiculed, or fired. Buffy is atypical in our society in that she is recognized as the unquestioned leader. No one doubts her authority, her right to make decisions when the stakes are high. She is the one who will suffer the most if the choice is a bad one, she must pay the cost of failure; therefore, she is given the right — the responsibility — to make the pivotal decisions [26–27].

In this regard, Buffy is the ideal teacher or better yet, the perfect candidate to be a building-level, or district-level administrator, and her "the vamp stops here" mentality means that she is willing to put herself on the line to fight for her students and teachers (better known as her family and her friends) to prevent each impending apocalypse.

In a sense, Christine Jarvis also echoes Thomas's claims even though Jarvis is speaking of Buffy's penchant for fashion and self deprecation as she writes further down the line in season four that, "Buffy's resistance to authority and hierarchy is also grounded in her gender. She uses stereotypically feminine approaches to fashion to establish identity and autonomy ... yet the viewer knows she is much stronger and more skillful than any of the soldiers" [in the Initiative] (6). In fact, this claim is also reinforced in Buffy's high-school years but, is best seen as the story plays out in season seven when Buffy becomes the teacher/administrator/ leader of an army of slayers (same-sex education).

Consequently, these two notions of gender and authority are tied together by Popular Culture specialist Cammie Sublette, who in a recent interview in discussing gender issues regarding Buffy's role as both student and teacher stated, "If part of the reason that Buffy isn't a traditional student is her gender, and part of the reason that she isn't a traditional girl is her authority, then she is something of an educational trailblazer—certainly an "engaged learner," but one who will only work with the system if it is amenable to her strengths." Sublette goes on to add, "I've long thought that one of the reasons that feminist philosophers tend to be so good (and trailblazing) in educational theory, especially anti-foundationalist educational theory, is that they never succeeded in the masculine educational paradigm—bell hooks says as much in her, *Teaching to Transgress*." Buffy seems to be the same kind of learner and teacher—she is engaged and engaging but she's not very good at sitting down, shutting up, and listening to a blowhard pontificate" (interview). Giles, unlike other members of the Watchers Council who try to control Buffy at one time or another, seems to recognize this characteristic in Buffy immediately and deems it is apparent that the "slayer's handbook" will do not good.

Buffy's conflict with learning to be a "better or more formal" slayer and her flirtations with academic endeavors is further obvious in early episodes of season one, just as are her traits of teaching and leadership. For instance, concerning the former, she leaves the library in a flash after her initial meeting with Giles, and later when Willow suggests that she and Buffy study together in the library, Buffy says, "That place just kinda gives me the wiggins." However, regarding the latter, as we all know, the library is precisely where Buffy receives her education and where in turn she delivers leadership, instruction, and guidance. It is where research is done, collaborative learning is achieved, and where realizations both good and bad occur. It is also the beginning and the ending of high school for Buffy, starting with her meeting with Giles and culminating with her destruction of the mayor and the school on graduation day. It is where high-stakes decisions are made and yet it is where Buffy has such practical revelations such as, "God, I'm so mentally challenged!" But, it is precisely moments such as this one where Buffy "turns the corner" and shows just how adept she is towards learning and leading, even as an unconventional student or teacher.

One strong example where Buffy shows an affinity for being a student with a different learning style occurs during the first episode where she meets Giles at The Bronze and he impresses upon her the need to be acutely aware of her surroundings. At this point, he presses her further to see if she can recognize a vampire in the crowd, and she does it almost immediately; however, not in the way that Giles believes a good slayer should spot a vampire by using honed skills and instincts. Instead, Buffy uses her sense of today's world commenting on the vampire's clothes and replying, "only someone living underground for 10 years would think that was still the look." Consequently, it is safe to say that Buffy is a resourceful student who relies on getting the right answer without regard to the process by which it arrives. In her world as a slayer — what does it matter as long as the bottom line is that bad guys get staked? The answer is the only thing that matters.

For Giles's part, he does have faith in Buffy's abilities to be a slayer, but her interactions with other teachers produce little in the way of encouragement towards Buffy's success in the classroom; however, there is one teacher during Buffy's sophomore year that shows faith in her academic abilities. In the episode, "Teacher's Pet," Buffy's Biology instructor, Dr. Gregory, takes an interest in Buffy on an academic level, offering her encouragement that she can do well in school and that she has the abilities to succeed in her efforts. Ironically, just as Buffy experiences this vote of confidence and faith from her instructor, Dr. Gregory is eaten by the "she-mantis" who becomes his permanent substitute teacher. Buffy is obviously hurt a great deal by Dr. Gregory's death because she cries when she learns of his passing; however, his death does not go to waste for in her moment of suffering, the roles of slayer and student intersect as Buffy pours her energy into the type of homework that Dr. Gregory encouraged and learns how to better kill demons who can do this type of damage to the people she cares about. Interestingly enough, it is Buffy who discovers the answer of how to stop the she-mantis and becomes the teacher, instructing Giles to record the sounds that will destroy it. On a side note there is an ironic twist here toward the entire educational system. In a sense there is a symbolic devouring that occurs within education. On one level, teachers devour students figuratively as they move from year to year hustling them in and out, and in this episode there is also a literal devouring of students by the she-mantis after she mates with them (an obvious reference to teachers who sexually prey on their students). Also, in another episode in season one entitled, "The Pack," we see the opposite type of feeding take place as a group of students turned hyenas literally devour Principal Flutie thus symbolizing how the public school system also feeds on those who both attend them and run them. But perhaps the most dramatic example of how schools and the people who inhabit them can have a devastating effect on students is seen in the episode, "Out of Sight, Out of Mind," in which a student named Marci Ross literally becomes invisible because she was a student ignored by students, teachers, and the system at large, and it takes Buffy, who ultimately had the best sense of how to see "the other," to recognize Marci's fate since she herself is an outcast in so many ways. Consequently, in the episode, "Teacher's Pet," as well as other episodes taking place at school in the first season, Buffy uses her personal sense and her academic skills in conjunction with her slayer abilities to save the day, and in "Teacher's Pet" by saving Xander from a horrible fate her work can be seen as ultimately paying tribute to the teacher who had faith in her as a "regular" student. In addition, in the later episode concerning the "disappearance" of Marci Ross, Buffy combines her slayer abilities with her own characteristics as the "other" (regarding her loneliness and despair in the inability to have a normal life) to discover what happened to Marci.

Buffy's unconfident and uncomfortable nature toward learning "bookish" things also comes into play regarding romance. In the episode, "Never Kill a Boy on the First Date," Buffy learns that sometimes cool guys do like smart girls, and she does her best to impress a boy named Owen, by telling him, "I love books; I really love books." And later, when Owen mentions the poet Emily Dickinson, Buffy says, "Emily Dickens; she's great." With her botched reference toward a classic poet, Buffy reaffirms that her worlds of slayer and student collide and that "saving and surviving" as the slayer takes precedence. As a student in the aesthetic and academic world she is simply not in balance, with the latter not receiving a great deal of significance and priority. Also found in this example, is the notion that Buffy only uses academic talk as a ploy to try and "get the guy." However, after saving Owen and the others, Buffy learns the lesson that the best thing she can do is to simply be Buffy, doing the best she can to balance her social, academic, and slayer roles. Coincidentally, in some ways readers can see a distinct similarity of Buffy's character to the character of Huckleberry Finn who also sees more value in the common sense approach in dealing with the world and his own survival rather than the quest of "literary things" which he leaves to his friend Tom Sawyer.

As mentioned, while Buffy generally eschews formal academic study, nonetheless she is a pragmatist, applying real-life scenarios with useful logic to assist her in her work as the slayer. For instance when training with a rod or staff with Giles, she questions why she is using this awkward weapon and says to him, "This is the 20th century; I'm not going to be fighting Friar Tuck." Formality has no place in her world — only the bottom line of how to kill the big bad will work. That is also the way it is with students with different learning styles and wherein how the American system has tried to label those who do not learn in one specific manner under the guidelines of federal programs and mandates. The real reason for Buffy is a bit more urgent — if she doesn't get the answer soon she may die and perhaps the world along with her. In other words, all that matters is the answer in real-life terms and not through abstract theory. And in returning to Laura Thomas's article we see how this notion reinforces why Buffy would be a good role model for teachers and superintendents who often get caught up in special programs or educational theory rather than looking at the real-life issues that face students and teachers. Additionally, we also see how Buffy the student gets easily lost in traditional lecture instruction. When Willow quizzes her, asking Buffy about Reconstruction after the Civil War, Buffy responds that, "Reconstruction began after the construction which was shoddy so that they had to reconstruct" ("Angel"). Additionally, in the episode "Nightmares," one of Buffy's horrible dreams is academic in nature in that she sits for an exam in history where her pencil continues to break and where time accelerates to the point where she has no time to finish the test.

Ironically, it is in the final episode of season one, "Prophecy Girl," that offers an interesting culmination of all of Buffy's worlds wherein Buffy defeats the Master while wearing her elegant "Spring Fling" dress, thus representing the ultimate statement of perseverance as she combines the slayer, the social, and the academic (in a sense) to defeat the big bad at the end of the school year.

Consequently, with the end of the first season, Giles, Buffy, and the Scooby Gang are well on the way to figuring out what could be in store for them in terms of fighting demons, yet they all have much more to learn about relationships, life, loss, and learning. They are also coming to know the "ins and outs" of the school, and the students have a marvelous ally/mentor in Giles who seems to be the type of educator that we are told to be in all those education classes. Regarding the students, Buffy, Willow, Xander, and even Cordelia, are outcasts, yet with Buffy, the issue is compounded with mythic responsibility grounded in real-life leadership and sacrifice — the qualities that we ask of our leaders today. Buffy makes choices based on what she believes is the best thing to do at the moment — that is also how she learns and how she saves the world (a lot). Ironically, it is Principal Snyder in one episode who does not have a clue about his role in the grand design of public education when he says to Giles, "Kids today need discipline. That's an unpopular word today, discipline. I know Principal Flutie would have said that kids need understanding. Kids are human beings. That's the kind of wooly-headed liberal thinking that leads to being eaten. I hate kids" ("Puppet Show"). Principal Snyder is the prime example of how the one in charge is often the most oblivious to his or her surroundings?

Joss Whedon did not place Sunnydale High School on top of the Hellmouth as a coincidence. To borrow the title from Tracy Little's article in terms of life for Buffy and her friends, "high school *is* hell." It ranges from antiquated institutions with boring ineffective teachers and useless classes and curriculum with an emphasis on standardized testing when it could just as easily be a place of empowerment and learning where dedicated administrators, faculty, and students try to make the world a better place, teaching and learning in the best manners possible. It seems as if Buffy Summers attends both types of schools at Sunnydale High, all the while having the awesome responsibilities of being cool, getting the right guy, making good grades, oh yeah, and there is that saving the world from apocalypse issue that she must contend with. Given all that, where is the time for English, Math, History, Science and the endless stream of worksheets? And, in understanding those choices, viewers see her perform as a student and slayer who is far ahead of the game. In fact, they see her as the type of student and leader that allows them to sleep safer with each passing night.

## WORKS CITED

Jarvis, Christine. "Real Stakeholder Education?" Lifelong Learning in the Buffyverse. *Studies in the Education of Adults*: Spring 2005, Vol. 37 Issue 1, pp. 31–46.

Little, Tracy. "High School is Hell": Metaphor Made Literal in *Buffy the Vampire Slayer. Buffy the Vampire Slayer and Philosophy: Fear and Trembling in Sunnydale.* Ed. James B. South, Chicago: Open Court, 2003.

Sublette, Cammie. Interview, 20 May 2008. University of Arkansas Fort Smith.

Thomas, Laura. "The Buffy Factor": What Educators Could Learn from the Vampire Slayer. *Education Week*: 11 June 2003, pp. 25–27.

Wilcox, Rhonda, V. "There Will Never Be a Very Special Buffy": *Buffy* and the Monsters of Teen Life. *The Journal of Popular Film and Television* 27:2 (1989):16.

Wisker, Gina. "Vampires and School Girls: High School Jinks on the Hellmouth." *Slayage 2* (March 2001).

# Keeping *Buffy* in the Classroom

## Tamara Wilson

As the television series text of *Buffy the Vampire Slayer* moves from popular culture to history, it becomes ancient and often embarrassing history for our students. Therefore brief references no longer bring Buffy into the classroom. In the fall of 2007, I brought an entire episode, "Never Kill a Boy on the First Date," to Eng 454 — Literature and Women at Flagler College, St. Augustine, Florida. The class is a senior level course, populated by primarily juniors and seniors who are declared English majors. This particular class was composed of twenty-three women and four men (the highest number of men so far in this bi-annual class). After studying *Madame Bovary, Sense and Sensibility, The Kitchen God's Wife*, Wollstonecraft's *A Vindication of the Rights of Women*, Rich's "Towards a Politics of Location" and Showalter's "Feminism in the Wilderness," among other texts, we viewed "Never Kill" together, engaged in a brief in-class discussion which was followed by online postings: fifteen women posted, but only two men wrote about their experience viewing *Buffy*. Their postings averaged two hundred words (the course requirement is two hundred-fifty words per week). Some students treated the episode with recognition, nostalgia; some "tuned" out. Happily, however, some students did indeed examine the episode in the context of literary analysis.

My hope was to offer this "chapter" of the *Buffy* text as a canvas for an academic response, building on Rhonda Wilcox's assertion that we should perceive episodes of a televised series as we do chapters in a novel (3). The students had access to the online journal, *Slayage*, but I did not specifically direct them to particular essays. My vision of this class's engagement, certainly, was highly influenced by Wilcox's workshops — but they, my students, aren't Buffyologists, so I was disappointed in the reception of the text; in part, it is unreasonable of me to expect them to respond as I do to the text of *Buffy the Vampire Slayer*, but a more effective presentation would have elicited a more energized response. Remedies can be concocted from student responses as well as from the generous feedback of my peers at the 2008 Slayage Conference. I will conclude this essay with a proposed course plan for presenting *Buffy* again.

"Never Kill a Boy on the First Date" is a very early episode in the Buffy-verse. I selected it precisely for its early date because I doubted any students in the class followed the series with academic intent. Most had not followed the series at all. I didn't want to spend a great deal of precious class time on back-story; however, one of the students of this class presented a paper on Buffy and the Gothic at the 2008 Slayage Conference, alongside the first presentation of this essay. She submitted her essay to *Slayage* later that summer. So, I had a teaching assistant in this budding Buffyologist; I should have used her more effectively to inspire the class.

In the first season of the series, in which "Never Kill" appears, the central characters are being defined, defining themselves, etc. Angel is still very much the mystery man and rather superiorly aloof, so Buffy focuses romantically on Owen, also mysterious (to her), but not nearly as inaccessible as Angel. However, she should be focusing on the Brotherhood of Aurelius— but she is "just a girl"— echoing the lyrics of the music that plays as she sees Owen dancing with Cordelia, her rival for Owen's affections, during this episode. Both Buffy's gender and youth are key issues. At the conclusion of this chapter, she feels responsible for Giles' near death and she discontinues her romantic pursuit of Owen because he wants to be "danger man;" she realizes he will endanger not only himself, but all the Scoobies.

I briefly prefaced the text with observations about the nature of a feminist icon, Whedon's assertions about the hero he sought to create and Wilcox's argument for television text as serialized novel. I also noted the issue of female duality, suggested they listen for double-voiced discourse within the text (polysyllabic) and touched again on the Venn diagram of Showalter's essay. Keenly aware I wasn't among fellow Buffyologists, I didn't wish to overwhelm my students with my interpretations, so my comments were no more than five minutes in length.

Immediately following the viewing of "Never Kill," class response was tepid. I do believe that they (and I) are far too seduced by the "boob-tube" aura of television. In other classes, when an entire film is viewed, students treat the experience with more academic rigor than they grant a "TV show." Still, some rallied, bringing forward a connection between Buffy's dilemma and the traditional texts of the course. They did not focus solely on dating, though it was mentioned and later discussed at length in several online postings; instead they quickly focused on examples of "double-voiced discourse" in the *Buffy* text.

This concept had been eagerly discussed in earlier classes as we worked our way through Elaine Showalter's "Feminist Criticism in the Wilderness." Showalter's section on "Women's Writing and Women's Language" notes that in "myths, the essence of women's language is its secrecy" (361); the text of

*Buffy*, rife with secrets, in this episode particularly secrets kept from Owen, vibrantly emphasizes Showalter's intriguing point. However, the most salient connection between Showalter's essay and "Never Kill" is with the final section of her essay — "Women's Writing and Women's Culture." The Venn diagram of two intersecting circles illustrating knowing and unknowing by gender was vastly intriguing to the class. Giles, for all his knowledge, cannot know what it is to be the Slayer. True, he did rebel from his "calling," but his rebellion never threatened to trigger the Apocalypse.

This "unknowing" is heightened in Owen, who, despite his desire to know (what women know). It is important to note his obsession with Emily Dickinson; an obsession that is repeatedly steered away from access to knowledge. Jowett observes, in her liner notes to the chapter titled "New Men," in her text *Sex and the Slayer*, that despite Owen's fixation on the works of Emily Dickinson, he doesn't "get" the bees. She suggests that this lack of understanding implies a "certain naiveté" (204). Once again, another man faces that unknown zone; perhaps the reason Buffy "almost feels like a girl" with Owen is because she is with someone who is almost a boy. Indeed, as my class perhaps already knew, it is hard to be a guy in this world.

In the text of *Buffy*, the fate of the world is intertwined with the challenges of becoming an adult. The complexities of maturation were not dealt with in any detail in any of the traditional feminist texts used in the Literature and Women course. The intensity of student response to this dilemma clearly indicates this is an issue the course should address. This is a promising discovery indeed for the continuation of *Buffy* in the classroom.

Paired with maturation, in the secretive aspect of the Buffy text we see illustrated one of the dilemmas of feminist critique Showalter noted as most worrying — the danger of exclusivism. In the opening paragraphs of her essay, Showalter quotes Nina Auerbach, "Feminist critics seem particularly reluctant to define themselves to the uninitiated" (354). Certainly, it is my hope, and one of the goals of this Literature and Women course, to address and ameliorate this exclusivism. While inclusion is our worthy goal, the image of the Venn diagram remains hauntingly in the background of our best intentions.

However, returning to the student response, those who spoke were lively; there was tittering about Angel and a collective feminine sigh about the challenges of dating, especially at that age; fifteen was treated by my students as "ancient and embarrassing history." However, I was disappointed that unlike other class discussions which usually ended only because the class time ended, this discussion petered out so swiftly and lamely. Perhaps I should acknowledge the understandable reluctance to discuss topics that are too close to students to allow comfortable academic distance. However, I don't allow my students to retreat; we must all, like Buffy, face our demons. I will try to give them better weapons in the future.

After that disappointing discussion, my expectations about the quality of the online responses was not high. However, they were, in general, positive and in the main, academic. The tittering was minimized and the challenges of dating dwelt upon with more energy than during class time—there are things we are clearly more comfortable saying in print than aloud—for girls, dating; as for the boys, one of them worked very hard to see into the no-man's land of the Venn diagram.

Throughout the semester we wrestled with the demands of society upon the women of the texts we examined—in the posts, several students returned to this issue of " the duality women struggle with at all ages. Doing what is required of us or what we have chosen to do and what society expects us to do" as one student expressed in her online post. Another student made a connection between Buffy and Judith Shakespeare of Virginia Woolf's "A Room of One's Own" (38–39), noting the dilemma of love and career for women; another saw the duality of Buffy's existence and compared it to Emma Bovary. This student went on to write her final essay on the topic of duality—but she didn't mention Buffy in her essay. Others were definitely impacted by the time lapse between the first airing of the text and their viewing (ten years), so they really didn't "get what the fuss was all about." To echo Phyllis Chelser in "Letters to a Young Feminist" I can only say, "you must not take [our feminist gains] for granted. (Although it is your right to do so—we fought for that too)" (5). However, one student was far from sanguine about the situation, intriguingly offering, "Buffy chooses safety of the society over a flimsy, teenage impulse. As a woman, I think Buffy will be seen as making the weaker decision NOT to go after Owen rather than heroic because if you have watched any other male-driven super hero show, then men are always considered heroic for not choosing love. Double standard?"

I should note here that a significant number of Flagler College's female students quite openly assert that they are in college to get a degree and then get married. While all choices are our own, societal demands must give us pause, as they did this thoughtful student.

On a slightly different track, one of the avid Buffy watchers recommended the episode "Halloween" in place of "Never Kill a Boy on the First Date." In "Halloween," there are numerous role-reversals as various characters experience how "the other half lives." Notably, there were, notably, no gender switches in that episode. Not until "The Killer in Me" in season seven, as Willow "becomes" Warren, does the series tackle that switch. However, the amount of back story required renders "The Killer in Me" too unwieldy for the time constraints of Literature and Women. Certainly, "Halloween" offers a depth of self-exploration that "Never Kill" lacked the maturity to create.

Finally, one astute, if qualified response: "I was more impressed than I thought I would be, especially the quick-witted dialogue and the feeling I got (maybe this is just me) that the show casts a critical eye towards itself in some ways, through simultaneously participating in and mocking cultural mores; I felt like I was being winked at while I watched." Certainly this student saw the power of Whedon's text that draws Buffyologists. Though I am not sure she enjoyed being winked at; after all, education is supposed to be a serious matter!

From the male perspective, (remember, only a 50 percent response rate), one student tried very hard to view the text from a female perspective, but asserted "...that the feminist implications are perhaps a bit more subtle than Dr. Wilson led me to believe; still, when I *found* them, they are there, strong, and well played." These comments constitute his "literature of witness" of his foray into Showalter's "no-man's land" of the Venn diagram. The other male student avoided the issue of feminism altogether by talking about how great it would be to have a class on television and literature.

In retrospect, I am fairly pleased with the class response to "Never Kill a Boy on a First Date." In pursuit of our goal to keep *Buffy* in the classroom, it is worth noting there was not one note of academic outrage from either my department chair (amused tolerance, yes) nor any student in the class. However, there is this caveat; Flagler College is a conservative institution, so it is unlikely I would be encouraged to offer an entire course on Buffy as some of my fortunate colleagues presently teach.

Also worthy of note here is that despite the fledging quality of this early episode, the pensive students diVenned the complexity of the topic at hand — for us, perhaps it is Whedon's "bring your own subtext"—for them, I hope it was a touch of Rich's "Notes Towards a Politics of Location"— indeed, "who is we?" (1106); how does that challenge balance against the feminine "literature of witness," as we find in Alice Walker's essay, "In Search of Our Mothers' Gardens," "...a personal account that is shared..."(328), so highly respected by many in the feminist movement, myself included? For it was that sympathy of first dates that drew many students into the text of this episode. However, for the men of this course, the challenging rethinking of a phallocentric worldview was, perhaps, their greatest hurdle — a bit harder to promote to my students was that women need to rethink as well. Assumptions and apathy are not gender-specific. Certainly Whedon's "open-image hero," as Early dubbed Buffy in "Staking Her Claim: Buffy the Vampire Slayer as Transgressive Woman Warrior," challenged my students (par. 30). Who do we want in a female hero? And how do the visions of Hollywood pair up with reality?

One male student was rightfully skeptical to challenge that all little girls could grow up to be Buffy, just as he will never grow up to be a basketball player. Clearly, there are limits to the "literature of witness" in fiction. However, it should be noted that Camron's observation from "The Importance of Being the Zeppo: Xander, Gender Identity and Hybridity in *Buffy the Vampire Slayer*," seems right in "how difficult it is—even with the best of intentions— to escape the prevailing hegemony" (par. 1). This effectively echoes Wollstonecraft's assertion that "it is vain to expect virtue from women until they are, in some degree, independent of men" (1133). Indeed, the class frequently wrestled with their frustrations about what they argued was the weakness of the female characters—often, they would say (both male and female), if I were Emma, Elinor or Pearl (*Madame Bovary*, *Sense and Sensibility*, and *The Kitchen God's Wife*, respectively), I would or would not do *x*.

In closing, I offer my final (so far) thoughts on the matter of *Buffy* in the classroom. Certainly the student-recommended "Halloween" episode has the potential for generating discussion about identity and role-playing. Or, building from Cocca's intriguing analysis in "First Word 'Jail,' Second Word 'Bait'": Adolescent Sexuality, Feminist Theories, and Buffy the Vampire Slayer," I consider "The Initiative," which holds this dialogue. Buffy, discerning that Riley holds a rather typical view, says, "You think that boys can take care of themselves and girls can't?" Riley, either unaware that the question is rhetorical, or perhaps, simply embracing the stereotypically masculine view, replies monosyllabically, "Yeah."

Riley, with his traditional mid-western value systems, offers a ready target, for discussion, of course. Indeed, Cocca notes:

> His black-and-white assumptions about gender and power feed into his feelings that she doesn't need him because she is the stronger and he is uncomfortable with that; his assumption is that she should need him and want to need him. As Vint points out, this is problematic for many adolescent girls as there may be some fear among boys about girls who compete with them, or even within society at large of such girls as threatening to an established "traditional" order. In a disruption of stereotypes of both gender and age, Riley feels like the weaker party in the relationship [par. 23].

Or I could widen my offering to something that will discuss the "women of the Buffyverse." Certainly Willow, Faith and Anya reveal a variety of feminist dilemmas. Cocca notes about Willow in particular:

> ... one can read Willow's relationship with Oz in more than one way. Liberal feminists might say she was the vulnerable party because she was the younger party; radical feminists might say the same because

of the "threat of the wolf," and sex radicals might say she was making well-considered decisions about someone she was very close to. But each of these aspects of a situation can be occurring at the same time. As Moss wrote, "Buffy displays the complexities of decisions that teenage girls must make, the tangled threat of their own sexuality they must learn to negotiate. Not content to be 'good' girls or 'bad' girls, the women of Buffy show teenaged sexuality to be the complex, sometimes strong, sometimes confused thing that it is..." [par. 4].

In a lecture I gave at a Unitarian Church in 2004 on *Buffy*, I was surprised by the young women who came up to me wanting to talk about Spike — I had braced myself for a similar onslaught in this class, but none came — as I am not quite sure what to do with Spike myself, I will not use "Seeing Red," powerful though it is as it deals with the, arguably, most tangible and offensive manifestation of masculine dominance, rape.

On the heels of my private investigations into the matter of *Buffy* in the classroom, my colleagues attending my presentation at the 2008 Slayage Conference made the following suggestions. In selecting a text for student consideration, both "Surprise" and "Innocence" were strongly recommended as texts which would spur student response. Both suggestions for guiding the students' investigations with directed readings from the online *Slayage* journal and ready-made handouts were generously offered.

However, I do find it intriguing to note that none of the episodes Buffyologists frequently examine together — "Hush" "The Body" "Once More With Feeling" would be my choice for this course. Is it that, despite Whedon's genius, he is "just a boy;" therefore he cannot enter that "feminine wilderness" effectively enough to have created a definitive "feminist" episode? After this round of investigation, I still have no definite answer, so that question will have to stand as it is.

I am a staunch supporter of academic studies of the Buffyverse, but if we cannot find a way to effectively provide students academic access to this powerful text, *Buffy the Vampire Slayer* will become an antiquated oddity upon which only we Buffyologists dwell. Our students will indulge us, but they will not follow us.

## WORKS CITED

Camron, Marc. "The Importance of Being the Zeppo: Xander, Gender Identity and Hybridity in Buffy the Vampire Slayer." *Slayage: The Online Journal of Buffy Studies.* 23 (2007). http://slayageonline.com/.
Chesler, Phyllis. *Letters to a Young Feminist.* New York: Avalon, 1997.
Cocca, Carolyn. "First Word 'Jail,' Second Word 'Bait'": Adolescent Sexuality, Fem-

inist Theories, and Buffy the Vampire Slayer." *Slayage: The Online Journal of Buffy Studies.* 10 (2003). http://slayageonline.com/.

Des Hotel, Rob, and Dean Batali. "Never Kill a Boy on the First Date." Buffy the Vampire Slayer. 15 March 1997. UPN.

Deshazer, Mary. *The Longman Anthology of Women's Literature.* New York: Pearson, 2005

Early, Francis. "Staking Her Claim: Buffy the Vampire Slayer as Transgressive Woman Warrior." *Slayage: The Online Journal of Buffy Studies.* 6 (2002). http://slayageonline.com/.

Eng 454 — Literature and Women. Flagler College, St. Augustine, FL. Fall 2007. WebCT.

Jowett, Lorna. *Sex and the Slayer: A Gender Studies Primer for the Buffy Fan.* Middleton: Wesleyan University Press, 2005.

Rich, Adrienne. "Notes Towards a Politics of Location." In Deshazer. 1095–106.

Showalter, Elaine. "Feminism in the Wilderness." In Deshazer. 353–74.

Walker, Alice. "In Search of Our Mothers' Gardens." In Deshazer. 324–31.

Wilcox, Rhonda. *Why Buffy Matters.* New York: Taurus, 2005.

Wollstonecraft, Mary. "A Vindication of the Rights of Women." In Deshazer. 1131–39.

Woolf, Virginia, "A Room of One's Own." In Deshazer. 16–72.

# About the Contributors

**Clinton P.E. Atchley** is an associate professor of English at Henderson State University in Arkadelphia, Arkansas. He received his B.A. and M.A. in English from the University of Arkansas, Fayetteville, and his Ph.D. in medieval languages and literature from the University of Washington, Seattle. His research interests include Old and Middle English literature and culture, medieval sermon studies, Arthurian literature, textual criticism, the history of the English language, and Shakespeare.

**Rebecca Bobbitt** is an adjunct professor of English at Middle Tennessee State University and is working on her dissertation—fairy tales in the *Buffy* and *Angel* universes. She has been lucky enough to be able to combine two of her passions—teaching and television—to write *Teaching in the Pop Culture Zone: Using Popular Culture in the Composition Classroom* with Allison Smith and Trixie Smith, along with the instructor's manual for *The Pop Culture Zone: Writing Critically About Popular Culture*. Her essay on Wesley Wyndham-Price was originally written for David Lavery's grad course, "Joss Whedon: Television Auteur."

**Elizabeth Bridges** came to *Buffy* thanks to the happy coincidence that, on the day in 2003 when she finally consented to spend her meager graduate student wages on cable, FX started over its cycle of *Buffy* reruns from Season 1, Episode 1. She completed a Ph.D. program in German and film studies at Indiana University. She teaches at Hendrix College in Conway, Arkansas.

**Leigh Clemons** is associate professor of theatre/women's and gender studies at Louisiana State University, where she teaches theatre history, dramatic literature, and criticism. A longtime fan of all things vampiric (she read *Dracula* when she was eight), this is her second published Buffy article. She has presented at Slayage 2 and 3.

**AmiJo Comeford** is an assistant professor of English at Dixie State College of Utah. Comeford enjoys utilizing Whedon studies as well as other popular culture figures, such as superheroes, as pedagogical tools in the classroom in a variety of contexts. She is focused primarily on nineteenth-century American literature, specifically American Civil War poetry and prose.

**Kevin K. Durand** teaches philosophy at Henderson State University and saw *Buffy* from the first episode. He continues to point out that Plato and Aristotle both thought the theatre of the day worthwhile grist for the philosophical mill. They were right then and now.

**David Fritts** teaches English at Henderson Community College in Henderson, Kentucky, and is working on a long-delayed Ph.D. in medieval literature at Ohio University. It was through the lens of medieval literature, specifically *Beowulf*, that David began to see the depth of the *Buffy* narrative. He began reading about *Buffy*, writing about *Buffy*, and, eventually, teaching with *Buffy*.

**Keith Fudge** is a native Arkansan who has earned a B.A. in English from Arkansas Tech University, and an M.A. and Ph.D. in English from the University of Mississippi. He has held teaching and administrative positions in traditional public schools and faculty positions at the Arkansas School for Math, Science, and the Arts and Henderson State University. He is currently an assistant professor of English, teaching courses in short story, novel, comp, Southern literature, and popular culture at the University of Arkansas-Fort Smith. He has published articles on William Faulkner and in the area of eighteenth-century studies, and his present research interests are in American popular culture, including *Buffy* studies, and the history or rock music and its application in the classroom.

**Brent Linsley** is completing his dissertation on contemporary interpretations of Shakespeare in film at Louisiana State University. He is particularly interested in the ways in which classical and canonical literature is reconfigured and re-presented in contemporary works. He has been given many opportunities to lecture on the nature of the *Buffy* canon and has found that it is a very effective way of convincing students of the importance of such questions—whether about *Buffy* or the Bard.

**Denise Tischler Millstein** has been fascinated by vampires since she first realized, too young, that death wasn't just something that happened to the elderly, but to everyone. She is an assistant director of first-year writing at the University of Alabama and also teaches courses on nineteenth-century British literature in the English department, specializing in Lord Byron, who had his own obsessions with vampires.

**Susan M. Payne-Mulliken** once offered to buy David Boreanaz a drink at a trendy Los Angeles bar. She based the thesis for her master's degree in communication studies on *Buffy's* final season after having been inspired by the powerful series finale, "Chosen." Valerie R. Renegar served as her master's advisor at San Diego State University and the essay here is derived from that thesis. Susan is working on a law degree at Pace University School of Law in White Plains, New York. (David turned down the drink but did engage in several minutes of polite conversation.)

**Valerie R. Renegar** is an associate professor in the School of Communication at San Diego State University and teaches courses in rhetorical research methods and feminist rhetoric. She has also published work concerning pop culture artifacts such as *The Big Lebowski*, and numerous articles concerning third wave feminist theory. She came to realize the significance of *Buffy* while serving as Susan M. Payne-Mulliken's master's thesis advisor.

**Lauren Schultz** wrote her thesis on *Buffy, Harry Potter,* and young adult media. She will be awarded her masters degree in literature from American University in spring 2009 and plans going straight into a Ph.D. program in literature. Besides film and television studies, she specializes in Anglo-American modernism and post-modern international literatures.

**Melanie Wilson** is a graduate student pursuing an M.L.A. at Henderson State University, where she is writing part of her thesis about Spike. She is compulsively drawn to all things medieval and gothic, even in their contemporary manifestations. She hopes to pursue her medieval and gothic research interests at the doctoral level.

**Tamara Wilson** teaches English at Flagler College. She has presented a number of papers for the International Conference of the Fantastic in the Arts and the Popular Culture Conference, among others, on a range of topics including classroom response to feminist utopias, female heroes, and *Buffy the Vampire Slayer*. She is a member of the Oxford Roundtable on Leadership and Women.

# Index